Industrialization and Democracy

Karl de Schweinitz, Jr.

Industrialization
and Democracy

ECONOMIC NECESSITIES AND
POLITICAL POSSIBILITIES

The Free Press of Glencoe
Collier-Macmillan Limited, London

LIBRARY OF CONGRESS CATALOG CARD NUMBER: 64–16967

COLLIER-MACMILLAN CANADA, LTD., TORONTO, ONTARIO

printing number
2 3 4 5 6 7 8 9 10

Preface

THIS BOOK is an essay in political economy. I have written it in the belief that the scientific bent which so dominates research in the social sciences today has tended to push aside important issues of economy and polity that do not lend themselves readily to quantification. Among these issues, none is more fascinating than the relationship between economic growth and democracy. In dealing with it, I have ranged widely in time and space and have placed great weight on economic forces as explanatory variables. The generalizations I have put forward, therefore, are provocative and, hopefully, will compel readers, whether they agree or disagree, to examine their beliefs about the economic basis of democracy and freedom.

The book was written during summers in which I received generous grants from the Ford Foundation and from the Comparative Politics Program of the Political Science Department at Northwestern University. For these I am most grateful. I am also grateful to my father, Karl de Schweinitz, Robert Freedman, Jr., Benjamin Nimer, and Stephan Thernstrom. Each of them read the entire manuscript and, though they are in no sense responsible for it, they made me more secure in my responsibility by correcting errors of fact and interpretation. To my colleague George I. Blanksten of the Political Science Department I owe a special debt. For three years we have jointly offered a graduate seminar at Northwestern University in the Politics of Developing Economies in which I have had an opportunity to expound my ideas on the political content of economics. He has been unfailingly tolerant and good-humored in what too frequently must

[v]

have seemed to be a presumptuous attempt on the part of an economist to straighten out political science.

Finally, I am indebted to the editors of *Economic Development and Cultural Change* for allowing me to use passages from my article "Industrialization, Labor Controls, and Democracy," which appeared in the July, 1959, issue.

KARL DE SCHWEINITZ, JR.

Evanston, Illinois
November 1963

Contents

Preface   v

Part One: The Argument

1   The Problem Posed   3

2   The Politics and Economics of Democracy   12

3   The Economics and Politics of Growth   35

4   Industrialization, Labor Controls, and Democracy   59

Part Two: The Evidence

5   The British Economy: Industrial Transformation and
the Evolution of Democracy   79

6   The United States: The Natural Haven of Industrialization and Democracy   129

7   German Industrialization: The Weakening of the
Democratic Impulse   158

8   The Twentieth Century Against Democracy: Russia
and Totalitarian Industrialization   187

9   Industrialization and the Prospects for Democracy in
the Underdeveloped Economies   234

10   Growth, Freedom, and Democracy in the Twentieth
Century   269

Notes   280

Index   303

Part One

The Argument

Chapter 1

The Problem Posed

IT IS WIDELY BELIEVED that the emergence of political democracy in the western world was intimately, even causally, related to industrialization. The industrial revolution, which in the second half of the eighteenth century accelerated the rate of economic growth in Great Britain, brought in its wake profound social and economic changes that could not be accommodated within the oligarchic political institutions bequeathed to Britain in the Glorious Revolution. The growing wealth of the middle classes, the concentration of an industrial labor force in urban areas, and the growth of the population at once destroyed the foundations of the eighteenth-century parliamentary government and created insistent demands on the part of the unenfranchised to be allowed inside the "pale of the constitution."

In Great Britain responsible political leaders gradually acceded to these demands in a series of franchise and parliamentary reforms extending throughout the nineteenth century, but in the United States political leaders acted with greater dispatch. During the Jacksonian era an increasing number of states dominated by the turbulent democracy of the frontier entered the union. And with the change in the relative political strength of east and west some of the defenses against the majority which the founding fathers deemed prudent to build into the constitution were attenuated. But the democratizing influence of the expanding west could not have become manifest without the powerful en-

gine of economic growth; this provided the means for constructing those internal improvements essential to the movement of
population and the circulation of trade from which the population made its living.

As the industrialization impulse spread out from Great
Britain to the European continent, it seemed to bring there similar political repercussions. The movement of France toward
democracy was, to say the least, frenetic. Republic, empire, and
monarchy followed one another in violent sequence until an uneasy political equilibrium was achieved in the Third Republic
at the end of the nineteenth century. The rate of economic
growth during these tortuous alternations of political systems
was not so high as in Great Britain, nor was the industrial transformation so dramatic. Nonetheless, it would seem that the revolutionary process in France was stimulated, if not touched off, by
the discontents of an increasingly prosperous middle class which
felt unconscionably constrained by the feudal restrictions and
aristocratic corruption of the *Ancien Régime*. Moreover, the
process of growth spawned the industrial proletariat whose revolutionary opposition to nonrepublican forms of government was
a characteristic feature of nineteenth-century French political development.

Elsewhere on the continent the tide of democracy ran strong
as economic development proceeded apace. If the German Hohenzollerns did not accept, or were not forced to accept, the
constitutional status of their British cousins, there were at least
many indications that the Prussian domination of Germany was
becoming less arbitrary. If World War I had not intervened it is
possible that the German political community would have continued to evolve in a democratic fashion. As for the smaller
countries of Europe, many of these had attained manhood suffrage within constitutional monarchies by the time of World
War I.

The negative evidence bearing on the relationship between
democracy and economic development is equally impressive. In
Europe the countries with the shoddiest performance by democratic criteria were precisely those that were least affected by the
advances of the industrial revolution—Spain, Portugal, Russia,

and the Balkan states. In Asia, Africa, and Latin America the story was the same in the nineteenth century: little, if any, economic growth; autocratic, feudal, and traditional political regimes.

Casual historical evidence of this sort undoubtedly has played an important role in influencing contemporary thinking about the problems of politics and underdevelopedness. American foreign aid programs since World War II, for example, have been predicated on the desirability of influencing the conduct of nations in international politics by making available to them the resources they lack but need for development. A crude rationalization of such programs conceives of aid as a means of making less developed countries beholden to the United States, much as the recipient of private charity is supposed to be grateful to his benefactor. A more sophisticated rationalization asserts that by staving off political systems hostile to democracy, i.e., communism, aid prepares the way for the underdeveloped economy along the path trod by the democratic nations in the nineteenth century. It is thus hoped that the United States will acquire new friends and maintain old ones by inducing foreign nations to develop in the image of its own political system and ideology.

Undoubtedly this is attractive doctrine and a significant improvement over nineteenth-century imperialistic notions of manifest destiny and the white man's burden with their heavy-handed disdain for indigenous beliefs and ways of life. Perhaps the objectives of contemporary doctrine are the same in terms of the realities of international politics, but few people in the democratic west would deny that it is preferable to manipulate the proximate conditions of development and hope that the underdeveloped nations themselves with greater autonomy and control over their own affairs come to accept the political ideology of the western democracies.

Historical evidence, however, is a frail reed to lean upon for the prediction of future events. Not surprisingly, no group is more keenly aware of this than the scholars who devote their professional life to the study of history. So far has the historian been impressed by the uniqueness of the past record of different societies that he typically is hostile to theories of change and development which might serve as the basis for anticipating the future. It is no accident that the men who have formulated such theories—Marx, Weber, Schumpeter—come from outside the ranks of professional historians.

The historian's insistence on the uniqueness of historical events cannot help but command respect when one examines the record of a country's development. Take, for example, the question with which we are concerned in the context of British experience. The political reforms which, starting with the Reform Bill of 1832, brought full democracy to Great Britain took place in the nineteenth and early twentieth centuries. But these measures were successful largely because of the gradual evolution of constitutional and parliamentary institutions in the centuries prior to 1832. When the political crises following the Napoleonic Wars were partially resolved by extending the franchise to the members of the upper middle class and by changing the basis of parliamentary representation, the political leaders who acquiesced to these reforms did so not in the interests of creating a democratic society, but in defense of the traditions of British government. Democracy was anathema to the members of the British oligarchy, all the more so because the French Revolution at the height of the Jacobin dictatorship had destroyed the illusion of democratic rationality disseminated by apostles of the eighteenth-century Enlightenment. But when the oligarchy felt that parliamentary institutions were threatened by civil disorder they chose to extend the ranks of the politically privileged rather than chance the destruction of the political system under which Englishmen had lived since time immemorial.

Looking at the eighteenth century, one becomes even more aware of the lack of any kind of democratic teleology guiding the growth of political institutions. Indeed, one can only be awed by the role which chance seems to have played. Suppose, for example, that George I had had a good command of English and had been more interested in the political process—suppose, in other words, that a man like George III had been the first Hanoverian monarch—would Robert Walpole have been able to establish the precedents and acquire the prerogatives which subsequently developed into the cabinet system of political responsibility? Again, would the House of Lords have allowed the House of Commons to acquire so much power in the Parliament if it had not felt that the restrictions of the franchise secured its authority against popular assault? Looking back even further, how is one to evaluate the role of dissent in the eventual emergence of democratic political institutions? When Henry VIII revolted against Rome, he had no intention of endowing a separatist movement within the liberated Church of England. Yet the necessary consequence of the unwillingness of all English clerics to defect with Henry called forth autonomous, independent and representative religious organizations whose subsequent role in disseminating the liberal and democratic spirit would be hard to overrate.

What strikes one forcibly is that so many actions and policies in Great Britain designed to achieve one end eventually had quite different and unintended consequences. To raise questions about the part chance played in the creation of British democratic political institutions is to wonder whether these institutions were a fortuitous by-product, what economists might call an external economy, of policies that had no immediate democratic rationale. Yet Great Britain in time formed the most successful democratic political system the world has yet seen. When England had established strong parliamentary institutions—but still excluded the great majority of Englishmen from exercising political rights— the French across the Channel created a society explicitly in terms of democratic criteria. The consequences of this experiment are too well known to belabor—France is still perhaps the most unstable democracy in the western state system.

But one need not give in to the apparent randomness and irrationality of historical data any more than one need endow them with a mystical inner meaning. However unique or fortuitous the actions and policies of specific people at particular junctures of history, the fact remains that in the western world the rise of the democratic political community has been associated with industrialization and economic growth. It is also true, as we have already mentioned, that many people presume that the process of causation runs from the latter to the former. Though these presumptions no doubt are based on the most tenuous evidence and may even be nothing more than articles of faith, we have no choice but to look for uniformities and constants in behavior which may provide us with a frame of reference for comprehending the world as we perceive it now and as we anticipate it tomorrow. In short, we cannot refuse to predict the future. The plea that history only proves the uniqueness of the past will not do, for it implicitly assumes that our own existence is unfathomable.

§   *A Methodological Note and the Nature of the Analysis*

Before outlining the scope of the analysis in this essay, it may be prudent to make some observations about its methodological emphasis. In recent years there has been mounting dissatisfaction with economics as a tool for explaining the problems of underdeveloped countries. Both inside and outside the economist ranks it is alleged that economics has little to say about why some countries have developed their economic potential while others have not.[1] Saving and investment rates, capital-output ratios, income and price elasticities, and the other constructs of economics may be useful for describing growth as a process, this view contends, but they fail to illuminate its sources. Because economics matured in historical circumstances where growth could be taken for granted, it has been unconcerned with the behavioral characteristics that generate growth. And because it has dealt with a range of phenomena more readily quantified than the phenomena of the other social sciences, it has work for many hands and little need to brood about the relevance of its behavioral assumptions. If one wants to understand the causes of growth, say these critics, one must delve below the organizational manifestations of economic systems into the psyche of the individual and the factors affecting the formation of his personality. Growth takes place in societies where individuals have a a need for achievement which can be satisfied in entrepreneurial activity. Where it does not take place, child-rearing practices and learning processes have failed to inculcate such a need in individuals. Growth, therefore, is less a function of external, environmental stimulants than it is a function of internal, personal needs.

One might well extend these remarks about economic development to political development and insist that the emergence of democracy may be explained by referring to the factors responsible for the creation of a democratic personality, if one may use such a phrase. Rather than viewing economic and geographical forces, for example, as having a political impact on a society composed of individuals with given behavioral propensities, one would look for their impact on society by way of induced changes in these propensities. In any society, the individual is the basic actor and the institutions which structure his existence must be created by him. What, therefore, could be more patent than that an understanding of the latter must start with an analysis of the former?

The methodological issue raised here really cannot be resolved. Whether one attempts to comprehend social processes by focusing on factors external or internal to the individual depends upon the purpose, skills, and interests of the analyst. No doubt an omniscient analyst would encompass both sets of factors and construct what perhaps is the goal of the social sciences—a science of society. But anyone who falls short of omniscience must economize time and energy and select a sector of society for investigation which he thinks will yield meaningful answers to the questions he raises. This necessarily means that many characteristics of society will be impounded in *ceteris paribus,* some advisedly and consciously on the grounds that they are unimportant, but others implicitly or unknowingly because of the limits of the investigator's knowledge.

In this book we will examine the relationship between economic growth and the emergence of democratic political institutions largely in terms of factors external to the individual. We shall be concerned with what may be called the macrocosmic—as opposed to the microcosmic—dimensions of society. The analysis will be partial in the sense that we will deal with conditions that are necessary to, though not sufficient for, democracy. Starting off with matters of definition and process devoid of specific institutional content, we shall deduce some political prerequisites for economic growth and the implications for political systems of different levels of income. Taking Britain, the United States, and Germany, we shall then analyze the influence of British-centered growth on political institutions in the late eighteenth and nineteenth centuries as facilitated by prevailing economic, technological, geographical, demographic, and ideological forces. Further, we shall observe the effect of these forces on Russian growth in the twentieth century. Finally, we shall discuss the relevance of these historical cases to the problems of the contemporary underdeveloped economies which are attempting to accelerate the rate of growth.

The conclusions to which this analysis leads are not especially hopeful as far as western democracy is concerned, and it might not be inappropriate to anticipate them. We find that with the passage of time the various forces affecting industrializing economies shift the initiative for development from the activities of autonomous individuals to the activities of the state. In the nineteenth century growth took place autonomously in Britain and the United States and to a lesser extent in Germany; in the twentieth century growth in Russia and in the newly developing countries has been induced by the state. The democratization process was historically stimulated by the independent growth of the entrepreneurial and laboring classes which placed persistent and ineluctable demands on nondemocratic political leaders for the extension of political rights. Now it is much more difficult for these classes to acquire an existence independent of the state. If the state is nondemocratic, as it is likely to be in impoverished societies, the growth process will not throw up those autonomous centers of power and pressure which in the previous century acted as vehicles of political reform.

Will such states, then, be as assiduous in reforming themselves and fostering political development as they are in fostering economic development? Doubt about the answer to this question necessarily raises doubts about the prospects for democracy in the newly independent states of the present century. One thing, however, emerges clearly from the subsequent analysis: the development of democracy in the nineteenth century was a function of an unusual configuration of historical circumstances which cannot be repeated. The Euro-American route to democracy is closed. Other means must now be devised for building new democratic states.

new democratic states.

Chapter 2

The Politics and Economics

of Democracy

DEMOCRACY is one of those troublesome words which means all
things to all people. Like motherhood and patriotism, it is
thought to be a noble condition and so is evoked by politicians,
publicists, preachers, and demagogues to prove their unsullied
intentions and just claim to popular support. In the communist
world the so-called people's democracies have established institutions which most people in the liberal democracies of the western
world would call totalitarian. Indeed the rise of these states has
led to the coining of a curiously anomalous, though no doubt
descriptive, phrase—totalitarian democracy.[1]

It will be useful to consider briefly the characteristics of totalitarian democracy, for such a state provides a stark contrast to
the kind of democratic society with which this analysis is primarily concerned. Its contemporary prototype, of course, is the political system of the Soviet Union, but it has roots deep in the
western tradition and its ancestry can be traced at least to the
French Revolution, and some would contend to classical Greece.
While totalitarian democracy may ultimately seek its rationale in
the interests and welfare of the individual, it denies the individual an autonomous existence apart from the state. The primary
purpose of government is not, as in the liberal tradition, the

establishment of social order through the adjudication of the conflicting interests of people who are free to determine their own ends and the means appropriate to them. Rather the purpose of government is the achievement of some goal of the state which transcends the preferences of individuals.

In the Soviet Union this transcendent purpose is the achievement of communism, a social state without historical precedent which originates in Marxian ideology. The justification for the conduct of Soviet government therefore inheres in the Marxian laws of historical development; these laws allegedly guide the progress of society through the various stages of growth prior to communism. Thus the Communist Party of Soviet Russia, which holds the reins of government, acts in the interests of the whole society as *revealed* by the eschatology to which it adheres. Translated into more mundane utilitarian terms—in the liberal tradition it is assumed that social welfare equals the sum of choices made by autonomous individuals, while in the Marxian system social welfare is derived independently of individual choice and then devolves upon individuals.

The inversion of the utilitarian welfare function casts an invidious light on any individual who chooses to differ with the established policy of government. His grounds for dissent must necessarily be immoral, since the party has determined the moral purpose of society according to the Marxian laws of historical development. The dissenter is not merely wrong, misguided, or deluded; he is evil and morally reprehensible because he interferes with the achievement of the very purpose of society. In the light of this totalitarian ethic much of the conduct of Soviet government, by western liberal standards incomprehensible and appalling, is quite consistent. The purge, the obeisance before party omniscience, the confession, the total and enthusiastic support registered by the delegates to the periodic party congresses are all part of the political process which identifies the party with the true purposes of society. This is totalitarianism, and all the more effective because it is designed to achieve for the individual the good life.

As suggested earlier, totalitarian democracy is not an invention of Soviet Russia, though it has experienced its greatest success there in the years since the Revolution of 1917. We need cite only one precursor in order to give it some historical depth. During the French revolution at the height of the Jacobin dictatorship Robespierre demonstrated with terrible clarity the totalitarian implication of Rousseau's concept of the general will. Influenced by the form of government in the small cantons of his native Switzerland, Rousseau envisaged the general will as being spontaneously generated by individuals who were in close and sympathetic association. Each individual would in a sense "will" the general will because in a small face-to-face community he would be conscious of what was in the interests of society and so in his own interests. When, however, the general will was writ large and became the presumed rationale of governmental action in the French Revolution, it inspired that messianic and moral fervor which, perversely enough, led to the killing of many innocent people. For the enemies of the revolution were not just opponents of Robespierre and the Committee of Public Safety; they were the opponents of the General Will and stood in the way of society's progress to the good life. The General Will was for Robespierre what the Marxian laws of historical development were for Lenin. It is hardly accidental that the Jacobin clubs displayed a strong family resemblance to the communist party in the ritual of their proceedings and in their compulsive need for unanimity and identification with the true purpose of society.[2]

Having introduced the concept of totalitarian democracy in the context of the Russian and French Revolutions, we should like now to drop the word democratic for societies of this sort. While there conceivably may be some merit in using the term to describe societies whose ends in a teleological sense allow individuals opportunities for free choice—in contrast to a totalitarian society of the Nazi variety which even in the longest of views did not anticipate individuals acquiring freedom outside of an organic relationship with the state—the grounds for doing so disappear when one examines the means espoused for achieving these ends. As means democracy denotes a system in which the problems of government are resolved on the basis of an appeal to the preferences of autonomous individuals. If individuals periodically have the opportunity through a voting mechanism to choose among alternatives, any one of which would lead to a policy different from those promised by the foregone alternatives, if the vote of each member of the adult population (suitably defined to exclude those who are mentally incompetent or not yet old enough to evaluate political alternatives) is weighted equally, and, finally, if the criterion for the determination of the preferred alternative is the majority of votes cast by eligible voters, then one may speak of a democratic political system. These conditions may be described as majority rule. They are preeminently lacking in the Soviet Union, but to greater or less extent have been achieved in many of the advanced economies of the western world.

The formal definition of the democratic process has a number of important implications which we now want to examine at some length. First of all, the ultimate sanction for governmental action arises from the choices that individuals make among policy alternatives (or symbols of policy alternatives, i.e., candidates). This does not necessarily imply that democracy means government by the people except in a remote sense. The actual formulation of policy alternatives and the administration of the policies decided upon must necessarily be the prerogative of a small minority of the population. In short, in democratic society one can still speak of the governed and the governors. But the governors cannot long ignore the preferences of the governed, because if they do they will lose the prerogatives of office, that is, they will be turned out at the next election.

Nor does ultimate sanction of popular sovereignty imply that the preferences of individuals are immune to all influences except those which emanate in some sense from the individual himself. On the contrary, it is essential that candidates for political office, private members of the community, business and labor leaders use the newspaper, radio, and the other media of communication to try to influence the voting behavior of the citizen. Otherwise alternative points of view and the evidence and information adduced in support of them will not be presented to the citizen, thus diminishing the stock of knowledge upon which choice depends. The communication requirements of mass society do, of course, raise some difficult problems for democracy. In so far as income and wealth are distributed un-equally, some individuals and groups will necessarily have greater access to the communication media and an advantage in the competition for the preferences of the voters. Does this mean that the autonomy of individuals in democratic society is spurious and that the system is really controlled by those who are in a position to dominate the editorial policy of newspapers, radios, and magazines? Is Marx's charge after all correct, that bourgeois democracy consists in "deciding once in three or six years which member of the ruling class was to represent the people in parliament"?[3] Answers to these questions would require an examination of the historical record. Here we simply want to suggest a condition which is necessary, though perhaps not sufficient, for entering a demurrer. The individual in a democracy must be rational in the sense that he is conscious of the ends he seeks and evaluates competing alternatives in the light of these ends.

At this point consideration of a similar problem in economics may be illuminating. When economists speak of consumer sovereignty, they mean a situation in which the choices individuals make in the markets for employment and consumer goods and services control the allocation of resources among firms. If this condition is to hold, resources must be mobile and capable of entering any line of productive activity. Similarly, individuals must be mobile in the sense that they know the terms of choice as manifested in relative prices and are capable of balancing at the margin the utility yielded by the various commodities offered for sale. Then one may say that under the compulsion of a profit system, if the demand for commodity A increases, the supply of commodity A will also increase. For the action of individuals as demanders will raise the rewards of the factors producing A, thus inducing individuals as suppliers to allocate additional productive factors to the industry. By the same token, if the demand for B decreases the supply of B will decrease, for the rewards of the factors in that industry will be diminished. Profits and losses, higher and lower wages and raw material prices all act to move resources to those occupations where the utility of consumers will be maximized.

The system in which consumer sovereignty prevails is

formally known as perfect competition. A feature of perfect competition which is relevant to our discussion here is the assumed independence of individuals within households and firms. The wants of consumers and their preferences are taken as given, an implied assumption that they are autonomously determined. This assumption is crucial for anyone who wants to make welfare judgments, that is, make choices between different situations in terms of better or worse. The reason for this is that the measurement of welfare requires a ruler whose units of measure will not change with changes in the values being observed. In this case the ruler is utility. If one can assume that wants and preferences are determined autonomously then one may say that, given the preferences of individuals, their welfare increases with a rise in their disposable income.[4]

The empirical basis of the assumption of the autonomy or independence of the consumer is, to say the least, tenuous. Far from being independent, casual observation of American market behavior might lead one to believe that the consumer is highly dependent on firms. The latter, at any rate, find the wants and preferences of consumers sufficiently malleable to warrant prodigal expenditures on advertising and promotional campaigns designed to influence the demand for output. To the extent that consumer preferences are molded by the firms producing output, the standards for making welfare judgments about economic organization are seriously impaired. For if preferences are not autonomously determined, the utility ruler turns out to be a stretchable piece of elastic. How can one say anything about the welfare of the consumer who has been made to like the new automobile he purchases every other year? One can say very little.

However much the lack of consumer independence may vitiate consumer sovereignty and attenuate the capacity of the economist to make welfare judgments, the market continues to function as a mechanism for allocating resources. No doubt it works imperfectly but it does provide opportunities for choice to all by fixing the responsibility for organizing economic activity on a few. Like the political system, the market system has its governors and governed. But where the governors of the political system are held to account by a voting system which operates periodically or intermittently, the governors of the market—the entrepreneurs or business men—are held to account by a voting system which operates constantly. A senator may lose his seat at the next election; an entrepreneur may lose his mandate any time the consumer is not willing to buy his product.

The analogy between political and economic governors cannot be pushed too far, but it is useful for the problem of the autonomy of the individual in a complex system of social organization. The consumer in a market economy is not able to call forth particular kinds of output. He can only choose among alternatives already existing in various markets. The power to introduce new commodities resides with the entrepreneur and there is no doubt that this is a very significant power. For the man or firm which innovates and markets a new commodity permanently affects the wants and preferences of the consumer. The automotive industry in the United States has created a new way of life as have the producers of the automatic kitchen and laundry equipment so characteristic of American homes. Yet having permanently affected the level of wants of households, the entrepreneur is still subject to the veto power that the consumer possesses. He has to obtain the approval of dollar expenditures. So long as consumers have choice, it is not important from this point of view whether they choose commodities they really want or only those that they have been made to want. What matters is the choices in fact made.

In the same way, the governors of the political system possess significant power because it is they rather than the governed who formulate the policy alternatives from among which voters choose at an election. And it is no doubt true that the alternatives in fact formed by political leaders influence the attitudes of the voter. At the time of writing the United States still had not recognized the government of mainland China. One would be hard put to prove that the policy of nonrecognition was formulated in response to the autonomous political preferences of the American voter. Rather, elites in and out of government established a policy which then became part of the political preferences of the voter as the issue was discussed and debated in the public forum. This example is perhaps unduly favorable to the point. The issues of foreign policy are often obscure and usually so far removed from the experience of the typical voter that it is difficult for him to evaluate them without making a special effort to acquire the requisite knowledge. But the issues of domestic policy, though perhaps not quite so obscure as the issues of foreign policy, are hardly less complex—witness, for example, the problems of price stability, growth, and employment—and voters, no matter how rational, cannot be expected to form opinions independently of the political and nonpolitical leaders whose views they have learned to trust and respect.

In the political system as in the economic system, the crucial consideration is whether or not alternatives are offered the voter. The voter can no more specify the dimensions of the policy he would like followed on a particular issue than the consumer can specify the characteristics of a special product he would like produced. If, however, he has a choice among competing candidates for political office who espouse alternative policies, his vote matters; in fact, it guarantees the continued operation of the democratic system, regardless of the forces which shape and form his political preferences.

§   *The Voting Paradox and Political Consensus*

Though surely essential to viable democracy, rationality presents certain problems of its own. These problems inhere in the difficulties which may arise in attempting to derive a rational social choice from rational individual choice. The dilemma raised here is by now widely recognized and we shall discuss it only briefly.[5] If choice is rational, the individual who prefers A to B and B to C, also prefers A to C. This same condition must hold if society is to make a rational choice. Suppose, however, that three individuals, 1, 2, and 3 are choosing among three alternative programs or policies, A, B, and C. Individual 1 prefers A to B and B to C and therefore A to C; individual 2 prefers B to C and C to A and therefore B to A; and, finally, individual 3 prefers C to A and A to B and therefore C to B. The choice of each individual is transitive and hence rational, but if one attempts to summate these choices to arrive at a social decision one encounters a difficulty. A majority (1 and 3) prefers A to B. A majority (1 and 2) also prefers B to C. A rational social choice therefore would require that a majority prefers A to C, but brief examination of the individual preferences reveals that this is not so. The majority (2 and 3) prefers C to A.

This formal example suggests rather strongly that rationality is not a sufficient condition for assuring the successful functioning of the democratic political system. If for A, B, and C we substitute communism, fascism, and democracy, and if the preferences of the voters are represented as above, we have described an electorate that is hopelessly divided and unable to make a rational social choice. Given the preferences of individuals on these issues there is no way of formulating a public policy consistent with individual choice. A majority decision can only be reached if one of the issues or one of the voters is removed from the electoral process, contingencies which necessarily involve the repression of the preferences of one-third of the electorate.

Democracy thus confronts a dilemma. On the one hand, full participation in the election leads to no decision, and, on the other, the repression of preferences alienates an important part of the electorate. If alternative C (democracy) were stricken from the ballot, a majority would prefer A (communism) to B (fascism), assuming that the removal of C did not alter the preference ordering of the voters. Yet it is hardly likely, given the nature of these issues, that supporters of B would stand idly by as policies were promulgated—the incarceration of Fascists, for example—to which they were inalterably opposed. Of course, the dilemma is in part a reflection of the gravity of the issues facing the voters. If for A, B, and C we had substituted peanuts, cashews, and almonds instead of communism, fascism, and democracy, we surely would have been credulous to expect disorders in society from disgruntled almond lovers.

There is, however, an important implication to be drawn for the democratic process from these disparate examples of issues which might be placed before an electorate. Some issues are more significant for the political community than others and on these there must be constraints on individual preferences which allow the formation of a consensus. The constraints may operate through the socialization and education of children in the home, school, church and other primary groups and may have the effect of ruling out certain alternatives, for example, communism and/or fascism as inadmissable and unwanted types of social systems. But lacking the constraints essential for a social consensus on fundamental issues, a democratic political system will not function effectively because the electorate, or the articulate political representatives of the electorate, will feel too much threatened by the possible outcome of elections. And if within the political community there are important groups fearful of the democratic decision-making process, they will not view it as a means of resolving problems facing the community, but as a means to be used or abused in defense of their position vis-à-vis other hostile political groups in society. In short, without consensus on fundamental values, it is difficult to legitimate the democratic political process.⁶

If there is consensus on fundamental values, many political conflicts may be resolved on a stable and continuing basis. Issues of lesser importance, as in our example of peanuts versus cashews versus almonds, may not raise serious choice dilemmas. In the first place, the fundamental consensus may itself impose constraints on the preferences of individuals with respect to these issues. For example, basic agreement on the desirability of maximizing individual choice through the political community precludes the consideration of tax proposals which have a confiscatory impact on racial, religious, or ethnic minorities. Tax proposals will be framed in such a way as to (1) permit the resolution of any differences through a voting procedure, and (2) make the outcome of the vote tolerable to those individuals and groups who find themselves in the minority.⁷ This implies that where consensus on fundamentals prevails, the issues confronting the electorate are likely to be marginal, marginal in this context referring to the differences among them and not to their general significance to society. Taxation obviously is essential to government, whether to provide revenue for needed community services or to prevent redundant expenditures from generating inflation. But the tax problem in a democracy is to determine which taxes to raise or lower and by how much and typically the percentage changes proposed are not great.

In the second place, many people who have preferences on lesser issues which if articulated might raise dilemmas for rational social choice do not bother to vote or to participate actively in the political process. Accepting the legitimacy of democratic government, they do not feel called upon to take action when it yields policy results at odds with their particular preferences.

Political inactivity, of course, does not necessarily reflect acceptance of the political order; it may reflect ennui or despair and a feeling of helplessness against forces too great for an individual to cope with. But this kind of political apathy is not characteristic of societies which have fashioned a strong democratic consensus. Now, the basis of a democratic consensus is the belief that individuals count as individuals and that it is the purpose of government to serve their ends. When people who accept democratic political beliefs are inactive politically the explanation is likely to be a crude utilitarian one, namely that it is not worth their time to get involved. This is another way of saying that they do not feel it will make much difference to their own interests how the issues before the electorate are resolved.

Finally, a strong consensus on fundamental values facilitates the growth of political institutions which accentuate the possibilities of majority rule and at the same time abort potential divisive influences in the community. A two-party system in which each party seeks support from the whole community (as opposed to a multi-party system in which each party appeals to special ideological or sectional interests) may narrow the range of choice open to voters at elections. Given the extensive basis of their potential support, these parties must so compromise their programs that they become broad generalizations of intent under which different voting groups may work together. In contrast, the party in a multi-party system is likely to appeal to a specific group with a specific program that cannot easily be reconciled with the programs of rival parties. Where the latter catapults the divisive forces of society to the center of the political arena and makes government depend on unstable coalitions of minority parties, the former keeps them, in a sense, at one remove so that a government based on a majority party strong enough to adjudicate them may be formed. Moreover, the party system necessarily affects the attitudes and values of the individual voter. The two-party system promotes conciliatory and accommodating responses from individuals who perforce must accept less desired alternatives on some issues in order to support more desired alternatives on others. That is to say, it fosters trading attitudes with regard to issues by compelling voters to rank their preferences about questions of policy so that they will know what their reservation price is in any particular instance. The multi-party system, however, does not induce any such accommodating attitudes, for the voter can more easily find a party which will completely reflect his preferences. And if he can vote for a candidate with whom he agrees on all issues, he will not need to compromise his position at any point.

§ Education and Democracy

Thus far we have argued that, since democracy is a political system in which issues are ultimately resolved by appeal to an independent electorate, it depends on (1) the rationality of the individual and (2) a consensus concerning fundamental values that is widely enough shared to make the outcome of the issues subject to majority decision. Granted that these are characteristics of democracy, do they in any way depend upon special social-economic conditions? Or is democracy a "free" political system that can be adapted by different societies with varying social-economic conditions?

A partial answer to these questions can be inferred from the characteristics themselves. Consider first rationality. There is no reason to believe that man is inherently rational in the manner required by the democratic system. On the contrary, rationality is acquired through education and the habits of

evaluative conduct learned from parents in the course of growing up. Without educational facilities for disseminating the
communication skills, man would not be able to comprehend the
issues and problems confronting the political community except
in a crude, instinctive, and unsystematic manner. He must know
how to read and write and he must be part of a social system
which motivates him to use these skills to accumulate the stock
of knowledge essential for active and spontaneous participation
in the political life of the community. Education not only must
impart the communication skills; it must also inculcate individuals with the attitude that their conduct matters, that the
environment of society takes shape in response to the actions of
individuals. In other words, individuals must come to believe
that they have control over their own destiny and are not simply
the pawns of mysterious and ungovernable forces.

The historical evidence more or less confirms this inference
about the necessity of education for the viability of the democratic process. To be sure, Athenian democracy in classical
Greece was not grounded in a literate population in the modern
sense. The typical Athenian citizen could not read or write, yet
was fully entitled to participate in the Assembly at its periodic
meetings. A period that inspired most of the original political
thought in the western world, all the more remarkable because it
took place at the dawn of recorded history, Athenian democracy
nonetheless must be regarded as an anachronism. The fact that it
did not survive is less important than the fact that it was the only
one of its kind. Perhaps it is for this reason that it has excited
so much admiration; in contrast to the oligarchies and despotism
of its rival city-states, to modern eyes it appears to be a paragon
of political virtue, Plato to the contrary notwithstanding. Moreover, since it was a small city-state, ideas could be effectively communicated by orators in face-to-face relationships. If he could
not read or write, the Athenian citizen could easily become con-
versant with the leading ideas and issues of his day by attend-
ing and participating in the discussions in the public forum.

However productive the political ideas and thought of
Athenian democracy, its problems were quite different from
those of democracy in a mass society. Not the least of these

differences is the burden of communication that devolves upon a society geographically large and populated by individuals who for the most part are strangers to one another. Under these circumstances education is an indispensable means of getting to know one's culture and of making possible the communication of the ideas on which democracy is based. It is no accident that the countries with stable democratic political systems—the United Kingdom, the United States, the Scandinavian countries, Belgium and Holland, Canada, Australia, New Zealand—also have highly developed educational systems and correspondingly low or zero illiteracy rates. Conversely, those countries with inadequate educational systems and high illiteracy rates—generally the countries of Latin-America, Africa, and Asia—are governed either by unstable democratic or authoritarian political systems.

We should add that we are not asserting that historical evidence proves causation between education and the rise of democracy. It is a necessary, but not sufficient, condition. One need only point to Germany which placed tremendous emphasis on the education of its citizens throughout the nineteenth century only to produce a formidable totalitarian state in the twentieth century. This chastening observation makes it worthwhile to distinguish two different aspects of education: (1) the techniques of communication and learning and (2) the substantive values it imparts. The former is neutral regarding the direction of political sanctions and control. Individuals who possess these skills may be able to communicate their preferences to, and make them binding on, those people who have assumed responsibility for the direction of the political community. On the other hand, the governors of the political community may be all the more able to dominate the governed through the manipulation of the ideas transmitted through the communication media. The latter aspect of education, then, is a crucial means of imparting to individuals a sense of their own importance to the community and their right to the privileges of political participation. In those societies in which citizens acquire communication skills through education only to be subjected to the litany of totalitarian omniscience, the chances of the emergence of democratic ideology are, of course, forestalled. Yet this is not the end of the matter. For the teaching of the communication skills may well breed a kind of independence among individuals which increases the resistance that must be overcome if the governors' values are to dominate the citizenry. The power to read and write is the beginning of the power to think and act independently. The German experience of the 1930's should temper one's enthusiasm about the democratizing influence of education, but it should not lead one to deny its profoundly important role in the performance of the successful democracies.

§   *The Level of Income and Education*

The importance of education in the creation of a rational citizenry establishes one of the links between democracy and the level of income it requires to function properly. A subsistence economy in which per capita income is barely high enough to support life does not produce a surplus that can be utilized for education and other investment purposes. The pressure on resources for present consumption is so great that few can be released for allocation to uses which will expand future output. Moreover, educational investment raises special problems, for the return on it is not easy to assess. This is so, not because it is necessarily low—on the contrary, it is probably significantly high —but because the pay-off takes place over a long period of time and in many unanticipated directions. There are, in other words, external economies associated with educational investment. It is difficult for individuals, except as a matter of philanthropy, to commit resources voluntarily to the construction of educational facilities.

The subsistence economy, therefore, is likely to be characterized by a population that is largely illiterate and is ruled by a small minority literate by virtue of its wealth and access to the advantages of educational institutions in more developed countries. With per capita income above subsistence, however, it is possible for an economy to increase not only the absolute amount of resources available for investment but also the relative amount as well. That is to say, net investment in a wealthy economy is a greater proportion of net national income than in a subsistence economy. With greater aggregate investment forthcoming, society can afford to devote more resources to the extension and development of its educational system. Furthermore, a high income economy not only increases the supply of resources available for educational purposes, but increases the demand for an educated population. The high-income economy is dependent on a productive labor force sufficiently skilled to handle and maintain the complex capital equipment which makes large output possible and sufficiently adaptable to meet the organizational requirements of a highly differentiated economic-social order. One may expect, paradoxically enough, that in the high-income economy the importance of the educational system will be more widely recognized than in the subsistence economy.

§   *Consensus and the Level of Income*

The income variable is also related to the problem of forming a consensus appropriate for democracy. In order to demonstrate this let us for the moment accept the materialistic notion that conflict, the antithesis of consensus, is basically an economic phenomenon arising in situations where one person's gain is another person's loss. If, for instance, two individuals are competing for possession of a fixed and nonrecurring sum of money, each one has an interest in obtaining as much as possible and, equity considerations aside, in seeing to it that his rival obtains as little as possible. Despite the fulminations of the Marxists against the market and transactions conducted under the aegis of the market, trade in goods does not typically involve conflict since each party to the trade gives up something he wants less for something he wants more. After a trade has taken place the utility of each trader is greater than it was before. The perfectly competitive system, far from being a model of conflicting rivalries, is a system for coordinating the economic choices of individuals so that by appropriate trades they can reach the highest possible level of satisfaction.[8]

But the trading relationships out of which markets are formed depend on the shares of income which individuals can obtain, and herein lies a source of conflict. While it is true that trade redistributes utilities, leaving everyone better off, the struggle over income shares may under certain conditions allow some individuals and groups to gain at the expense of others. (Workers view wage rates as income and employers view them as costs; higher wage rates mean lower profit shares.) And the nature of conflict over income shares will vary with the level of income.

Let us first examine the kind of conflict which is likely to arise in a subsistence economy. Where workers are producing little above their maintenance requirements, they have few resources other than land to work with. Capital-labor ratios are extremely low and the population is engaged primarily in agrarian occupations. Since each household consumes the substantial proportion of what it produces, it has occasion to enter into trade relationships only on a local and limited basis, i.e., with neighbors or merchants. As a result, a subsistence economy is likely to consist of many small economies which have but tenuous links with one another. The output of any given household, and its share of the national income, will depend upon the quantity of land it possesses. The use of capital is not a feasible alternative because the subsistence economy does not generate a surplus for investment and, further, local custom is not likely to motivate farmers to experiment with productive methods requiring new kinds of investment. Labor is usually amply supplied by the household. But if land is a scarce factor and fully owned and occupied, then no household can improve its status except at the expense of other households. Nonetheless, with the level of income very low there will be insistent pressures for each household to try to do so, for what it needs above all is more subsistence. This is a highly conflicted situation.

One can perhaps now better appreciate the feudal system as a political institution for maintaining order. By ascribing status to the various members of the community and by associating the distribution of land with status, the feudal system was able to mobilize the full force of custom, tradition, and class in the containment of economic conflict potentially capable of debilitating society. It was, in short, a device for inducing people to accept the status quo with respect to the distribution of income—and the acceptance of the status quo might well be referred to as a consensus. Serfs may have accepted their invidious status as part of the necessary order of society; there may have been some kind of shared agreement about the necessity of separating society into different social classes. But such a consensus is a far cry from a democratic consensus which starts from the belief that the individual *qua* individual is the primary unit of society and that his preferences provide the rationale of community or governmental action. In the feudal society, the preferences of the individual were subordinated to the collectivity. Indeed, the feudal system's success as a political instrument depended upon its ability to constrain the individual aspirations that members of the subsistence economy may have harbored.

One may doubt, however, that a feudal consensus was widely held, that the member of the feudal community spontaneously and autonomously accepted the necessity of his status. In Europe, at any rate, peasant revolts were not uncommon during the feudal period. There were enough Jacqueries to lead one to believe that the conflicts nurtured by a subsistence economy with a limited land supply never lurked far behind the façade of rights, obligations, and duties formalized in feudalism. Moreover, when there were no group peasant revolts, individual peasants could and did manifest their discontent by fleeing to the towns where they were allowed a greater degree of autonomy.

Consider now a high-income economy. Working with large amounts of capital, the labor force produces more than it consumes, giving rise to an investment surplus. The high-income economy therefore is a growing economy. It is also an interdependent exchange economy. High capital-labor ratios lead to the concentration of production facilities and population. Workers can no longer consume what they produce and must enter into trade relationships in order to satisfy their wants. They thus have no alternative but to cooperate with other

members of the community who similarly labor under the necessity to trade.

But the cooperation called for here does not necessitate the
direct and immediate compromising of one person's preferences
with another. The volume of trade in the high-income economy
is so large that bargaining among individuals is too costly a
procedure for consummating the many transactions necessary to
move commodities through markets. Individual consumers take
prices as given and adjust the margins of their expenditures to
obtain the highest possible level of satisfaction. Though these
actions make possible and are made possible by the similar
actions of others, the consumers are not conscious of their dependence on the actions. It is as if the market were a vast
machine with levers,—prices—the pressing of which brought
forth goods. If some levers are harder to press than others, individuals may pull any combination of them in order to accommodate their preferences for goods to their stock of strength.
Any animus they might feel because of their inability to pull a
particular lever can be directed only against the machine and
not against the human agents who construct and stock it with
goods. In short, the market for goods in a price mechanism
allows individuals to maximize utility with their share of the
national income while it minimizes the personal hostilities which
might arise in the course of doing so.

Paralleling the coordination of individual behavior in the
marketing of goods is the coordination of behavior in the production of goods. The high-income economy with its technolog-
ically complex capital structure and socially complex division of
labor depends upon timing and sequence in the flow of resources.
Machines and assembly processes compel regularity, however
much human beings might wish to follow less exacting schedules.
Under the discipline of modern production, individuals acquire
habits of punctuality and dependability, making their behavior
more predictable and hence easier to coordinate with others.

Moreover, since consumption is so far removed from production in the high-income economy, the need for cooperation
among workers in securing their livelihood is self-evident.
Though awareness of the necessity for technological coordination

may well be submerged in the habits of industrial discipline, the need for group action in influencing the terms of employment will be consciously recognized. Since they do not own the means of production, and, more significantly, do not produce, except in rare cases, directly consumable output, workers are solely dependent on money wages in obtaining their share of the national income. They can therefore be expected to use informal and formal methods of organization in order to maximize money wages.

This, of course, brings us to an obvious source of conflict—the struggles between capital and labor, between management and trade unions. When the representatives of management and workers sit down at the bargaining table, they are engaging in a struggle for the shares of income that are created by the firm. What one side is able to gain the other loses. If, as a result of bargaining, wage rates rise, profit rates must fall, at least in the short run. One may wonder whether in essence this conflict situation is any different from the conflict over the distribution of land in a subsistence economy. But it is different and for a number of reasons.

First, the high-income economy is growing and the bargaining over shares of income does not necessarily involve the increase of one group's income at the cost of an absolute diminution of another group's income. The bargaining concerns the increment to income, that is, the distribution of the productivity gains which have accrued to the firm in the course of its operations. So long as income grows, the conflicts arising over its distribution will not be so threatening to the contestants and there will be greater opportunity for accommodating the interests of all of them.

Second, the relative urgency of the wants to be satisfied by a high-income economy is not so great as in a subsistence economy.[9] Conflict is therefore more negotiable and its occurrence does not pose the threat to the stability of society that it does where the stakes involved are higher.[10] Finally, the high-income economy increases the number of dimensions in which bargaining takes place, thus increasing the possibilities of amicable settlement. Wage rates are but one factor. The length of the working day, the conditions of labor, the number of days of paid and unpaid vacation, retirement benefits, and so on, will also be fair game in negotiations. As the number of relevant considerations increases, so do the opportunities for trades and compromises among them which will prove satisfactory to the contesting parties. In short, with the scope of bargaining broader there are more possible routes to settlement.

We can now relate these contrasting patterns of economic conflict in the subsistence and the high-income economies to the problem of creating a democratic consensus. In the subsistence economy where production and consumption are intimately and directly associated and where land is the most important resource, economic conflict is potentially so debilitating that a stable society cannot tolerate it. Social institutions, such as feudalism to which we alluded previously, may then have to perform the function of containing and restraining conflict by proscribing some kind of behavior and generally prescribing the norms of conventional conduct. These proscriptions and prescriptions, however, achieve their purpose by inducing individuals to accept the inevitability of subsistence and the social and economic relationships built upon it. It will then be difficult, if not impossible, for a consensus to arise which is based on a belief in rational individual conduct. For here the very harshness of the economic problem prevents people from breaking out of the conventional mold. In such a world people's loyalties are likely to be focused on family, clan, or manor because the identity of production and consumption seals them off from a larger community. To the extent that parochial loyalties provide the dominant stabilizing values in a person's life, he will be inclined to be hostile and suspicious of other communities which do not conform to the familial characteristics of his own group. Subsistence economies produce blood feuds and vendettas more easily than they produce a widely shared consensus on values which cut across family and local commitments.

In the high-income economy, however, though the economic problem persists, it is not so ineluctably tied up with the struggle for existence. Conflicts over shares of income may be brought to full light without threatening the survival of the society, and individuals may be permitted to seek consciously for ways and means of resolving them. Thus society, instead of trying to repress economic conflicts within the matrix of its social institutions, may try to erect new institutions capable of reconciling opposing interests when and where they occur. The institution of collective bargaining, for instance, does not repress conflict, but establishes orderly procedures and rules for mediating it. It does not prevent conflict, it assuages it. If one may be permitted to draw upon psychoanalytic concepts for an analogy, the repression of economic conflicts in the subsistence economy induces a kind of neurosis which alternately yields supine subservience to convention and authority and violent revolt (Jacqueries and so on). The overt recognition of these conflicts in the high-income economy allows individuals to understand them, recognize them for what they are, and make a rational adjustment to them.

The fashioning of institutions for resolving conflict is immeasurably aided by the destructive impact the high-income economy has on parochialism. We have already mentioned its effect in coordinating the activity of individuals as consumers and producers. This diminishes the importance of the indigenous values of households in motivating behavior by bringing into the household a larger community with its greater emphasis on universal values and goals. Having been disciplined to the requirements of the industrial order, individuals are all the more ready to accept the rules and procedures which are worked out to accommodate the conflict which must rise in the struggle for income shares. Oddly enough, conflict between labor and management may be a major vehicle for promoting a stabilizing consensus in society, for it can lead to the acceptance by the contending parties of the ground rules under which the contest will be conducted.

Moreover, the demonstration of the efficacy of accommodating conflicting interests in one context yields external economies elsewhere. The settlement of the differences of labor and management in the give and take of collective bargaining establishes a presumption in favor of compromise as a value relevant to other phases of life. Where collective bargaining is successful one may expect the dissemination of attitudes and expectations which are favorable to the successful functioning of democratic political organization. For it is easier to maintain intransigent, hostile, and irreconcilable views about one's opponent when one does not have to negotiate with him. Though far from conclusive evidence in support of this contention, the experience of the German Social Democratic Party in the period prior to World War I is certainly suggestive. No party was more militant in its hostility to capitalism and capitalists, no party was more dedicated to the revolution and the destruction of the bourgeoisie, and no party had greater support among the working classes. Yet with the rise of income in the last quarter of the nineteenth century and the growth of the trade union movement, the revolutionary ardor of German Social Democracy noticeably abated. The trade unions had come to have too great a stake in the existing order and its members were finding that they could win many objectives by negotiation and compromise. Without the intervention of World War I the German political system might have evolved even further on the road to democracy.

In the light of this discussion it seems abundantly clear that in answer to the question raised previously democracy is not a "free" political system. The requirements of rationality and consensus cannot be obtained under all social-economic conditions. They most certainly will not hold in a subsistence economy; they *may* hold in a high-income economy. This poses the problem which is the central concern of this book: how may economic growth which is the process by which an economy passes from a subsistence to a high-income status democratize political systems which initially are nondemocratic? We noted in the previous chapter that during the industrialization of the western world in the nineteenth century economic growth seemed to have this effect. Will it also have this effect in the twentieth century? May we say that the creation of high-income economies today *will* bring in its wake the requisites of democracy? In order to develop systematic answers to these quesions, we turn in the next chapter to a consideration of economic growth and its political implications.

Chapter 3

The Economics and
Politics of Growth

ECONOMIC GROWTH may be defined as the process which gives rise to an increase in per capita, or average, income, Admittedly, this definition will not do for everyone. The analyst who is trying to measure economic welfare may complain that income is much too broad an aggregate and that two economies with identical per capita income may nonetheless produce disparate welfare, depending on how each allocates income among the sectors producing it. Others will object that since the definition is couched in terms of averages, it implies that those economies which have increased aggregate output, but then have had to support a larger population, in consequence have not grown. Surely, these people would argue, an economy that is able to feed, clothe, and shelter more people is not standing still, even though it is not able to raise the average income of households.

However valid these objections are for some purposes, for the problems with which this book is concerned they are not critical. In the previous chapter it was observed that the democratic political system will not function in subsistence economies, but may function in economies with high per capita income. The concern here is with the political consequences of the economic transition from one stage to another, rather than with the measurement of economic welfare. To repeat, then, economic growth in this discussion will mean the process generating increases in per capita income.

The proximate requirements for economic growth may be stated quite briefly: increased employment of resources per capita and/or increased efficiency in the employment of existing resources. The spelling out of these requirements in greater detail reveals why they are not easy to achieve.

In order to increase per capita income, an economy may increase the quantity of land, labor, or capital that it utilizes per capita. Given the supplies of other resources, if there is an increase in the quantity of mineral resources (land) available to an economy, per capita output may increase. If the supply of labor from a given population increases because the existing labor force chooses to work longer hours or because a change in preferences induces previously idle members of the population to work, output may similarly increase. Finally, per capita output will rise if the quantity of capital with which the labor force works increases.

In contrast to these forces which affect output by increasing per capita input, there are those which do so by increasing the efficiency with which given inputs are utilized.[1] Innovations alter production functions by changing the amount of land, labor, or capital required per unit of output. These may take the form of land-saving, labor-saving, or capital-saving invention. In any event, output will be increased either by the industry adapting the invention or by other industries which utilize the resources released by the innovating industry.

Whether growth is achieved through the increased use of inputs per capita or through increased efficiency, one process stands out as being crucially important—investment. Investment may be defined as an addition to plant and equipment and/or inventories. It involves the production of that type of output which expands the capacity of an economy. Obviously, when an economy grows through the accumulation (the increase) of capital, investment is taking place. Perhaps less obviously, investment also is basic to growth through an increase of the other resources—land and labor.

Normally, land and labor do not increase autonomously. They become available in larger quantities because of investment activities. The development of new supplies of oil resources is preceded by geological survey and oil prospecting. The discovery of oil must be followed by investment in pipelines or other transportation facilities before the oil can be produced and marketed. The opening of new agricultural land depends upon investment in roads and fences and frequently in irrigation or in drainage. Similarly, the labor supply is affected by investment in transportation, education, and housing. It may even influence employment by changing the terms of choice between work and leisure. That is to say, investment in home laundry equipment may so lighten the household duties of women that they look to employment as a means of relieving boredom. Finally, investment activates the technological changes which increase the efficiency with which given supplies of resources are utilized in production.

Since investment plays such an active role in generating the appearance of those forces which meet the proximate requirements for economic growth, it marks out the specific path of development that an economy will follow. If the agricultural or industrial or export sectors of an economy are to lead its advance from subsistence to above-subsistence status, investment must give rise to the concrete additions to capital which will direct the flow of resources to the leading sector. Agricultural productivity cannot rise unless resources are applied to land reform, the production of fertilizers and plows, or experimentation with new strains of crops. Investment, in other words, is the active ingredient in economic growth to which other forces more or less adjust. Where it leads, in a manner of speaking, others will follow.

§   *The Rationale of Investment and the Nature of Entrepreneurial Activity*

The paramount importance of investment in economic growth necessitates further inquiry about its rationale and the conditions which make it possible. Who invests and why? What is the nature of the decision-making process which induces some individuals to commit resources to the expansion of future output? Do all investment decisions involve uncertainty? How are the benefits of investment distributed?

In attempting to answer these questions it will be convenient to distinguish between private and public motives for investment. Assuming that a private individual maximizes profit, he will invest if he anticipates that his income will increase at least as much as the added costs he incurs. One can imagine the hypothetical entrepreneur who contemplates the purchase of a new asset, calculating its present value by discounting at an appropriate rate the future income stream it will yield and its costs and comparing the rate of return with the prevailing rate for borrowing capital. He will then invest as long as the internal rate of return—the marginal efficiency of investment—is equal to or greater than the market rate of interest.

The public motivation for investment is similar, but with this difference: a public authority, in calculating the feasibility of an investment project, balances social income against social costs and will carry out the project only if he expects a greater return *to society* from resources in the contemplated project than in alternative uses. Where the private investor is maximizing values derived from his own utility function, the public investor is maximizing values derived from a social welfare function.[2]

The distinction between the private and public motive for investment is necessary because there are particular kinds of output, crucial to the process of economic growth, that may not be produced in great enough quantity if one relies solely on private motivation. Some kinds of output yield income over such a diffuse area of economic activity that it is difficult to calculate, though in aggregate it may be quite large. This is the problem of external economies in production.[3] Where they exist, private entrepreneurs cannot easily internalize a rate of return because they have no way of calculating the net income stream which the asset in question will yield. Education is a case in point. The expansion of plant and equipment in primary and secondary schools and in universities enables society to increase the supply of skilled mechanics, technicians and engineers, professional and administrative personnel. This increased supply does not yield a rate of return to educational institutions, but to the many industries which have occasion to benefit from the skills. An increase in the ratio of doctors to population may be expected to raise the standards of public health. Industry may gain advantages through lower rates of absenteeism or a heightened capacity for exacting and sustained labor. Similarly, transportation, housing and what may generally be called social overhead capital yields external economies which inhibit their production by private entrepreneurs.

While some kinds of output spread external economics throughout many industries, other kinds of output impose external diseconomies on society. The production and testing of atomic bombs affect unborn generations through the genetic impact of the fallout on the present generation. Large-scale production in the steel industry concentrates population in urban centers, which apparently gives rise to higher proportions of juvenile delinquency. Just as public motivation for investment may have advantages in capturing the external economies of production, so private motivation for investment may have some advantages in excluding the external diseconomies of production. We shall come back to this point later. Here we can just indicate briefly what we have in mind. Some kinds of investment cause dislocations and human strains which, if given full consideration in the context of a social welfare function placing great weight on "human values," might lead to cancellation of projects on the grounds that the anticipated social benefits are not large enough to outweigh the anticipated social costs. Yet the projects might be crucial for economic growth. Under these circumstances, private investment, which would reduce the range of costs calculated, might be a stimulus to economic growth.

Though private and public investment are motivated by different rationales, they both focus on the expansion of future output and, therefore, have characteristics in common. First of all, to greater or less extent the decision to invest is made in the face of uncertainty. This is least in the expansion of capacity called forth by the demand for existing output and greatest in the creation of capacity for producing new output. Where there already is a market for a commodity, price and cost data provide entrepreneurs with clues about the future shape of the market. Where there is no such market and the entrepreneur has to predict, for example, the state of consumer preferences which are as yet unrevealed, the uncertainty attendant upon the decision to invest is all the greater.

One may infer from its inherent uncertainty that investment requires a person with rather uncommon, if not unique, characteristics. He must have the capacity to calculate his chances of success on the basis of signals that the existing economic environment flashes to him. He must have the ability to obtain and organize the resources for constructing additional or new plant and equipment. Above all, he must have confidence that the future will validate his present choice of action, which is to say that he believes that he can manipulate the environment to achieve the ends he has set for himself. We enumerate these characteristics because they suggest that entrepreneurial talents will not be widespread in any society and will be particularly limited in a subsistence society.[4] For the latter tends to obviate problems of uncertainty by adhering to customary or traditional patterns of performance. The typical individual in a subsistence economy then will not be accustomed to change, and still less to the notion that he can influence the shape of the environment by his actions.

The inference that entrepreneurs are a minority group is further supported by a second characteristic that private and public investment have in common, namely their dependence on the withdrawing of resources from present consumption. The restriction of consumption, that is saving, raises issues which are particularly germane to our analysis, for they relate to problems of conflicts in preferences. In a subsistence economy, the members of the community will necessarily try to consume all output produced. No matter how they may feel about the virtues of allocating resources to investment, they have no choice, given the immediacy of the struggle for existence, but to maximize present consumption. In short, their propensity to consume approaches unity. Yet growth requires that resources be released from present consumption for allocation to investment.

How can this impasse be surmounted? In general there are two answers to the question. One, income can be distributed in such a way that a disproportionate share is placed at the disposal of those who will be willing to refrain from consuming it. This method, of course, involves the generation of saving through an unequal distribution of income. Two, government may impose taxes on households which reduce the level of disposable income available for consumption. Neither with the one alternative nor the other does the mass of individuals make an unencumbered choice between consumption and saving. In both cases they are forced to save, in the one through the medium of capitalists, in the other through the medium of government officials.

Let us restate the problem now in terms that will bring out the essential preference conflict involved in growth at low levels of income. In a subsistence economy, the time preference of the overwhelming majority of the population will be so high that no monetary reward, however great, can induce them to forego present consumption. If growth is to take place, some members of the community with a low enough time preference to allow them to calculate the advantages of future versus present output must gain title to resources. In short, the preferences of a minority must take precedence over those of a majority.

The crucial question then becomes the following: Where does the entrepreneurial minority with the appropriately low time preference and the requisite abilities to cope with the organizational problems of expanding future output in the face of uncertainty come from? Is there some random process of selection which draws entrepreneurs from all ranks of society? Or is there some kind of social constraint which singles out particular groups for bearing the responsibilities of entrepreneurial activity? Economics, as a deductive system based on certain assumptions about behavior, has no answers to these questions— or, rather, it suggests an answer that very few people would accept, that entrepreneurship is an alternative freely open to anyone who can acquire title to resources in excess of his consumption needs. But this formal statement explains very little, and it is abundantly clear that one must turn to the historical evidence for clues to the answer.

§ *Noneconomic Influences on Entrepreneurial Behavior*

Historical evidence strongly suggests the need for some kind of force exogenous to the economy that reinforces the incentives for entrepreneurship which arise from within the economy. We shall cite two bits of evidence from different societies at widely different points of time.

During the Industrial Revolution in England from the middle of the eighteenth to the middle of the nineteenth centuries, a disproportionate number of the innovations in the textile, iron and steel, power, and transportation industries was carried forward by Protestant dissenters who were not members of the Anglican Church and accordingly were denied access to many privileged positions in English social life. One may place two interpretations on this prominence of dissenters. One, already implied, is that the disabilities suffered by dissenters, their inability, for example, to matriculate at Oxford or Cambridge and acquire the privileges of professional status, compelled them to turn to activities in which they were not disbarred because of their religious beliefs. Manufacturing and industry offered them untrammeled scope for their abilities and the means of gaining status in Britain through the accumulation of wealth. The significant exogenous factor in this interpretation was the minority position imposed upon dissenters by the state-sanctioned privileges of the Anglican majority. A second view, and one preeminently associated with Max Weber,[5] is that through their religious training dissenters had internalized a set of values which induced them to accumulate and to acquire wealth as evidence of their elect status in the eyes of God. In the manner of David Riesman's inner-directed man, they pursued their goal with a single-minded devotion which allowed them to overcome the barriers set in their way by an environment hostile to their efforts.[6]

Whichever interpretation is the more reasonable or relevant, either one can be understood as the lowering of the time preference of an identifiable social group in English society. The subsequent effect was that the supply of people willing to trade present consumption for the possibilities of greater future output increased. While greater future output may be viewed simply as a conventional economic end—the desire to expand one's level of consumption—its force in motivating what at a time of low income appears like deviant behavior is much greater when it is reinforced by some value or goal inspired by institutions outside the economic system.

Now consider for the moment post-revolutionary Russia. Unlike England, the supply of autonomous and indigenous entrepreneurs was very limited and one can say that the entrepreneurial function was performed by the state through the organization of economic activity in the five-year plans. There is very little doubt that the passage of the Soviet economy through the five-year plans imposed on the members of Soviet society a greater sacrifice than they would have voluntarily chosen. The leaders of the Communist Party had such a low time preference that they were willing to sacrifice the present generation of Russian citizens to future generations.

This is difficult to explain solely in terms of economic criteria, but if one introduces the exogenous variable of Marxian ideology the behavior of communist entrepreneurs appears more comprehensible. Marxian ideology has built into it a progressive ethic which implies a low time preference. According to the doctrine, as society evolves through its various stages, people are becoming better off. The optimal welfare for society consists of achieving the highest stage of development, namely Communism. Thus when he evaluates the future, the Marxist does not assume that there is reasonable choice between the present and the future, involving different time paths of consumption and production. He *knows* that the future is better regardless of the preferences of individuals and therefore is willing to evaluate it as if there were a very low rate of discount. Clearly ideology of this sort was just as much of a stimulant to investment in Soviet Russia as the Protestant Ethic was to investment in England.

To summarize: While economic growth may be caused either by increased utilization of inputs per capita or increased efficiency, investment is the dominant and central force in the process. Whether undertaken by public authority or private individuals, it leads an economy along the path of development by allocating resources to the expansion of capacity in particular industries and sectors. Though the economic system itself throws up cues and signals which facilitate the making of investment decisions and offers enticements and rewards to the entrepreneurs who are able to carry these decisions out successfully, a great thrust for investment comes from outside the economic system in the form of forces which create particular minority social groups with low time preferences and a compulsive need to perform the duties of entrepreneurship.

§ *Economic Obstacles to the Industrial Transformation*

With these notions about investment before us, we come now to the crucial issue of economic growth. We know that a subsistence economy hardly invests more than the amount necessary to maintain the value of its meager capital stock, reflecting a set of social institutions which maximize traditional and customary values. We also know that high-income economies invest a high proportion of their national income and have acquired the kinds of institutions and attitudes which more or less automatically sustain the saving and investment processes essential to growth. How, then, in the words of Professor Lewis, does an economy change from a situation in which it is investing less than 5 per cent of its national income to one in which it is investing more than 12 per cent?[7] Or, to quote Professor Rostow, how does an economy achieve "the take-off into self-sustained growth"?[8] The take-off, or the period in which the net investment rate of an economy for the first time accelerates to a higher level, is of considerable importance to our analysis of growth's impact on the emergence of democratic political institutions. We shall therefore treat it with special care.

Let us first consider the basis of the ratios which Professor Lewis uses to distinguish the subsistence from the growing economy. An economy with a population growing at the rate of 2 per cent per annum and a marginal capital-output ratio of 3–1 would have to invest 6 per cent of its net national product if per capita income were just to be maintained, and, of course, a larger proportion if per capita income were to increase. If, however, the rate of population growth were 1 per cent per annum, the economy would only have to invest 3 per cent of the net national product to maintain per capita income. On the other hand, if the rate of population growth were 2 per cent per annum and the marginal capital-output ratio were 4–1, then the economy would have to invest at the rate of 8 per cent to maintain itself. Professor Lewis' investment ratios, therefore, are put forward on what seemed to him reasonable assumptions about rates of population growth and marginal capital-output ratios likely to prevail in contemporary underdeveloped economies.

While these figures seem plausible, they are difficult to confirm empirically because of the problem of measurement, particularly the problem of measuring capital-output ratios.[9] Nonetheless, the capital-output concept is a useful means for suggesting the dimensions of the tasks confronting an economy which intends to rise above the subsistence status. What is at issue here is the amount of investment that is required on the average to produce a unit of output. The lower the capital-output ratio the more rapidly a given amount of investment will give rise to increased output.[10] The concept understandably has strong attraction for planners and others concerned with problems of growth acceleration, for if they could know the capital-output ratio for the economy, they would have a strong clue about the proportion of the community's resources, given the rate of population growth, they would withdraw from consumption and allocate to investment in order to achieve a given rate of growth of per capita income.

The capital-output ratio has undoubtedly raised expectations of planners and others only to frustrate them with the difficulties of measurement. This is hardly surprising for it is a massive aggregate which, when disaggregated, reveals its dependence on technology that covers the whole gamut of productive methods from those that are labor-intensive to those that are capital-intensive. Moreover, the capital-ouptut ratio is likely to be a highly unstable relationship because it varies cyclically with the level of income and employment and with the skill of the labor force in maintaining capital assets.

If there are reasons for being doubtful about the meaningfulness or usefulness of attempts to measure capital-output ratios at a given moment in time, there is no reason why one cannot apply the concept in mapping the course of an economy's development over longer period of time. In particular, it would appear to be a reasonable hypothesis that when a subsistence economy enters upon a stage of development in which its rate of net investment rises to a permanently higher level, marginal capital-output ratios at first rise and then subsequently fall. The reasons for suggesting this hypothesis are as follows. Technical capital coefficients tend to be highest in the transportation, communication, and utility sectors of an economy and lowest in manufacturing. This is to say, it takes a greater amount of capital to produce one unit of transportation than it does to produce one unit of manufactured goods. When, however, an economy first starts to grow it may allocate to transportation and the other utilities a disproportionate share of its investment. This is done in order to construct the social overhead capital which provides manufacturing concerns with the means for marketing output and employing inputs. Accordingly, one would expect capital-output ratios to rise during this period of utility construction. Subsequently when this sector of the economy does not require a disproportionate share of the community's investment, the output of sectors with lower capital-output ratios may experience a relatively greater expansion, thus leading to a decline in the overall capital-output ratio. Furthermore, during the early stage of growth when the labor force has not yet acquired the habits of industrial discipline, a given stock of capital will not yield its maximum output because of absenteeism, excessive turnover, and because of improper and inadequate capital maintenance. These problems will be resolved as the industrial labor force comes of age, leading to labor's more efficient utilization of the existing capital stock.

If this hypothesis is correct, it suggests that "the take-off" is characterized not only by a proportionate rise in net investment, but by a period in which there is a longer than "normal" wait for the appearance of the increased output contingent upon investment. Consider what this means in more concrete terms. During the take-off, or what conventionally is called an industrial revolution, railways, canals, roads, harbors, steel plants, and other facilities essential to an interdependent industrial economy are being constructed. The limit to the development of the economy is the availability of saving rather than the existence of investment opportunities.

Indeed, so great is the pressure on resources for the construction of industrial and social capital that not all demands can be satisfied simultaneously. Something has to give. In the face of capital scarcities some projects will be postponed, or, if undertaken, constructed with materials that economize capital. Thus it may be the case, for example, that urban housing is not expanded at a fast enough rate to take care of the influx of workers from the rural sector of the economy leading to overcrowded conditions in cities. Or perhaps additional housing is constructed from flimsy, nondurable materials which deteriorate rapidly. Urban communities may neglect their health and recreational services. Factories may be constructed with inadequate safety devices.

While the economy is cutting corners on some kinds of investment and refraining from other kinds, the investment being undertaken yields its return slowly. This is attributable partly to the technical constraint under which utility construction labors, namely high capital coefficients, and partly to the external economies which it must release before society benefits from it.

A few comments about this latter point are in order. Though the construction of a railway may well increase the community's satisfaction directly by giving it a sense of accomplishment and an awareness of its greater opportunities for mobility, the real pay-off depends on the increased output of goods it makes possible.[11] By reducing transport costs, railways increase the size of the market, inducing the expansion of existing output and the production of new output as new resources for the first time become marketable. But these latter output effects do not take place immediately. If they did, the construction of railways would not create external economies; they would merely take advantage of the existing degree of market specialization (as when railways are constructed between well developed commercial communities). In an economy on the threshold of an industrial revolution, however, the expansion of the rail network lowers transport costs for industries yet to be built and for labor skills yet to be trained. Until the transport-using output is produced, the output of consumers' goods cannot increase. But each mile of track laid adds to the net national product. In short, the expansion of consumable output will be delayed pending the diffusion of external economies throughout the economy.

§   *The Population Barrier to Growth*

The take-off during a society's industrial revolution is widely recognized as requiring an extraordinary effort on the part of the society. Such terms as "the big push," "the hump," or "critical minimum effort" have become part of the jargon of economists and others who concern themselves with problems of economic development.[12] The most commonly discussed barrier to growth, the surmounting of which seems to require the expenditure of a concentrated dose of social energy, is the possible population explosion it induces. In a subsistence economy birth rates and mortality rates are both relatively high. If with the onset of economic growth mortality rates decline before birth rates, then the rate of population growth will increase. If it increases rapidly enough, it may abort per capita income increases and, indeed, may even lower per capita income. The reasons why output growth and population growth may be functionally related are well known. The increased production of subsistence goods such as grain may lower mortality rates by improving diets and increasing resistance to disease. The draining of swamps and the use of DDT reduce the incidence of malaria and yellow fever. Increased educational opportunity facilitates the spread of higher standards of public health and hygiene. While the expansion of the output of consumers' goods and/or investment goods may decrease the mortality rate, the birth rate, at least for a time, remains insensitive to these changes. Only when households come to recognize family limitation as a desirable goal and have the knowledge for and means of doing so will birth rates fall. Since this view represents a fundamental change and reorientation of values, economic growth can be expected to induce it, if ever it does, only after the passage of a considerable length of time. In the meantime, mortality rates decline and population explodes.

§ *The Welfare Problem During the Industrial Revolution*

The take-off, then, raises a formidable standard of living, or what for shorthand purposes we shall call a welfare problem. This early stage is in contrast to subsequent stages of development when capital-output ratios may be declining, certainly not increasing, and the external economies of utility construction have been appropriated, thus rendering the expansion of the output of consumers' goods relatively easy. The take-off stage is characterized by forces which tend to prevent marked improvement in the standard of living of the masses of people.

"Standard of living" and "welfare" are extremely slippery concepts, and at this point we must make clear what our argument purports to say; equally important, we must clarify what it does not say. We are not using the standards of modern welfare economics in making this assertion about the standard of living of the masses during the industrial revolution. Though welfare economics has the great virtue of rigor and compels one to distinguish between scientific and value judgments, it so circumscribes the concept of welfare that it becomes useless. The Paretian optimality criterion enjoins the making of positive statements about welfare except where it can be shown that an anticipated change in the organization of resources improves the condition of at least one person while leaving no one worse off, a restriction, incidentally, that economists have conspicuously honored in the breach. Since interpersonal comparisons of utility lack scientific objectivity, it is impossible to balance one person's gain against another person's loss and derive a net change in social welfare. In the very strictest sense, without making some sort of ethical postulate, one can say nothing about a situation in which hundreds gain and only one loses. Accordingly, we use the welfare concept in an old-fashioned sense, basing it on the utilitarian ethic that each person counts equally, i.e., each person's capacity to enjoy the fruits of income is the same.

Given the utilitarian idea of welfare, there are three factors affecting it which we consider particularly relevant to our analysis, two relating to supply conditions and one to demand conditions. Consider first the level of income and employment. If a subsistence economy fully employed available resources including labor and produced enough only to provide the members of society with a minimal standard of living, then a rise in the rate of net investment would imply a decrease in the output of consumers' goods and a decline in short-run welfare.[13] For in order to expand the capacity of the economy, resources would have to be saved, withdrawn from present consumption uses, leading to an absolute diminution in the output of standard-of-living commodities. The assumption of full employment, however, does not appear to be especially valid in the conditions of a subsistence economy. First of all, there is likely to be a surfeit of population with many workers unable to find full-time employment under the existing organization of production. Second, many workers who are ostensibly employed may not be contributing much, if anything, to output. In other words, there may be an inefficient utilization of resources in that the marginal product of labor in some occupations is zero, or even less than zero.[14] Unemployed labor, whether overt or covert in inefficient employments, permits the expansion of investment without an absolute decrease in the output of consumption goods. Railways, roads, or canals may be constructed by workers who other-

wise would add little to the output of welfare goods. The proportionate rise of net investment, therefore, comes out of an increasing rather than a given income.

While the conditions of aggregate investment during the
industrial revolution do not preclude increases of welfare, the
allocation of investment—the second supply factor—raises some
problems for which there is no easy solution. As indicated previously, capital scarcities during the period will compel the
cutting back or holding back of certain types of investment projects. The priorities given to competing projects, however, have a
grave impact on welfare. Suppose, for example, that urban housing and recreational facilities receive a low priority and therefore are not constructed in large enough quantity to keep pace
with the demands of the growing industrial labor force. If, however, at the same time there is an increase in the supply of subsistence goods, say bread and cotton cloth, are people better or
worse off? This is the so-called index number problem, the
magnitude of which is likely to be greater, the greater the structural changes which an economy is undergoing.[15] When there are
marked changes in the availability of commodities and their
relative prices, the meaningfulness of the value aggregates which
one might compare before and after is open to question. The
industrial revolution is such a period of marked change. The
industrial-manufacturing sector with its particular configuration of commodities grows relative to the agrarian sector with
its configuration of commodities. Does the peasant turned worker who moves from country to town, trading less crowded housing and inferior clothes for more crowded housing and superior
clothes, improve his status?

One answer that immediately comes to mind is that so
long as the move from country to town is voluntary, individuals
must think that their status will improve. Otherwise they would
remain where they were. The evidence of history in this connection is quite impressive. Since the start of the industrial revolution in the western world there has been an irrevocable
drift of population to the towns and cities. People in diverse
societies with varying customs and traditions all seem to agree

on one thing: They prefer to look at the country and live in the city.

In raising this question we have introduced the third factor affecting welfare, namely the subjective element of demand, preferences, and expectations. The person who decides to move from country to town has formed some kind of image of the new universe he intends to inhabit. It is composed of information, misinformation, superstitions, rumors about reality, and thus contains the ingredients which form his expectations. A number of things may happen to people's expectations during the period of the industrial revolution. As workers move into the industrial community, their image of reality more adequately reflects conditions as they are and they become aware of the shortcomings of their new environment in concrete terms. Prior to moving, rumors of high wages may have subordinated rumors about crowded housing facilities. After moving, high wages become a particular bundle of goods and services that urban society affords the workers. If the welfare component of this bundle of goods and services during the industrial revolution is constrained by investment priorities necessitated by growth, then the expectations formed at one remove from the industrial-urban environment are likely to be frustrated.

This might not be a matter of great moment if it were safe to assume that expectations of people were quickly and easily adjusted to circumstances as they found them. When housing turned out to be worse than expected, if people simply devalued the housing component in their utility function, there might be no difficulty. But this is most unlikely. Indeed, expectations may be raised under the influence of new preferences and demands acquired in the industrial-urban community. We are referring to the impact of the so-called demonstration effect. As first formulated by Duesenberry, the demonstration effect related to the propensity of people when confronted by a decline in disposable income to try to maintain the highest standard of living they had attained in the past.[16] Here it refers to the tendency of people to acquire higher consumption aspirations when they come in contact with a standard of living higher than that to which they have been accustomed. The urban-industrial community is an active disseminator of the demonstration effect. If people live in squalid and cramped gerrybuilt houses, they can observe others who live in sumptuous quarters. If they cannot pay the price of admission to the theater or other forms of urban entertainment, they at least know something about the entertainment that is available. To put it another way, in the urban community the inequality of wealth and income is more visible than in the rural community and therefore acts as a greater stimulant in the formation of new preferences among the less privileged members of society.

The welfare problem of the industrial revolution may be contrasted to the problems which J. K. Galbraith sees afflicting the Affluent Society. In the latter the basic wants have been more or less satisfied and production is geared to the satisfaction of wants of less urgency. Since the capacity of the economy to produce goods and services is so great, there is a marked tendency for production to run ahead of the wants of the community. Industry therefore must use increasing amounts of resources on marketing, advertising, and promotional campaigns in order to induce people to want the commodities it produces. In such an economy goods are often designed to catch the eye and compel attention rather than to fulfill the functional requirements of consumption; automobiles stress fins and chrome rather than safety.

On the other hand, the opposite problem holds for the economy entering upon the early stages of development. Wants increase faster than the output of consumer goods, for while the structural capital of an industrial economy is being built, the wants of the community grow without the special effort and blandishments of the advertisers. So basic are they that when people become aware of higher standards in their satisfaction, they can quickly revise their preferences and acquire greater expectations. One can easily see now why the welfare problem at this stage of development is so formidable. If, for instance, one chooses real wages as his index of welfare and shows that during this period real wages rose, one cannot conclude necessarily that the state of well being of the population has improved. For if the rise in real wages is accompanied by an even greater rise in expectations and standards, workers by their own subjective estimate might even be worse off.

We are not trying to resurrect the famous Marxian immiserization *(Verelendung)* hypothesis. The hypothesis probably had some validity during the period Marx observed English capitalist institutions,[17] but he projected an observation about a particular stage of development without qualification or reservation to the future course of capitalist growth. We limit our hypothesis about welfare to the formative period of an industrial economic order. Moreover, there is a considerable difference between welfare being impaired by a decline in the physical volume of subsistence goods available to society and by a rise in the subjective estimate of the population with regard to what they would like or think they should have. Where the one may cause ennui, despair, and apathy, the other may give rise to active and persistent attempts to obtain higher rewards in the system. This latter reaction is of special interest to us.

§ *The Individual and Collectivist Response to the Welfare Problem*

Another aspect of the "hump" implicit in our discussion of the welfare problem during the industrial revolution suggests an important link between economic growth and the problems of the political system. If wants expand more rapidly than the output of consumers' goods, it is reasonable to expect that the people whose expectations are frustrated and who do not receive what they think they are entitled to will attempt to do something about it. This is all the more true because as markets encompass a larger part of a person's existence they stimulate a kind of rationality and calculating behavior which is not so typical of the subsistence economy with its routinized activity and deference to traditional standards of behavior. Generally, one may distinguish two quite different responses. One, individuals might accept the economic order as they see it with the goals it represents and the drives it maximizes and try to acquire the perquisites of the privileged members of society by their own individual efforts. If entrepreneurship is the route to wealth, so be it. Alternatively, individuals might band together in organizations in order to improve their status in society. Working through trade unions, they might try to raise wage rates and influence other conditions of labor through the exercise of their collective strength. Similarly, they might engage in political activity to achieve a change in the institutional environment favorable to their interests, e.g., minimum wage legislation.

Though the first response is the fabled path taken by Richard Arkwright, Matthew Boulton, James Watt, Andrew Carnegie, John D. Rockefeller, and other less illustrious capitalists, it is not open to the majority of those who are enmeshed in the growth process. Entrepreneurship requires a rare combination of qualities, the capacity to evaluate the uncertainties of the future, a belief in one's ability to manipulate and control the environment, and command of scarce capital resources. These qualities only fall to a minority. The majority, therefore, may react to the frustrations of the industrial revolution by turning to some kind of collective action.

This does not mean that every member of the industrial labor force becomes a participating member of the labor movement. It only means that if they are going to respond actively to the frustrations and discontents of the period, they are more likely to turn to collective action than to individual entrepreneurship. Most people in fact may do nothing at all but knuckle down to the regimen of an industrial existence. Moreover, collective action is not natural and spontaneous any more than entrepreneurship is. It is a learned type of behavior. When workers first join a labor force they may neither perceive the need for collective action nor have the necessary forbearance to abide by the constraints that organization imposes on the individual. Thus we are not asserting that a labor movement necessarily rises full grown with the start of the industrial revolution, but only that there will be found dissatisfaction and discontent among the workers which may stimulate the organization of trade unions and political action groups.

§   *The Political Problem of the Industrial Revolution*

We are now at a point in our analysis where we can state the essence of the political problem raised by the process of economic growth. Whatever the specific institutional factors which trigger it, a small group of men assume responsibility for the investment projects which mark out the path of the economy's development. While this group has first claim to the increased output generated in the early stages of growth, a far larger number of people is thrust into circumstances where their wants start to run ahead of the capacity of the economy to satisfy them. The resulting discontent and dissidence may manifest itself in disorders—riots, strikes, mob demonstrations—which threaten the political stability of the society. Governmental leaders, therefore, as a necessary part of maintaining the prerogatives of office and political power, must deal with these disorders and attempt to maintain social order in the community. But in performing this task there is one thing they cannot do, if they are concerned with facilitating the continued growth of the economy: they cannot try to solve the political problem by acceding to the demands of the masses of workers and granting them rights commensurate with the rights of the privileged members of society. For growth at the early critical stage of the take-off is a discriminatory process which favors the few who are able to take the steps necessary to raise the rate of net investment. If the political system chooses to support the consumption goals of the many against the growth goals of the few, then growth, if not aborted, will surely be slowed down.

Suppose, for example, that trade unions are able to organize effectively as rapidly as workers move into the urban-industrial sector of the economy and therefore can bring pressure on entrepreneurs for increased wages. Profit rates will fall diminishing the volume of retained earnings which at early stages of development very likely are the most important source of saving. Or, perhaps more significantly, suppose trade unions are able to impose on entrepreneurs rules and regulations with respect to the employment of workers which inhibit the ability of the former to experiment with different uses of capital. Growth through increased efficiency in the utilization of resources might then be so far restricted. Again, consider a political branch of a labor movement which is well organized to pressure government into granting workers the many benefits of the welfare state. The resulting old age, health, and unemployment measures may divert resources away from the construction of the utilities essential for subsequent growth through their effect on the distribution of income. If taxes on entrepreneurs rise to finance these programs the funds available for the accumulation of real capital will be decreased.

Granted that the aspirations and demands of dissident workers must somehow be contained or repressed in order to preserve the conditions for further growth, how can governmental authorities be sure that the measures they take do not also kill off the democratic potential to which the organized activities of workers give rise? The subsistence economy, we have argued, cannot sustain a democratic political society and one of the things which must happen to foster development towards democracy is the dissemination of the idea that individual action does matter and that individuals can influence the state of the community through participation in political life. The dissidence and discontent of the early stages of the industrial revolution are among the influences which may lead individuals to acquire democratic attitudes. Irritated by the circumstances in which they find themselves and no longer able to believe in the immutability of an environment which is visibly changing, workers may be induced to remedy their own condition rather than accept the writ of tradition and authority. The answer to the question raised at the beginning of this paragraph, of course, is that governmental leaders at early stages of development are not themselves particularly interested in fostering the democratic potential of workers. They are not trying to create a democratic society. Rather they are trying to maximize their tenure of power by taking the steps necessary to retain office. The question then can be rephrased: How can nondemocratic governmental leaders cope with the tensions of the industrial labor force in such a way as to allow economic growth to continue to take place without destroying the democratic tendencies which growth may contain? We will seek the answer to this paradoxical question in the experience of the industrialization of the western world. First, however, we must pose a hypothesis about growth and democracy which relates the emergence of the latter to the point or period in history when the former takes place. This will be the subject of the next chapter.

Chapter 4

Industrialization, Labor
Controls, and Democracy

A HIGH-INCOME ECONOMY stimulates the development of the consensus essential to the democratic political process by maximizing the cooperative element of trade and exchange and minimizing the conflict over the distribution of income. During the take-off into economic growth, however, conflicts over the distribution of income may be exacerbated by the frustration of many people's consumption aspirations. Moreover, at this particular stage of growth, society cannot afford to yield to the consumption demands of the greater part of the population as it tries to contain these conflicts and maintain social order. In this chapter we shall examine the various controls that government can use to perform this political function in order to identify those controls most consistent with the eventual emergence of democratic political institutions. Further, a hypothesis will be put forward about the historical circumstances in which these controls are most likely to be used.

Governmental policies towards labor may be thought of as a continuum; at one end lies the policy of permissive control and at the other the policy of totalitarian control. In the first there is a minimum amount of direct and overt control of labor by government. Workers may establish friendly societies, organize trade

unions, and form political parties. The effectiveness of these independently created working-class institutions is, however, limited
by a hostile legal environment. Collective labor action is resisted
either because it circumscribes the use of labor's offensive weapons—the strike, picketing, boycott—or because its discriminates
in favor of private groups—for example, employers—who have
an interest in attenuating labor's organized strength. Yet such a
policy is nonetheless permissive in that within the constraints of
the legal environment labor organization can develop independently of the government. Membership of trade unions can
increase, and as their number and financial strength become
greater they may even exert pressure on government in order to
obtain favorable changes in the legal environment.

In the second type of policy, as opposed to the first, there is
a maximum amount of direct and overt government control of
labor. Workers have little opportunity for independent expression of discontent. They are prohibited from organizing independent unions and political parties. If they belong to working-
class organizations these are dominated by officials whose purpose
it is to train workers to the tasks and discipline of industrial
production and who, accordingly, do not serve the function of
articulating discontent. Under a policy of permissive control, independent enclaves of labor power may develop in the interstices
of the legal system, but under a policy of totalitarian control
there is no opportunity for such a development.

The labels given these two policies leave no doubt which is
more consistent with the emergence of democratic political institutions, but it is important to look beyond the labels and understand the reasons. Democracy evolves from nondemocratic society; on the face of it that is a paradoxical statement. Why should
governmental authorities who have legitimatized their political
authority on the basis of some set of non-democratic values yield
to the democratic aspirations of some members of the community,
especially since those authorities are seldom motivated by the
desire to maximize popular participation in government? Moreover, their power and tenure of office may well be threatened by
the extension of political rights to a larger group of people in
society. The question may be answered formally as follows: If in

assessing the demands for the extension of political privileges, governmental leaders calculate that they jeopardize their position of authority more by refusing to accede to the demands than by suppressing them, then they may yield to them.

The relationship of permissive labor controls to the emergence of a democratic political system may now be stated more explicitly. By allowing labor organizations some autonomy, even though circumscribing the area of their legitimate activity, permissive labor policy gives scope to the growth of groups which have an existence independent of government and may constitute a threat to the security of government leaders. In the extreme, the threat is one of revolution, but it does not have to be so dire. The important point is that the emergence of democracy is expedited by the development of autonomous groups whose members, while performing roles essential to the functioning of the community, feel strongly entitled to the political privileges presently denied them.

In contrast, totalitarian labor controls achieve their purpose by limiting the autonomy of workers and binding them to the objectives of the state. Without the opportunity to develop representative institutions for dealing with their problems, workers are not likely to acquire the skills and techniques of using their collective strength for embarrassing government. They will not acquire that feeling of moral indignation, so important to protest movements, which characterizes individuals who do not think they have rights commensurate with their responsibilities and accomplishments. If workers are treated like wards of the state, they may in fact lose the capacity for independent action and learn to behave "spontaneously" as required of them by the totalitarian labor policy.

Thus it may be seen that the labor policy that government formulates to contain the unrest characteristic of the early stages of industrial development is an important guide to the type of political community that may eventually emerge.

The hypothesis underlying the substantive portion of this book may be stated, then, as follows: Since the classical industrial revolution in England during the latter part of the eighteenth and the early part of the nineteenth centuries, the passage of historical time has so altered the relationship among certain key variables, shortly to be specified, that countries now undergoing a similar process may not be able to rely upon labor policies which lie near the permissive end of the control spectrum. That is to say, permissive policies feasible under the conditions prevailing in the nineteenth century are not so feasible in the twentieth century. These conditions may be divided into two broad categories, those affecting the capacity of government to exert controls over the population, and those affecting the magnitude of the discontents and response to them during the industrial revolution. The remainder of this chapter will set out the *a priori* reasons for believing that these conditions are relevant.

§ Governmental Control of the Civilian Population

The ability of government to control behavior inheres in its police power, based ultimately on the wielding of the weapons of destruction, and its indoctrination powers, based ultimately on the manipulation and domination of the communication media. The more divisible the techniques of destruction and communication, the more difficult it is for governmental authorities to control behavior and, conversely, the easier it is for individuals to maintain autonomy from government. If the weapons of police power are divisible, governmental authorities will have difficulty in maintaining an absolute monopoly in producing, allocating, and using them, and to that extent there will be limits to the effectiveness of the state's police power. The private citizen who can acquire arms that bear a close parity to the weapons possessed by government will be more independent in articulating his grievances than the citizen who is confronted by a government with a monopoly of highly efficient means of destruction. The risks of independence are smaller in the age of rifles and horses than in the age of machineguns and tanks. The right of citizens to bear arms or to form a militia, therefore, is most especially a significant democratizing force in the former age, for in the latter, the weapons of destruction are too complex for the ruled to mobilize them without the permission and assistance of the rulers. With the development of weapons technology, the possibility of effective opposition to the police policies of government tends to pass from the population at large to the men who direct the mobilization of the armed forces, i.e., from the private citizen to the commanding officer.[1]

That there is abundant evidence in the contemporary world of violent conflict with and revolt against constituted political authority does not in the least contradict this proposition. The nationalist revolts and guerilla activities that have disturbed the political stability of many countries since World War II have been military campaigns conducted less by citizens bearing arms than by professional soldiers. Indeed the great stock of modern weapons that governments can draw upon to control the population and the increasing efficiency of their destructive power have tended to make opposition a career requiring special skills and extraordinary dedication. It has become increasingly difficult with the passage of time for private individuals, acting within the limits of civil society, to pressure governmental authorities into extending political rights to wider segments of the population. Or, perhaps more realistically, governmental authorities find these pressures less compelling because of their increasing monopolization of the means of destruction.

As the police power of government becomes stronger with the development of weapons technology, its powers of propaganda and indoctrination similarly become greater with technological advances in communication techniques. As long as ideas are communicated primarily on a face-to-face basis and with the aid of relatively simple printing methods—as long as communication techniques are highly divisible—literate and articulate private citizens are not at a disadvantage vis-à-vis governmental authorities in influencing attitudes and values of diverse groups in the population. They can seek support for unorthodox and heretical views with about the same degree of efficacy as governmental authorities can urge conformance to traditional patterns of behavior. But when communication becomes technically complex and highly concentrated, when the publication of a newspaper or the operation of a radio station necessitates a substantial commitment to fixed capital, most citizens are cut off from the means of influencing their peers. Those who do possess adequate resources for operating the communication media may find that they can only gain access to them with the consent of governmental authorities.

The technology of communication reinforces the effect of the technology of destruction. With passing time, the cumulative strengthening of these control techniques raises the power of governmental authorities in relation to the autonomy of private citizens. The demands for democratic concessions which the latter might place on the former may no longer elicit a democratic response, since governmental authorities have at their disposal effective means of maximizing their tenure of power without broadening the basis of the consultative process.

§   *The Discontents of the Industrial Revolution*

A number of conditions must be considered in regard to the magnitude of the discontent during the industrial revolution. First, the relationship between increases in output and increases in population affects the size of the groups caught up in the process of economic development. Population may increase because of the impact of factors—for example, the use of DDT—exogenous to the economic system on birth and/or mortality rates, or because of the impact of endogenous factors—that is, increased output. The passage of historical time increases the likelihood that population will increase ahead of output by extending the influence of exogenous factors on the crucial rates affecting population growth. One may conceive of a world inventory of mortality-reducing commodities which becomes larger as more economies step up the rate of growth. The countries which first industrialized had to build up this inventory themselves, which of course meant that to that extent decreases in the mortality rates were endogenously induced. The exogenous factors affecting mortality rates were natural conditions, for instance the persistence of weather favorable to the harvest, over which man then had little control. Countries starting to industrialize now not only may find their mortality rates affected by these natural conditions but also by the output of more advanced countries which has added to the world inventory of mortality-reducing commodities. If population does increase ahead of output, society will face an employment problem which will exacerbate the discontents arising in the early stages of development.

Second, the technological conditions relating to the utilization of resources constantly change over time. Resources which could not be used in one period become available in a later period because of scientific and technological advances. It is frequently remarked that for this reason latecomers to industrialization have advantages that were denied the pioneers.[2] The former do not have to bear the burden of creating new technological frontiers; they have before them the experiences of the more advanced economies, acquired at the cost of many blind alleys and many experiments that yielded little additional output to the economy. Moreover, the latecomers have a wide choice among production functions. They may use capital-intensive or labor-intensive methods of production. If they are attempting to establish communication facilities between two areas in their economy, they may consider road, rail, or air transport and within each category of transportation choose among technological alternatives, for example diesel-powered or coal-burning engines in rail transportation. In contrast, the pioneering country may be compelled to utilize the technology it developed itself beyond that technology's optimal life because of the large and indivisible investment in fixed assets tied up in it. Thus railways with their bridges, tunnels and terminal equipment built in one technological era may not be readily altered if in a subsequent technological era it is found that engines should be larger and the track gauges wider. A change in one component of the rail system requires a change in all other components.[3]

These very advantages for the latecomer from a technological point of view are likely to turn out to be disadvantages from a social point of view. The investment choices made are likely to embody a technology which during the period of the take-off places a severe strain on the resources available to the economy.

The pioneering economy cannot be tempted by a technology which is too complex for existing labor skills and too demanding of scarce capital simply because it does not exist. But the late-comer can easily aspire to the technological accomplishments of the advanced economies. Nor are such aspirations devoid of economic reason, though with some interpretations they do not make much sense. It is argued, for instance, that countries with a surfeit of labor should not adopt a capital-intensive technology because this economizes the factor labor which is in abundant supply. Adherents of this view would contend that it is far more appropriate to use labor-intensive techniques in order to obtain optimal use of the economy's scarce capital resources. Instead of importing the latest techniques of refining iron ore, these economies should expand labor-intensive output, increase their exports to foreign markets, and with the foreign exchange earned buy the steel they require. This argument has much merit, but it is not one which meets the problem of growth, for its major premise is that an economy should maximize output from *available* resources. But growth, above all, is concerned with increasing the quantity of available resources; with this goal in view, there may be good reasons for utilizing existing stocks of resources in less than optimal fashion. The adaptation of a technology too advanced for the given skills of the labor force may be worthwhile if it induces workers to acquire new industrial skills and habits, even though in the short run the output of the economy may be smaller than it would have been had a less ambitious technology been used. The peasant accustomed to horse and plow will probably not know how to operate a tractor and harrow and certainly will not know how to maintain them. But he cannot learn to use them properly until he has been given the opportunity to observe the breakdowns and mechanical failures which improper maintenance brings on. One may argue that a modern steel plant is an essential means for instilling the habits of punctuality and disciplined cooperation and attuning labor to the functional requirements of a machine society, while recognizing that for the time being output might have been larger if the techniques of production were less subversive of the time pattern of an agrarian and traditional society.[4]

But the latecomer in the industrialization process who, when confronted with a wide range of technological possibilities, opts for capital-intensive methods of growth may prolong the gap between total output and the output of consumers' goods, thus rendering the objective basis of discontent during the take-off more obdurate. If instead of using additional labor to expand the output of agricultural commodities, it is used to build railways to hitherto inaccessible deposits of minerals, which in turn will be allocated to the expansion of domestic steel output, the output of consumers' goods may in the short run come off second best. Consumers then may be compelled to defer the gratification of more wants than is consistent with their time preferences.

While the argument of the previous paragraph has been couched in terms of choice, it may be that the country approaching the threshold of growth late in historical time has relatively little choice if it wants to raise itself above a subsistence level. On the one hand, it may accept the existing international division of labor and adapt its allocation of resources to the demands emanating from the world market, producing agricultural raw materials and minerals as the advanced economies of the world require. In its status as a primary-output producing economy, its standard of living would depend on circumstances largely outside its control—the level of income in the advanced economies, the terms of trade, changes in industrial technology, and so on. On the other hand, it may decide to break out of the extant pattern of international specialization and create domestic markets capable of sustaining a growing economy. This alternative may require simultaneous investment in complementary industries so that domestic markets for output will grow along with the capacity to produce output. It is not enough to expand the output of steel; there also must be industries capable of absorbing steel. Where the first alternative makes the standard of living in the less advanced economy depend on the characteristics of growth in the more advanced economies, the second alternative jeopardizes the existing standard of living through investment demands designed to break through such dependence.[5]

To the extent that this notion of balanced growth has validity, it points up the severity of the "hump problem." The technological advances which proceed apace regardless of the levels of income of the various economies in the world, increase the scope and extent of the external economies which must be captured by investment before growth can be established on a self-sustaining basis. The production of hydro-electric power with the related industries that supply it with input and provide a market for its output absorbs a greater volume of resources than does the production of steam power. Yet the subsistence economy which bypasses the latter because of technological developments still has to start from scratch. Though its choice may be wise in the long run, in the short run it increases the strain on the economy's scarce resources.

A third factor affecting the magnitude of the discontent during an industrial revolution is the demonstration effect. The factors already discussed related to the objective circumstances in which discontent takes roots and grows; the demonstration effect disseminates the standards by which people judge whether they are well off or badly off. Again the passage of historical time would appear to work hardships on the society undertaking industrialization late. The early comers expand economic activity against the background of historically given wants. Though the process of growth necessarily raises consumers' expectations as population moves from a relatively static agrarian sector to an urban-industrial sector, the gap between expectations and realizations is nonetheless restrained by the internal character of the demonstration effect. The country which is in the forefront of world economic development cannot aspire to higher standards of economic well-being, for they do not exist. If the wants of the population expand it is because of the impact of the growth process itself on the formation of wants. The latecomer, on the other hand, must produce in response to the historically given wants at a time when it is relatively easy for individuals to be aware of standards of consumption and material well-being in countries with high per capita income. Wants therefore may expand at a much faster rate than they possibly can be satisfied. It is one thing to provide workers with cramped housing quarters when they have little evidence that workers had ever lived any other way; it is quite another when they know that people in roughly their same social position in other societies have achieved some of the amenities of material welfare. The expansion of wants ahead of output may consequently exacerbate the discontents afflicting societies which embark upon industrialization late.

§   *The Weakening of the Individualistic Response*

If the discontent engendered by industrialization in the late-comer is potentially greater than in the early comer, it also is the case that in the former there will be a less resilient individualistic response and therefore a greater need for overt governmental control of discontent. The dissatisfactions which arise in the growth process would raise no difficulties if people simply worked harder as individuals with the opportunities afforded by the economic system to achieve higher status. Economic growth, after all, takes place because some people are dissatisfied with the existing state of the economy and attempt to change it. If growth itself did not create dissatisfactions there would be none of the struggling and striving for higher standards of material attainment which is the essence of the process. But if discontent leads to the formation of extra-economic organizations whose functions are not consistent with growth objectives, then these objectives may indeed be jeopardized.

The worker who finds himself frustrated by his present economic circumstances and wants to improve them through the exercise of individual initiative may do one or both of two things: (1) engage in entrepreneurial activity, or (2) change jobs by moving into a different market. The first alternative becomes increasingly difficult with every advance in technology. The barriers against entry into industry rise as the capital and knowledge required to build and operate industrial assets become greater. If industry is small and not technically complex it is possible for workers to acquire the requisite knowledge for operating a firm by observing the production process. However, when expanding technology subdivides the production process into many minute operations, it is no longer possible, or at any rate is very difficult, for workers to acquire the necessary technical competence. Moreover, as capital costs rise with technological change, it becomes more difficult to organize production, even if one possesses the requisite technical expertise. The finding of capital itself is a task which cannot easily be performed and requires skills over and above those of the engineer.

Even if many people possess the knowledge and capital necessary for entrepreneurship, their activity as autonomous individuals will be inhibited in the country industrializing late by the external economies of production. No matter how willing and able the potential entrepreneur may be, he cannot undertake a project which depends for its pay-off upon the simultaneous carrying out of complementary projects or the development of the whole economy. In other words, external economies increase the optimal-sized decision-making unit beyond the competence of an individual's purview. The economic system therefore does not throw out meaningful clues and signals to which private individuals can respond.[6]

It is important to note that this does not mean that in the country industrializing late private autonomous investment is impossible, but only that during the period of the take-off when the conditions for self-sustained growth are being established private investment is not likely to be able to bear the full burden of the responsibilities of construction. Mineral, power, and labor resources are not close enough at hand in the right quantity and quality to sustain private entrepreneurship. The difficulty, of course, is that the particular factors which prevented the development of an economy's resources in the past also stunt any private entrepreneurial potential it might have contained. If for technical reasons it could not develop during the steam or electric ages, it may have lost or repressed the private entrepreneurial talent for which subsequently there was plenty of scope when the atomic age made the development of its resources technically feasible.

While it is difficult in the country industrializing late for the individual to sublimate his discontents in entrepreneurship, it is also difficult for him to search out better conditions in another society. Although there are few, if any, transportation barriers to the movement of population, the increase in world population since the start of the industrial revolution has been so great that most desirable land has been claimed and man-made obstructions have been placed in the way of population migrations. The frontier has disappeared and there is less opportunity for those who feel dissatisfied by their present circumstances to try a new start in another society. In contrast, at the start of the industrialization process in the west there were still large quantities of cultivable land in the middle latitudes of the western hemisphere to which people could migrate. The barrier to population movement was technical and as successive innovations throughout the nineteenth century lowered the cost of land and ocean transport this barrier was gradually lowered. Where in the twentieth century an industrializing country has to bear the full burden of increases in population, in the nineteenth century it was possible for an industrializing country to shed some of its increased population to other lands.

Summarizing the argument thus far, the discontent engendered now by industrialization during the take-off is likely to be more persistent than it was in the previous century because the "hump" which has to be overcome to achieve self-sustained growth is greater. Yet it is more difficult for individuals to respond to this discontent either in entrepreneurial endeavors or by migrating to another society. Moreover, the technology of controlling behavior has advanced so far that governments have at their disposal police and propaganda techniques which place them at a marked advantage vis-à-vis private citizens. The implications of this are evident. Governments in countries embarking upon industrialization today are not so willing to stand aside and allow individuals to articulate their discontents in autonomous organizations, for the conduct of the latter is likely to jeopardize the success of the growth process itself. Rather these governments incline toward totalitarian control of labor to mute the protest function of labor unions, for example, and to accelerate the commitment of labor to an industrialized order which necessitates sacrifices in the present to the prospects of growth in the future. In the nineteenth century the governments of the early starters in industrialization were more willing to apply permissive policies of labor control, partly because the discontent did not pose so much of a threat to the economic objectives of society, and partly because the technical means for controlling a mass society were not as efficient as they subsequently became.

§   *Trade Unions During the Industrial Revolution*

There remains one question to be considered before turning to the substantive historical evidence of industrialization. How does discontent actually manifest itself? What role do trade unions and labor parties play, and how do they get organized? These questions are similar to one that consumed a considerable amount of the intellectual energy of the socialist movement in the nineteenth and early twentieth centuries. In the debates of the social democrats the question ran as follows: Would workers spontaneously recognize their interest in socialism and themselves take the steps necessary to attain this end? Or would they have to be led out of the labyrinth of capitalism by specially endowed leaders who could follow the trail to socialism? The debate was a crucial one, for as it turned out the opposed views on the question distinguished the revolutionary from the evolutionary socialists, and, most significantly, the Bolsheviks from the Mensheviks in Russia. It is not necessary here to follow the tortuous twists and turns of the debate, but the point at issue is relevant for our analysis. Lenin believed that spontaneity would only lead to the economism of trade union policy, that if the workers were left to their own devices they would seek short-run solutions to bread-and-butter questions, settling for the scraps from the capitalists' table and losing sight of the ultimate goal of socialism. Accordingly, he conceived of the Russian Social Democratic party as a group of men dedicated to achieving the true purpose of the workers' existence, tireless in their efforts to wean them away from the control of trade union leaders and to implant in them a consciousness of socialism.[7]

Even though Lenin's views were almost always rationalizations for revolutionary action and seldom the product of an objective, scientific appraisal of social conditions, his views on the trade unions in capitalistic society merit respect, though his views of trade unionists do not. For Lenin realized that the trade unions as they developed during the industrialization of the nineteenth century were basically bourgeois institutions. Created to countervail the bargaining power of the private business firms which were leading the advance through the industrial revolution, trade unions took on some of the characteristics of the organizations they originally arose to bedevil. Their leaders became, appropriately enough for a commercial age, cost-benefit calculators, balancing the advantages of higher wages against the advantages of shorter hours and estimating the time that might possibly be lost in strikes in trying to enforce demands for either one. The apocalyptic goals of Marxian socialism could not easily be cast in the balance and therefore did not loom large in the calculations of trade union leaders. Indeed they were often actively hostile to socialists as they feared that the visions of the latter would lead to precipitous action that could only weaken, or even destroy, the organizations which they had worked so hard to form.

Given the policy of permissive labor control during the first century of industrialization, trade unions tended to grow at the top, in a sense, and trickle downwards. First skilled workers were organized effectively, and subsequently semiskilled and unskilled workers, but there was nothing spontaneous about it. It took time for workers to recognize the need for organization and it took time to create the leaders who could fashion an amorphous group of workers into a cohesive union. Moreover, the success of unionism of the bread-and-butter variety depended upon the existence of a negotiable surplus. Income had to be high enough to permit bargaining over wage shares and the demonstration that after all unions could work. But at the dawn of the industrialization process there was sufficient inertia resisting the organization of unions, paradoxically enough, to give scope to the growth process which subsequently permitted the gradual organization of workers from the top downwards.

Now, however, the hiatus between the formation of an industrial labor force and the organization of a labor movement may not be so great as it once was. Though workers themselves may have little concept of what organization involves and may be no more capable than they ever were of spontaneous action, there will be no lack of leaders from outside the ranks of labor anxious to take workers in hand and right the injustices to which they are subjected. Nineteenth-century industrialization not only created a group of indigenous labor leaders—workers from the ranks who assumed initiative and leadership in the formation of trade unions—but a prodigious output of theories, prescriptions, ideologies about how labor ought to behave to achieve its due. Just as technological innovations pioneered in one economy can be adapted into a less advanced economy, so the accumulated stock of labor ideology founded on the experiences of the industrialized economies can motivate and guide the behavior of would-be labor leaders in the industrializing economies. Thus the discontent inherent in the acceleration of growth at the early stages of development may be used and abused by intellectuals who are conscious of the widening gap between the standards of living in the industrialized and industrializing economies, who believe in some political or economic nostrum for saving mankind, and who would like to embarrass the existing political authority. Moreover, since the latecomer to industrialization is beset by peculiarly difficult problems, it is not likely that economic growth will yield quick returns. It will therefore be difficult to demonstrate the practical advantages of bread-and-butter unionism, making the realm of politics and political action appear to the dissident intellectual labor leader all the more attractive. But this is the kind of activity which must be foreclosed if growth is to take place. Permissive labor controls, then, may allow the articulation of too much discontent. Justice, for the time being at any rate, may have to take a back seat to growth objectives while the labor force is consciously fitted into the industrial mold.

In the chapters that follow we shall attempt to give these abstract notions about growth and labor policy some historical content. We should then be able to evaluate more effectively the impact of growth on the emergence of democratic political institutions.

Part Two

The Evidence

Chapter 5

The British Economy:
Industrial Transformation
and the Evolution of Democracy

In the middle of the eighteenth century on the eve of the industrial revolution, England was far from being a democratic society. Few people possessed the political privileges which today are assumed to be central to the democratic tradition. The forty-shilling freehold in the counties restricted the franchise to the aristocracy, gentry, and wealthy landowners; in the boroughs freemen were similarly held to a property qualification which denied the great majority of urban residents voting rights. Though the electors were few, those who could sit in Parliament or hold office under the Crown were even fewer. The men privileged to be part of this aristocratic oligarchy had no intention of bringing the masses of people into the councils of government. Whether Whigs dominated the central government at Westminster and Tories were in ascendancy in local government, they were in fundamental agreement with the political settlement of 1689 which, while establishing the supremacy of Parliament over the Crown, repressed the democratic impulses that had become manifest in the abortive republic of the mid-seventeenth century.

Yet compared to her European contemporaries, England was without doubt a more advanced political community. At a time when the Bourbon monarchs of France through inept and tyrannical rule were preparing the way for their own demise and that of the effete French aristocracy, the British were continuing to develop the constitutional traditions of government. Resisting Stuart despotism during the turbulent seventeenth century and finding the Cromwellian Republic not to its liking, Britain in the eighteenth century once and for all caged the arbitrary will of the monarch and gave free rein to the growth of parliamentary government.

While the creation of the party system and cabinet government was not the work of the common man, his welfare could not help but be affected by the curbing of the monarchy. In its struggle with the crown, the Commons necessarily stood for the rights of the people it represented over against the privileges of the king. Whether they disputed fiscal or religious matters, the Commons held that in issues affecting the private purse or conscience of its members it should not only be consulted, but should have the last word. The triumph of the Commons at the end of the seventeenth century, therefore, was the triumph of civil rights. Even though by modern standards those rights were truncated and limited in their application, the precedent for constitutional liberties had nonetheless been firmly established. The rights of the politically privileged members of English society were significantly greater than those of the common man, but it became increasingly difficult, given the traditions of British constitutional development, to justify the difference. Under any circumstances the rights of the meanest Englishman, regardless of the class of society to which he belonged, were more respected than those of his peers on the continent who typically lacked strong parliamentary champions of the cause of constitutional liberties.

With the advantage of hindsight it is not difficult to see those elements of the British political system in 1750 which subsequently burgeoned into a democratic order, but here we are interested in the processes which caused the metamorphosis of these elements. How did it come about that a parliamentary system through and by which a small oligarchy in midcentury controlled the political community in Britain transformed itself into a vehicle for the creation of a democratic political order? In order to answer this question we shall examine the nature of economic growth in Britain during the industrial revolution.

§   *Economic Organization Prior to the*
   Industrial Revolution

The industrial revolution in Britain was a preeminent example of what we shall call autonomous growth. Autonomous growth stands in contrast to state-induced or, more
briefly, state growth. In the latter, the agents of government take
the initiative in bringing about the changes that stimulate the
growth of income, while in the former private individuals, for
motives independent of the convenience of state, take the initiative. In either event government plays an important role in
growth, if only because, as a minimum, it must establish the
order and political stability essential to economic activity. What
is particularly relevant in this context is the source or origin of
that behavior which led to the commandeering and allocation of
resources to growth projects.

As a well developed commercial economy prior to the industrial revolution, Britain had always given considerable scope
to private entrepreneurs. But this had been at the largess of
a government which concerned itself with many details of
economic life and, no doubt, would have concerned itself with
many more if it had been technically capable of doing so. Mercantilism was nothing if not a system of state economy. Wage
and price controls, export bounties, import restrictions, production specifications, and consumption proscriptions limited the
freedom of action of private citizens. Directed toward the aggrandizing of state power, mercantilist policy was designed to
manipulate the economic universe in order to accumulate the
precious metals at the disposal of government. Such policy, held
up to obloquy by Adam Smith and generally thought to be
self-defeating by classical economists, may have made some sense,
as John M. Keynes pointed out, in an economy plagued by a

shortage of money, for it may have allowed the quantity of money to be greater and interest rates to be lower than they otherwise would have been.[1] Whatever the effect of mercantilism on interest rates, it is doubtful whether growth occurred during this era in England; prior to the latter part of the eighteenth century output did not grow significantly faster than population.[2]

Though economic growth, as we have defined it, did not take place, some of the preconditions for growth were firmly established during the mercantilist period. The expansion of trade throughout the world, the building of empire and markets in the East Indies and in North America confronted Englishmen with circumstances which generated investment skills. A merchant dealing in linens and cottons from India and tobacco from the American colonies necessarily had to calculate risks and weigh these risks against the expected returns he might anticipate if his cargo survived the hazards of traffic on the high seas. He had to make calculations in universal categories which transcended the parochial characteristics of local markets. Where local merchants survived by adapting their conduct to the idiosyncrasies of suppliers and customers they knew personally, merchants working in world markets had to rely on a complex organization of agents, representatives, and factotums tied together by the cash nexus of money and prices.

If expanding trade during the Mercantilist era disseminated a commercial milieu congenial to entrepreneurial activity, it also raised practical problems by straining the productive capacity of the British economy. Both in agriculture and in manufacturing traditional methods of organization imposed limits on the extent to which output could expand. In the counties the open field system tied up arable land in communal patterns of usage and made the waste lands subject to traditional peasant pasturage and fuel rights. The improving landowner or landlord therefore was frequently frustrated by practices which subordinated the use of his resources to the traditions of the community. It proved difficult to experiment with new breeds of livestock, for example, if there were common pasturage rights enjoyed by both peasants and lords living under the jurisdiction of the manor.

Manufacturing was organized in the putting out, or domestic, system in which merchants owning raw materials moved them from household to household for processing until they were ready for marketing as finished products. Located in the counties households frequently performed their manufacturing duties as an adjunct to their agricultural occupation. But a system that was feasible to operate at one level of output raised many problems at a higher level of output. As the volume of raw materials that had to be processed increased, transport costs in the domestic system became too great. Moreover, the difficulty of coordinating production increased. This was particularly true in the textile industry as technical inventions in the eighteenth century, affecting the carding of wool and cotton, the spinning of yarn, and the weaving of cloth, disrupted the synchronization of these processes.

The bottlenecks to production inherent in the organization of agriculture and manufacturing were further aggravated by the diminution of wood resources in the eighteenth century, by the technical problems of keeping the coal mines free of water and gas, and by the impoverished state of the transportation system. The disappearance of the forests threatened to cut short the supply of charcoal on which the iron industry depended for a fluxing agent. The deepening of the mines, in consequence of centuries of use, not only increased the hazards of an already hazardous occupation, but raised the costs of bringing coal to the surface. Internal transport facilities had not been attended to in Britain since the Roman occupation, and, although the durability of Roman roads was proverbial, by the eve of the industrial revolution they no longer were adequate for the needs of the economy.

While commercial expansion thus strained the British economy, there was wide spread recognition of the need to solve these problems of organization and production in order to expand capacity. There were monetary inducements for doing so, for the growth of aggregate demand pressing down upon limited capacity raised prices in the latter part of the eighteenth century and buoyed up profit prospects. There was, then, no lack of economic stimuli for entrepreneurial activity.[3]

§   *Noneconomic Influences on Entrepreneurial Activity*

We know from the plight of today's underdeveloped economies that economic stimuli are not enough to set in motion the process of economic growth. The raising of prices and profit prospects does not automatically call forth entrepreneurial energies. There must be in addition extra-economic stimuli which drive men to achieve the material rewards offered by the economic system.

There was no doubt that in eighteenth-century England many men possessed the necessary drives. The scientific tradition as it gradually emerged in Europe culminated in the eighteenth-century Enlightenment and the widely-held belief that, contrary to tradition and the received authority of the past, the environment could be manipulated in order to improve the condition of man. For some this was a revolutionary belief leading to the advocacy of revolt against the feudal and oppressive institutions which blocked mankind's opportunity for rational enlightenment. For others it contained no such social message, but simply acted as a catalyst in the process of experimentation. The gospel of progress, in effect, condoned the tinkering with the techniques of production. James Hargreaves' spinning jenny, Richard Arkwright's water frame, Samuel Crompton's mule, and James Watt's steam engine were not isolated phenomena, but the most successful of a great outpouring of innovations which inundated England in the latter half of the century.[4] Some of these inventions were the result of tinkering in a rather literal sense; others, as with Watt's steam engine, were the consequence of analysis which diagnosed a problem and specified a solution prior to embodying it in a physical contrivance. However much the inventors and entrepreneurs may have responded to the stimuli thrown up by the economic environment, they also were driven by the new beliefs of the age to experiment with productive processes just for the sake of manipulating and improving, as they believed, the physical environment.

As an ideological and intellectual phenomenon, the eighteenth-century Enlightenment affected most directly the educated classes. In addition to manufacturers, the gentry and wealthy landowners who were anxious to improve agricultural yields came under its influence. The dissemination of the principles of scientific agriculture and experimentation with new crops and new methods of breeding livestock eventually led to an increase in agricultural productivity without which the industrial revolution could not have taken place.

If entrepreneurial activity was stimulated by the ideological influences of the Enlightenment, it also was advanced by a social structure and political system which discriminated against certain marginal groups. We are referring, of course, to the position of Protestant dissenters in Britain in the eighteenth century, a subject on which we commented briefly in Chapter 3.[5] The settlement which ended the disastrous religious controversies and battles of the seventeenth century granted dissenters the right to worship as they saw fit, but denied them access to many of the privileged positions in British society so long as they refused to take the sacraments of the established church. The dissenter could not matriculate at Oxford or Cambridge, which closed to him careers in the professions. He could not be a minister in His Majesty's Government. Manufacturing, however, offered him unlimited opportunity for his talents. Further, as a means of accumulating wealth, it was a path to worldly success and social recognition. England was too much the commercial nation to allow religious dogma to stand in the way of its appreciation of the man who through ingenuity and hard work had acquired wealth.

§ *The Central Role of Textiles in British Industrialization*

The economic and noneconomic stimuli to entrepreneurship created vibrant forces in eighteenth-century England for engineering economic growth during the industrial revolution, but they could not achieve full expression in the mercantilist structure of the British economy. The constraints by which the government attempted to maximize mercantilist objectives tended to limit opportunities for experimentation and therefore held back the technological changes which were the essence of industrialization. Nowhere was this better illustrated than in the textile industry. For generations the manufacturing of woolen textile products had been the national industry of Britain. The whole process from the raising of sheep to the marketing of finished broadcloth was supervised with lavish care by an attentive and paternal government. Not only were the wages and prices affecting the production and sale of woolen products controlled, but the technological specifications of the productive process were set out in some detail. Moreover, the government stood ready to bail the industry out when and if it was beset by difficulties that could not be met by existing policy. Early in the eighteenth century the industry found itself competing with an inconveniently large market, developed partially at its expense, for the fine calico products of India, then the largest producer of cotton cloth. The woolen interests were able to obtain the passage of parliamentary acts, in 1700 and 1721, which prohibited the importation of cotton goods from India and other eastern countries and the use of calico cloth by British citizens. These acts did the woolen industry little good and ultimately proved to be a boon to the domestic cotton textile industry in Britain, but they epitomized the mercantilist propensity to maintain an advantage by forestalling the competition that might render its protected output and technology obsolete.

Restricted by the proscriptions and prescriptions which made up the economic milieu in the older textile centers, the entrepreneurs who transformed the cotton textile industry tended to work outside the jurisdiction of the mercantilist order in Lancashire and Yorkshire. Manchester, the capital of the new industrial system which subsequently arose in England, was an unincorporated town and so was not bound by the regulations of the guilds and the government as were the textile centers in the south of England. In a very real sense industrialization was fostered by new firms building new production sites and opening up new markets. The mechanization of spinning and weaving, the harnessing first of water and then of steam to the power requirements of the industry, the building of factories took place in the north of England and relocated the geographical center of manufacturing activity.

From the vantage point of the twentieth century it may perhaps seem curious to lead off a discussion of industrialization with these remarks about the textile industry. Today industrialization evokes images of steel mills, machine tools, and in general the accoutrements and apparatus of heavy industry. The textile industry would hardly appear to be a likely candidate for leading the advance of an economy to an industrial system. Here, however, we are concerned with the unique circumstances in which the industrial system was created for the first time and the sequence in which industry developed is important to the points we wish to make. Today it is no doubt true that the industrialization of the production of textiles, since time immemorial a household occupation in every society, may not contain a significant impulse for economic growth. Yet in the latter part of the eighteenth century the other industries which we associate with industrialization were themselves either not yet developed or only in the early stages of development. The steel age was not to arrive until the second half of the next century when Henry Bessemer's converter (1856) and Sir William Siemen's open hearth (1866) effected a revolution in the processing of iron ore, made all the more spectacular by the Gilchrist-Thomas process (1879) for refining phosphorous-bearing iron ores. At the start of the industrial revolution the iron mongers of England were still learning to use the process invented by Abraham Darby early in the eighteenth century for smelting iron ore with coke. Steam railroads did not come to England until the second quarter of the nineteenth century. The transportation improvements which first revitalized the British communication system were confined to canal and road construction. The chemical, aluminum, and electrical industries had not yet been conceived. In short, in eighteenth-century England the alternative routes to industrial development were sharply limited. Indeed, the only one available was that opened by the pioneering entrepreneurs in the textile industry.

§ *Factors Minimizing the Problem of the "Hump"*

The expansion of output in the cotton textile industry in response to the technological changes in the spinning and weaving of cotton could not have occurred without an increase in other kinds of output. We have already mentioned some of these. The development of the transportation system with the construction of turnpikes and canals made what had previously been primarily a coastal economy into a well knit internal domestic economy, thus increasing the size of the market in which textile products could be sold. The perfection of the coking process in the smelting of iron ore released the industry from its dependence on wood and charcoal, assuring the continuous supply of good iron for the makers of the metal parts in textile machinery. Watt's steam engine made possible a more effective system of keeping coal mines clear of water, thereby stimulating the growth of output of the coal needed for the power requirements of the textile industry. Productivity increases in agriculture released workers for employment in manufacturing. In other words, the performance of the cotton textile industry during the industrial revolution depended on the more or less simultaneous development of industries producing output which it used as inputs and of markets capable of absorbing the output it produced.

These output and input interdependencies constitute what in Chapter 3 we called the problem of the hump in economic development. A capital-scarce economy which must expand output on a number of fronts in order to attain a level of income from which economic growth will be self-sustaining may find itself hard put to find the necessary resources for investment. The problem, moreover, will be all the greater if mortality rates decline with initial increases in output, causing population to grow at the same rate as the growth of output. In England the problem of the hump was minimized by the pioneer role performed by the economy in the process of industrialization. British entrepreneurs were not adapting a technology which had been fully developed by a more advanced economy. In a sense, then, they were not completely aware of the capital costs of the projects they were undertaking; they had no evidence before them which would allow them to make such an evaluation. They experimented with new technology to the extent of the resources and knowledge that were immediately available to them, and more often than not these came out of firms which they themselves owned and operated. Furthermore, the innovations which brought on the industrial revolution were very largely confined to the methods of producing existing types of output. Watt's steam engine increased the efficiency with which mines could be kept clear of water, thus reducing the cost of mining coal. Indeed, Watt and his partner Matthew Boulton first sold their steam engine on contracts which yielded them income only when it had demonstrated its capacity to reduce costs. The series of inventions which mechanized the textile industry reduced the costs of spinning and weaving and eventually allowed the British cotton masters to produce as fine a cloth as had been produced traditionally in India. Thus while the capital costs of innovation were held back by the limits of man's knowledge of technology, the returns to technology became manifest relatively quickly in a reduction of the costs of producing existing output.

The problem of the hump was also minimized for the British economy by its favorable location and the supply and availability of resources. Lying just off the northwestern corner of the European continent, favored by a mild and damp marine climate, and standing athwart the sea lanes between northern Europe and the rest of the world, Great Britain possessed incomparable advantages which became increasingly evident after the voyages of discovery opened the oceans to commerce. Its insular position gave Britain a ready-made water highway at a time when it was extremely difficult to carry any kind of goods over land, and impossible to carry bulky commodities. The construction of canals and roads increased the size of the domestic market by joining the interior of England to the coastal economy, already well developed commercially because of its access to the sea. The climate gave England a long growing season and went far to explain the position of self-sufficiency in agriculture from which England embarked on the industrial revolution. Location and climate thus minimized the volume of investment required to equip the economy with adequate transportation and to provide it with a food supply capable of feeding the labor force. Neither massive irrigation works to increase the supply of arable land nor overland transport facilities to break its isolation from world commerce were required to set the stage for industrialization. Moreover, the compactness of the British Isles and the close juxtaposition of coal and iron ore minimized transport costs for the basic resources of industrial development.

§ The Wide Extent of Private Entrepreneurship and of Entrepreneurial Values

Because the hump problem was minimized by England's pioneer position in industrial development and by favorable natural conditions, it was economically possible for individual private entrepreneurs to assume the chief responsibilities of engineering the growth of income in the latter part of the eighteenth century. Because the state stood for a system of economic organization which, however productive of mercantile success, tended to inhibit technological change, the new economy innovated by entrepreneurs matured outside of government in the interstices of the mercantilist system. It was the genius of Adam Smith to catch and assess the significance of this change in the structure of the British economy. Though far from being a prophet of industrialism, he saw in advance of his time that the new forms of enterprise opening up in the north of England represented a break with tradition and that the wealth of nations depended directly on the freedom of action with which these enterprises bought and sold goods and resources in the markets surrounding them. His name justly deserves to be linked with laissez-faire, individualism, and the coming of the new economic age.

There are a number of further observations about the entrepreneurial character of the industrial revolution in Britain which are relevant to our analysis. Though the notion of entrepreneurship most often brings to mind a picture of manufacturers adapting new techniques into industrial processes, it is important to note that it is a function that may be performed in any part of an economy. In the England of the industrial revolution entrepreneurial activity was widespread and not just confined to industry. The landowners and gentry who undertook to raise yields in agriculture by applying the principles of scientific farming to the breeding of livestock and the cultivation of grain were agrarian entrepreneurs. Different though they no doubt were in political outlook and social background from their industrial peers, they nonetheless similarly had to create new production functions as they broke down the resistances and antipathies to agricultural innovation. The acceleration in the pace of enclosures around the middle of the century, for example, was occasioned by rising grain prices and the impediments to innovation and experimentation placed in the way of improving landowners by the open field system. That Parliament was usually quite willing to accommodate the interests of the gentry by passing enclosure bills does not change the character of their activity. Indeed, it points up an important role that government may perform in the process of autonomous growth. The enclosure movement, which increased the average size of land holdings in Britain and was instrumental in raising agricultural productivity, was not instigated by government. It was facilitated by government at the behest of agrarian entrepreneurs. In other words, government responded to pressures brought to bear on it by persons external to it. It was not initiating action to solve an "agricultural problem."

Outside industry and agriculture, there was equally active entrepreneurship in those commercial and financial occupations which provided the services essential for facilitating the movement of goods and resources from the locus of production to the points of consumption. In the middle of the century, financial institutions were not organized effectively to provide industrial firms with the short-term and long-term capital required to support a rapidly growing economy. The fields of insurance, commercial banking, investment banking, and security marketing needed Watts, Boultons, and Hargreaves as much as did the textile and power industries. Someone or some group of people had to create a securities exchange, find means of increasing the quantity of money, and devise institutions for sharing the risks of enterprises. These services were perhaps less dramatic than the technological innovations in the production of physical goods, but they were no less essential to the process of industrialization. Typically, we do not have as clear a sense of the growth of financial institutions as we do of industrial firms. In comparison to the entrepreneurs who gave concrete shape to the latter, the leaders of the former tend to be shadowy and amorphous. We can put our finger on James Watt as a crucial figure in the development of steam power, but who was the James Watt in the development of the money supply? That we are hard put to answer such a question does not mean that there was no entrepreneurship in the growth of the banking system. Rather it suggests that enough people were involved to overshadow the performance of most individuals.

If entrepreneurship was found throughout the British economy, entrepreneurial values were disseminated even more widely throughout the society. As indicated in a previous chapter, the skills and resources required for entrepreneurship are such that under the best of circumstances only a small portion of the population may be expected to perform the function. Though restricted in number, their influence in society may be much greater by way of the values they represent. In England economic conditions were favorable to the spread of these values. The new technology developed in the textile, iron, coal, and power industries was embodied in new firms which came of age with the maturing of the technology itself. Entrepreneurs necessarily worked closely with their labor force, since not the least of their problems was the training of workers to the new skills demanded by the new technology. As in many underdeveloped economies today, the limited supply of skilled workmen inhibited production. Today the skills required are known and may be imparted through formal institutions such as trade schools, but in England these skills had to be innovated on the spot in the firm which was pioneering the new technology.[6] The distance between master and worker therefore was not great. The complex administrative hierarchy through which top management communicates to, and organizes the activity of, its labor force was the progeny of a later and more advanced technology. At the turn of the nineteenth century workers and entrepreneurs still knew one another. While the latter were not for this reason necessarily any more solicitous of the welfare or interest of workers—we have it on the authority of Ashton that the eighteenth century iron mongers, for instance, were a hardbitten and hard driving group of men who would not put up with any nonsense from their men[7]—the former were nonetheless in a position to appreciate and respect the tasks that the entrepreneurs were attempting to perform.[8]

The close relationship between master and workman facilitated the spread of entrepreneurial values in the following ways. First, firms being small, it was possible for a worker, if he possessed the requisite intelligence, to comprehend the process of production by participating in it and observing it. A skilled worker could conceivably carry in his head the design of the machines which made possible the transfer of cotton spinning from household to factory.[9] And if he could not do this, he could set them up and supervise their operation. In other words, it was possible for workers to acquire the requisite knowledge on the job for entry into industry on their own account. It was an awareness of the skilled worker as a carrier of the secrets of the new technology which induced the British government to continue the mercantilist prohibition against the emigration of skilled workmen until late in the industrial revolution. Second, even those workers who lacked the personal qualifications to become independent entrepreneurs themselves could in the intimacy of the small firm come to accept the values of the master. Undoubtedly in such a milieu opportunities for arbitary conduct were great. Where there were no institutions as in a modern unionized plant for regulating the behavior of employers towards workers, employers could vent their prejudices on individual workers, discriminating against some and favoring others. But it was precisely this kind of personal attention, harsh though it often was, that frequently led to acceptance of entrepreneurial domination in the production process. It is when firms grow large and the anonymity of workers increases that they are likely to feel less of a community of interest with their employers. During the industrial revolution in Britain firms did become larger, and, as we shall see, disorders and unrest swept the labor force threatening the consensus on which the British political community was based. But these firms had to grow from smaller origins in which it was possible to maintain some kind of personal rapport between employers and workers.

§   *The Ideology of the Rising Middle Classes*

Let us now consider the implications of the autonomous growth which transformed the British economy in the latter part of the eighteenth century for the development of the British political system in the nineteenth century. The individuals who created the new wealth of the industrial revolution had strong proprietary interests in the fruits of their entrepreneurial activity and a growing feeling of frustration and impatience with the discrimination that the existing political system imposed upon them. The relative growth of population in the northern industrial counties further distorted a system of representation long infamous for its rotten boroughs, pocket boroughs, and the manipulation of elections in open balloting. One may well imagine the indignation of the frugal and accumulating entrepreneur when required to pay taxes by a Parliament in which he was not directly represented, in support of expenditures which too often turned out to be sinecures for the aristocracy and its retainers.

However deeply the entrepreneurial classes may have felt morally entitled to some say in the determination of the nature of the political community in which they conducted their business affairs, they were not especially articulate in expressing their views. Because their energies were so completely devoted to the building of their businesses, they had little time to acquire either elegance in thought or expression or political skills. Because to them the justification of their views was self-evident, they were not likely to see the need for presenting them in terms that would be acceptable to wider social groups in society. The industrialist therefore was frequently an inept political protagonist. If the political salvation of the middle classes in England had depended on the heroes of Samuel Smiles, it would have been a long time in coming.[10]

The new economic world, however, that the industrialists were creating inspired a bounty of pundits and theorists from outside the business community who could argue forcefully and with great eloquence that the welfare of England, and not just the welfare of a few individuals, was inextricably associated with the growing enterprises being pioneered in the Midlands and the north of England. We have already referred to Adam Smith, the first herald of laissez-faire and the market economy. In the first quarter of the nineteenth century the system of classical political economy was rounded out with the contributions of David Ricardo and his close friend and disputant, Thomas Malthus. Rigorous and precise where Smith had been vague and contradictory, Ricardo fashioned an economic model which of its kind was a masterpiece. If one accepted the premises of the model, one was led irrevocably to accept the conclusions derived from it. Given the level of technology, diminishing returns to land, and the tendency for population changes to keep wages at a subsistence, the accumulation of capital on which the progress of society depended would eventually be jeopardized by declining profit rates. Along with the growth of population, the cost of producing subsistence would increase as land of poorer quality was brought into cultivation or as land already in cultivation was worked more intensively. Rents received by landlords would rise with the rise in the price of subsistence as would money wages. But since money wages and profits moved in opposite directions, the latter necessarily declined as the former rose. Thus the motive for entrepreneurs to accumulate capital was threatened by engrossing landlords whose rising share of the national product left little enough to the former as compensation for the trouble they incurred in organizing productive activity. In the hands of the pamphleteer or propagandist who wanted to blacken the eye of the gentry and landed interests these were powerful arguments. For they suggested that hard-working capitalists were being done in by profligate landlords whose only contribution to the economy was the mere chance of land ownership. One need only recall the persistent and successful campaigns of the Anti-Corn Law League. Among the first organizations to develop and exploit the techniques of mass propaganda, the League based its opposition to the corn laws firmly in the principles of classical political economy. Indeed, to Bright and Cobden these amounted to fundamental laws which a nation could ignore only at its peril.[11]

If classical political economy provided a meaningful justification of the role being performed by the rising entrepreneurial classes, Utilitarianism disseminated the most powerful welfare goal the world had yet contrived and an unrelenting call for political reform—the greatest good of the greatest number. Moreover, the means to this end then espoused by the Utilitarians were eminently consistent with the new economy being created by the rising middle classes. Asserting that man was motivated by the twin sovereigns of pleasure and pain, they argued that welfare could be maximized only if individuals were free to respond to these stimuli. For the greatest good of the greatest number consisted of the summation of the net advantage of pleasure over pain that each individual was able to gain in pursuit of his own interests. Since each individual counted equally in the Utilitarian world, society ought to be so structured that everyone had an equal opportunity to respond to the stimuli of pleasure and pain. Thus, monopoly, aristocratic privilege, and feudal rights were all anathema to Utilitarians, for each tipped the balance in favor of particular groups before the pursuit of self-interest could even start. Utilitarianism, therefore, was a strong corrosive agent for wearing away the ideological defenses of the mercantilist community out of which industrial capitalism emerged in Great Britain.[12]

The combination of a rising entrepreneurial class and a social and economic ideology elegantly expressing its interests eventually gave form and structure to a middle-class political movement which sought to remedy its second-class status and attained its first fulfillment in the Reform Bill of 1832. Prior to that time entrepreneurial groups were either not represented in Parliament or were represented at one remove by members of the Commons who could be prevailed upon to champion the cause of industry. For the greater part of the industrial revolution, however, the Parliament, especially the Lords and only slightly less so the Commons, was made up of men who represented the older social-economic order which was being subverted by industrial capitalism. This is not meant to suggest that no manufacturer or industrialist made his way into the politically privileged councils of British government. Far from it. The English social structure was by no means closed to the man who aspired to higher status. Indeed one of the strengths of the British aristocracy was that it was relatively young and tended to be replenished from below. The exigencies of both war and civil conflict from the fifteenth through the seventeenth centuries took their toll of noble lives; hardpressed monarchs in need of support from influential and wealthy groups in society were not loath to ennoble successful mercantile families. In the more settled eighteenth century, the manufacturer might gain political influence by acquiring a country estate and the perquisites of the gentry. He might even manage to marry an eligible daughter to an impecunious son of an aristocratic family. But the point is that, prior to the nineteenth century, if he were to become politically privileged, he had to acquire the coloring of the old society. He could not attain political rights in his stature as a manufacturer and industrialist. Inevitably in the process of worming his way into the gentry, the manufacturer lost the political urgency of his vested economic interest in compromises with his new interest as landowner and country gentleman. Moreover, he might even find that once inside the establishment it was eminently desirable to protect it from the incursions of other parvenu. The Peels, of course, were the most brilliant example of a family that rose from humble manufacturing origins to the pinnacle of political power during the industrial revolution. One might well explain the capitulation of Sir Robert Peel to the free traders and the consequent smashing of the conservative party in Britain as a reflection of his inability to repress the political propensities of his middle class origins. But the fact is that the son of a wealthy cotton textile manufacturer became prime minister as a Tory member of the House of Commons.

§ *The Welfare Problem During the Industrial Revolution*

We have stressed the private entrepreneurial characteristics of the industrial revolution because as a creative process giving rise to an accelerated rate of economic growth it was the handiwork of the men who assumed the risks and responsibilities of adapting a new industrial technology and new forms of production into the economic order. We have also pointed out that the Britain of the eighteenth century, because of its previous mercantile success and because of its pioneer position in the industrialization process, was peculiarly amenable to the dissemination of entrepreneurial values. One cannot infer, however, that entrepreneurial activity was engaged in by a majority or even a substantial minority. The majority of people lacked the resources, ability, and inclination to create new production functions. Yet the majority of people was profoundly affected by the industrial revolution. What of them? What role did they play in the transformation of the British political community? If the entrepreneurial classes performed their functions outside the pale of the constitution and consequently came to have strong moral feelings about being entitled to political rights, what of the people who were even further removed from constitutional privileges though every bit as much enmeshed in the changing industrial world? The answers to these questions depend on one's evaluation of what in Chapter 3 we called the welfare problem during the passage of the British economy over the hump of industrialization.

This problem is extraordinarily difficult because there is little reliable data about the condition of the working classes during the industrial revolution and still less agreement about how these data should be interpreted. The standard of living of the British workers has been a perennial favorite of economic discourse since the start of the revolution itself, and from the very beginning there have been sharp differences of opinion about whether it rose, remained the same or fell. That there was such a controversy, of course, was significant, for prior to the industrial revolution it never occurred to anyone that workers could get more than subsistence. Contemporary investigators of the problem were not completely satisfactory by present-day standards; they tended to be anecdotal and to base their judgment on fragmentary evidence. Not surprisingly, then, their views varied from the pessimism of Friedrich Engels in his *The Condition of the Working-Class in England in 1844* to the optimism of Andrew Ure in his *The Philosophy of Manufacturers*. Subsequently, Karl Marx gave the controversy added piquancy by generalizing the evidence drawn from the reports of Royal Commissions, Poor Law Commissioners, and factory inspectors on the state of workers into his famous immiserization (Verelendung) hypothesis. Ever since, the battle lines have been drawn, and if Marx was aided and abetted by the work of Arnold Toynbee and the Hammonds, he sustained severe blows from the work of A. L. Bowley and G. H. Woods and J. H. Clapham.[13] Today, the issue is still with us, though on a less polemical plane. T. S. Ashton has recently affirmed the notion that the standard of living of the British workers rose in the period following the Napoleonic Wars.[14] E. J. Hobsbawm, however, has published some indices of food consumption during this period which cast some doubts on the validity of Ashton's position.[15] W. Arthur Lewis has suggested that the average standard of living of the workers could have risen, provided workers were moving from a subsistence sector into a capitalistic sector that offered higher real wages, even though the latter might not have changed significantly over time. This, of course, leaves open the question of what happened to the standard of living of workers in the capitalistic sector.[16]

In general, two opposed views emerge in the discussion of the previous paragraph on the standard of living of workers. The optimists believe that the condition of workers improved.

Having no illusions about the economic status of workers and peasants in the mercantilist economy, stressing the greatly expanded output of consumers' goods brought about by the industrial revolution, and applying relatively narrow economic criterion of welfare, the optimists adduce evidence of rising real wages to show that the status of workers tended to change for the better. The pessimists, on the other hand, placing the welfare problem in a broader context, incline to the view that the status of the workers probably did not improve, for, while they may or may not have experienced an increase in the purchasing power of their wages, they moved from a society, which, however harsh its economic basis, gave them the security of stable social relationships, to one in which they were deprived of all security in the uncertainties of the market. Needless to say, these opposed views often are associated with correspondingly opposed normative views about competitive industrial capitalism, the one seeing it as solving more problems than it raised, and the other as raising more problems than it solved.

A reasonable position falls somewhere in between the views of the optimists and pessimists. In the first place, it is difficult to make meaningful welfare judgments on the basis of wage indices no matter how accurate they might be. In the second place, it is no less difficult to assign responsibility for the condition of the working class during the industrial revolution, whatever it might have been. While one cannot agree with the views of the early British socialists, for example, that the competitiveness of capitalistic institutions was brutalizing the workers, neither can one accept the view of Nassau W. Senior that the welfare of workers and society in general depended on the extension and purification of competitive capitalism. The relevant point here is that *economic* welfare, the well-being derived from the consumption of goods and services produced from scarce resources, depended upon the ability of the British economy to surmount the hump of industrialization and raise income to a level from which self-sustained growth would continue to take place. As shown in Chapter 3, the process of achieving this goal contains costs irrespective of the specific type of institutional structure in which it is embedded. The raising of the rate of net investment at low levels of national income depends upon the imposition of constraints on consumption which may be all the more galling if at the same time the demonstration effect works to raise individual consumption aspirations. Whether private entrepreneurs or governmental officials gain title to the use of resources for investment, the community as a whole must defer gratification of many wants until the capital stock being accumulated starts to yield income. If, therefore, during the early stages of industrialization there is a welfare problem, it is largely attributable to the exigencies of economic growth rather than to capitalism, socialism, or some other form of economic organization.

Since this proposition is central to the analysis of economic growth and its relationship to the emergence of democratic political organization, a few observations should be made, somewhat parenthetically, about the light it casts on what clearly has always been a disturbing ethical question for British society. Though there was no lack of representatives of the optimistic view of the welfare problem during the industrial revolution, the pessimistic view in a sense more deeply and accurately reflected the fundamental ethical concern of British society. Both from the left and the right social philosophers and moralists fulminated against what they thought was the dereliction in the duties of responsible men toward their fellow citizens in the emerging world of industrial capitalism. With a humorless persistence which eventually made him the greatest bore of his age, Robert Owen trumpeted the environmentalist message to anyone who would listen and to many who would not. The depravity of human behavior in early factory towns was not the fault of individuals but of the institutions in which they lived. If responsible men would create a cooperative commonwealth, individuals would be molded into ethically unimpeachable citizens. Possessing none of Owen's radical propensities but sharing his basic concern for the moral condition of man, the so-called Tory Radicals excoriated the new manufacturers and industrialists for not assuming the obligations toward their workers that the possession of wealth in the best tradition of the landed aristocracy required. The brooding presence of Thomas Carlyle was a perpetual reminder of the unheroic qualities of the new social order.[17] There were even disquieting reservations about capitalism that emanated from within the very citadel of classical political economy. At mid-nineteenth century John Stuart Mill was discouraged about how much the revolutionary changes in the British economy of the previous fifty years had benefitted the condition of the common man. During his early years, he had looked to the spread of democracy as the means of bringing about the salvation of the working man, but at the end of his life Mill tended to place his hope in some form of modified socialism.[18]

Not only does one sense a profound concern about the industrial order from contemporary writers, but also from present-day scholars who look back at the period. One would expect socialists to impugn the origins of the system which they have traditionally opposed. But historians, dedicated to objective historical fact and wanting to be labeled neither pessimists nor optimists, sometimes give the impression that the material advances of the industrial revolution were exacted at a cost which could, and might better, have been avoided. Thus in a recent economic history of Britain W. H. B. Court observes of the period that "it came about that, while the influence of the new science helped to clear away mistaken views and the ancient lumber of the statute book, it also dangerously weakened the content of social and economic law. Great Britain entered upon an age of swift transition, under the handicap of an inadequate, in some respects a mean and ignoble, conception of the State."[19] The query that immediately comes to mind is: How can the state be anything but mean and ignoble during a period of transition? The resources available to the economy are not adequate for meeting all the new demands being placed upon them during such a period. The conflict between the goals of equity and growth poses a trying choice for the responsible leaders of society. They must somehow contrive to induce the present generation to forego satisfactions in the interests of increasing the welfare of future generations.

§ *The Impact of the Welfare Problem on the*
Laboring Population

When the characteristics of British social and economic life
which disturbed the conscience of sensitive observers are
considered, the harshness of the conflict becomes especially clear.
The housing for the expanding population, crowded into the
northern industrial cities during and after the Napoleonic War,
was woefully inadequate. Gerrybuilt at minimum cost, the
houses of many workers lacked sanitation facilities, and had
little if any, ventilation. Though they were no meaner than the
hovels in which the poorer agricultural workers lived, they became fine conveyors of disease. Death rates in the new towns
were higher than elsewhere in England and in the towns themselves death rates were highest in the working-class sections.
Moreover, the towns offered few diversions to entertain the working population. The income of workers was not high enough
to provide a market for many of the amusements which we now
associate with urban life. Private firms therefore had little reason to devote resources to the production of working-class entertainment. The exception, of course, was the production and
sale of alcoholic beverages, the consumption of which, however,
caused moralists grave concern for the welfare of the nation.
While the pubs of the nineteenth century perhaps did not ener-
vate the poorer classes in the manner we are led to believe the
eighteenth-century gin mills did, they nonetheless seemed to be
an apparent cause of immorality, rioting and other conduct
inimicable to the stability of the British community. If the private economy did not provide suitable diversions for the working-class, neither did the public economy. An age inspired by
private entrepreneurship did not look kindly upon great public
spectacles. There was no place in Britain for the public forums
and circuses which entertained Roman citizens in the days of the
empire and presumably helped to relieve the drudgery of existence in a subsistence economy. On the contrary, land that had
once been open to public use in the towns frequently was en-
closed for private use as the towns grew into industrial cities.

Indeed private consumption itself among those who were accumulating industrial resources for the British economy was frequently so inconspicuous that less fortunate citizens had difficulty even in participating vicariously in the enjoyment of the new wealth of the age.

However drab the life of individuals in the households of the new industrial towns, their life in the new firms was hardly better. The hours of labor were long and arduous. In the textile mills the working day was twelve hours and sometimes as much as fourteen. In the coal mines it was no less. The danger of industrial accident was high not only because the factories and mines were not equipped with proper safety devices, but also because long hours fatigued workers and made them less capable of taking the necessary precautions to protect themselves against accident.

Furthermore, whole families were frequently involved in industrial labor, rendering them under the new conditions of employment a less cohesive unit.[20] Where under the domestic system of production the activities of all the members of a family were coordinated around a production process carried on in a home, under the factory system they were subjected to equally long hours of labor demanded by the regimen of machine technology. Children were often the first entrants into the textile mills. Before the widespread adoption of steam power, the first factories in the cotton textile industry had to rely on the water power of the streams of Lancashire. Being removed from the towns and centers of population, these factories were confronted by a shortage of labor which was at first overcome by the employment of pauper children. Later as the source of power changed to steam and the developing factory system undercut the less efficient domestic system of production, families sent their children to the mills. Reluctant themselves to take employment that seemed to bear the stigma of the workhouse, but nonetheless pressed by the exigencies of economic necessity, men often placed their children in mine and factory while they themselves tried to make their way with their old skills in the old domestic employments.

Compounding the problems of life in the home, factory,

and mine was the instability of aggregate income and the consequent uncertainty of the subsistence earned by workers. Since
the industrial revolution was spawned by increasing investment
in manufacturing, mining, and transportation, the stability of
aggregate income depended increasingly on the kind of expenditures made in anticipation of future earnings. The durability of factories and railroad facilities necessarily meant that
entrepreneurs had to calculate costs and revenues over a longer
period of time. Accordingly, expectations played a more important role in the making of investment decisions. Since expectations were subject to the vagaries of a wide variety of social,
economic, and political factors, which seemed to affect entrepreneurs at any given time in a similar manner, the volume of
investment tended to fluctuate over time. That is to say, if one
entrepreneur felt disinclined to invest because of the way he
evaluated these factors, there were likely to be others who reacted
the same way. Hence aggregate investment fell off. On the
other hand, if one entrepreneur was encouraged to invest by
the prevailing market milieu, then others were also, thus causing a rise in aggregate investment. Alternately rising and falling
investment through the multiplier or respending effect, was
magnified in changes in the national income and in output and
employment.

Under the best of circumstances in a capitalistic economy
relying largely on the initiative of private individuals, the uncertainties plaguing the investment decision make the flow of
income uneven. In England during the industrial revolution
these were made more ineluctable by imperfections in the
monetary system. The first country to industrialize, England had
to devise means of providing a circulating media capable of
financing and facilitating the production and exchange of a
higher and growing level of output. Not surprisingly in a private enterprise economy, greater output called forth an increasing number of private banks. While these banks came into
existence for the express purpose of increasing the quantity of
money, they did not automatically bring with them a governor
for controlling the aggregate money supply. Central banking,
in other words, did not precede the industrial revolution, but

was born of painful monetary experiences during it. We need not go into these experiences in any detail. It is sufficient to suggest that their effect was to make the money supply at once more inelastic and elastic than it should have been. Declines in real income tended to be accentuated by sudden and sharp drops in the quantity of money. Conversely, an expansion in investment went further than desirable for the stability of income because of an unbridled expansion in the quantity of money. Particularly after the Napoleonic Wars, Britain passed through crises that, with hindsight, one can say were both more frequent and more severe than necessary. In the first half of the nineteenth century, she was beset by economic crises in 1811, 1816, 1819, 1826, 1830–32, 1837, and 1847–48.

It was without doubt a gross injustice that workers, living close to subsistence and working in drab surroundings, should be subjected to loss of job or decline in wages because of periodic crises in the economy. The people who could least afford to be idle were the first to lose their jobs and those who could live in idleness never lacked for employment. But if one considers the plight of the worker in the context of the problem—that of overcoming the hump of industrialization—then one may see why matters of equity take second place. Consider, for example, the poor housing and entertainment facilities provided for workers in the urban centers of Britain. At a time when the demand for capital was so great that the supply of saving could not meet all needs, some types of investment had to be forestalled and others had to be carried forward with production techniques that economized the use of capital. The construction of libraries, recreational halls, and athletic centers for workers necessarily had a lower claim on the scarce resources of the British economy than the construction of textile mills, engineering equipment, and railroads. Though the former might indirectly have increased the capacity of the economy by raising the morale and the productivity of workers, the latter had a more direct and calculable effect on future output. If workers' houses had been built with a greater regard for the amenities of living, resources would have been drawn away from the construction of other kinds of capacity with greater potential for the expansion of future output. Similarly, the absence of suitable safety devices in the early British factories reflected the fact that a capital-poor economy had more urgent uses for those resources that were available for investment. In short, the capital for generating self-sustaining growth in the industrial revolution was acquired at the expense of the standard of living of the British workers.

While drab social conditions, made all the more unpalatable by periodic unemployment, excited the sympathies of sensitive observers, the entrepreneurial classes were fashioning a competitive economy in which such conditions were not relevant to the making of investment decisions. From the point of view of maximizing profits, welfare was external to cost and revenue data. If, for example, employers had to build housing in order to attract workers to their firms, they built houses which were suited to this purpose alone and not houses which achieved other objectives as well, say, the elevation of the moral and psychological stability of family life. Robert Owen, whose mills in New Lanarck were a showpiece of the industrial revolution precisely because he tried to minimize the external diseconomies of production in the cotton textile industry, was certainly atypical. Surely one can doubt whether the British economy would have grown as rapidly as it did had his colleagues been persuaded to follow his example.[21]

Furthermore, unlike Owen the typical entrepreneur did not unduly trouble himself about the impact of long hours of labor on the physiological condition of his workers. Neither did he worry about the relationship between his investment decisions and the level of income and employment. The universe in which he carried on his business was bound by the markets in which he purchased resources and the markets in which he sold output. If these did not reflect the diseconomies of expanding output, they did not inhibit production.

To summarize, the passage of the British economy over the hump of industrialization was facilitated by capitalistic organization that permitted entrepreneurs to exclude variables from their calculations which, if considered, might either have aborted investment projects or drawn resources away from projects with high growth potential. It is almost as if blinders were placed on entrepreneurs so that they would not be frightened off the road of growth by the social costs that were becoming manifest in the surrounding country. These social costs constitute the welfare problem, an equitable solution of which was sacrificed to the competing demands for scarce capital of an economy on the threshold of accelerated economic growth.

§   *Slow Rise of a Labor Ideology and Labor Movement*

The welfare problem was the handmaiden of economic growth. The reaction on the part of those who bore the burden of it was crucial to the rise of democratic political institutions. Because it was so important, we shall reiterate briefly some general characteristics of the reaction discussed in earlier chapters which are requisite to the emergence of democracy.

First of all, the response of workers to the welfare problem cannot be so strongly and persistently organized in collective action that it jeopardizes the process of growth itself, for the attainment of a high level of income—income above subsistence —is a necessary condition for the development of democracy. Secondly, it must be articulated in such a way as to threaten the ability of governmental leaders to maintain social order under the existing, and nondemocratic, political system.

The position of England at the beginning of the industrialization process had consequences in these regards that are hard to underestimate. Consider the position of labor in the society in which the industrial revolution first took place. Eighteenth-century Britain was mercantilist in outlook and among the privileged classes it was generally believed that the lot of common man was labor and that he had little reason to expect from his labor more than subsistence. This, of course, was a belief entirely appropriate to the economic conditions which prevailed in England and throughout the world prior to the industrial revolution, for, in fact, except for a precious few, subsistence was the fate of man. In the minds of some pundits, however, subsistence and labor were causatively related. No one expressed this belief more effectively than that indefatigable traveler and rapporteur Arthur Young: "Everyone but an idiot knows that the lower classes must be kept poor or they will never be industrious."[22] The Reverend Joseph Townsend heartily agreed and had very dark forebodings about the prospects for the more delicate members of society if labor aspired to more than subsistence:

It seems to be a law of nature, that the poor should be to a certain degree improvident, that there may always be some to fulfill the most servile, the most sordid, the most ignoble offices in the community. The stock of human happiness is thereby much increased whilst the more delicate are not only relieved from drudgery, and freed from those occasional employments which would make them miserable, but are left at liberty, without interruption, to pursue those callings which are suited to their various dispositions and most useful to the state. As for the lowest of the poor, by custom they are reconciled to the meanest occupations, to the most laborious works, and to the most hazardous pursuits. . . . When hunger is either felt or feared, the desire of obtaining bread will quietly dispose the mind to undergo the greatest hardships, and will sweeten the severest labours. The peasant with a sickle in his hand is happier than the prince upon his throne.[23]

The harshness of life in a subsistence economy thus tended to be mirrored in a harsh attitude toward labor. There being no example of a society in which labor had achieved a standard above subsistence, it was not possible for the demonstration effect to disseminate normative ideas about the welfare of labor which were sharply at odds with the existing condition of labor. Life, in short, was expected to be difficult, and the welfare problem perhaps did not seem to be as unjust initially as it subsequently appeared to later observers.

While the upper classes typically held obdurate views about the working classes, the latter themselves had little political ideology from which they could draw inspiration and gain guidance for their own efforts to meet the problems of subsistence. Until the very end of the eighteenth century there was no systematic social philosophy directed to the problems of the most numerous members of society. The Civil War of the seventeenth century had, to be sure, produced on its left fringe the

Levellers and Diggers and the unforgettable plaint of Thomas Rainborowe that "the poorest he that is in England hath a life to live as the richest he."[24] But these manifestations of discontent among the lower classes were a primitive equalitarianism, focusing on ends rather than means and thus lacking in well thought-out programs of political action. The significant ideologies arising out of the Civil War were the contrasting systems of Locke and Hobbes. Their appeal lay primarily with the growing commercial middle classes and those who still clung to the ideas of royal absolutism. While Lockean philosophy constituted a magnificent defense of civil liberties and the priority of individual conscience and property over aggrandizing state power, it did not meet the problems of a working class whose members were ineffectual as individuals because of their lack of property.

And even the dramatic events of the French Revolution did not turn up a peculiarly proletarian philosophy. Thomas Paine proclaimed the Rights of Man and with admirable prescience delineated the outlines of the welfare state. No doubt in the activities of the Jacobins and in the abortive Babeuf conspiracy, one can see the future events affecting the labor movement casting their shadow before. Like the English revolution preceding it, however, the French Revolution was primarily a middle class upheaval, and while it waxed violent on the fury of the nameless Paris mob which stood behind the leaders of the Mountain, its democratic ideology was fathered and broadcast by the aspirations of the middle class. Coming as it did in the midst of the industrial revolution, it inevitably had a profound impact on British society and particularly on the attitude of the upper classes towards the lower classes. Edmund Burke, whose polemic against the Revolution inspired its defense by Paine, most surely reflected the deep concern of the aristocracy and the landed interests for the political stability of Britain, a concern that manifested itself in a series of repressive measures which the government of the day took to restrain the conduct of the disenfranchised and politically underprivileged.[25] The French Revolution thus exacerbated divisions in British society, but did so by way of its democratic ideology, and not by way of the incipient strains of socialism that it contained.

One may say that the industrial revolution in Britain had run half its course before there began to appear those ideas, philosophies, and ideologies which were directed to the problems and frustrations of the working man. In the period following the end of the Napoleonic Wars there was a babble of voices raised in defense of labor's right to a stake in the new world it was creating. We have already mentioned some of these voices to show that the conscience of sensitive observers in Britain was disturbed by the welfare problem. But as the industrial revolution proceeded apace there were increasing demands and declamations that labor itself look to its condition and organize itself for action, both on the economic and political fronts. Where a man like Carlyle thought that noble and generous leaders should bestow on labor the just reward of its status, William Lovett thought that labor itself should organize and through its own efforts claim its due.[26]

The organization of collective action by workers, then, in response to the welfare problem was delayed by the hiatus between the start of the industrial revolution and the appearance of a proletarian ideology. If, for example, Marx had created his system fifty years earlier, a group of leaders directing their energies to the organization of labor in trade unions and political parties would also have arisen earlier. As it was these institutions had to wait upon the process of growth itself to create conditions in which an indigenous labor movement could develop. Not only did workers have to be concentrated in industrial areas, but they also had to perceive the need for organization and the rationale for allocating some of their limited income for the support of working-class institutions. When the habits and discipline of organization are learned from within the ranks of labor it takes a longer time and the resulting labor movement assumes a different character from that which arises when leaders outside the ranks of labor attempt to ride herd on the collective energies of workers.

The problem of organizing workers in Britain was further inhibited by the inertia which carried over from the older re-

gime, from which industrial capitalism had emerged.[27] While
there were cases of unions being organized and strikes conducted,
the prevailing spirit of Britain in economic relationships during the eighteenth century was paternalistic. Whether in the
domestic system of manufacturing or in the manorial control of
agriculture the emphasis in social relationships was on status in
a hierarchy of statuses, each one of which had its perquisites and
responsibilities. Though the guilds declined as the state took
over many of their regulatory functions, the notion of master
and servant each in his place was widespread. Whether industrial
workers came from a rural setting or manufacturing occupations
they were likely to bear the attitudes appropriate to the old
world. Far from being militant workers very much conscious of
their identity and interests as industrial workers, peasants newly
arrived from the country were confused, perhaps even frightened, and likely therefore to cling with great tenacity to some
of their old beliefs and customs.

Prior to the nineteenth century, then, economic growth in
Britain was not encumbered by a labor movement. The lack
of a proletarian ideology, the persistence of habits and patterns
of thinking among workers inherited from a paternalistic world,
the high proportion of women and children among factory
workers combined to abort the appearance of unions on a wide
scale and the undemocratic nature of the political system prevented the formation of labor parties, if indeed this had even
been contemplated by the early industrial workers. Entrepreneurs thus were able to conduct their affairs in the new firms they
were organizing without too great solicitude for the welfare of
their employees. They provided the minimum essentials for at-
tracting a labor force, but they were not distracted by the problems that an active and militant group of workers can raise. The
firm was sufficiently insulated from the enervating demands of
consumption-oriented workers to become a prime source of accumulation. At a period when capital markets were not yet
well developed and the saving that did accrue annually was
typically held in government securities or the shares of the
great trading companies, it was of no small importance to the

growth of the new economy that the potential force of these internal pressures on the resources of the firm was minimized.

§　*The Ambivalent Status of Trade Unions in the Nineteenth Century*

Notwithstanding the occasional flurry of union activity and the growth of friendly societies in the eighteenth century, the labor movement really started in Britain during the nineteenth century. Perhaps it can be best dated with the passage of Combination Acts in 1799 and 1800. It did not, however, loom large in the British social scene until the end of the Napoleonic Wars and the relaxation of the restrictions of war. Before the end of the war King Ludd had raised his battle cry and the stockingers and other domestic workers, threatened with displacement by new technology, responded by smashing and breaking up the new machinery, the ostensible cause of their discomfort. The unsuccessful march of the "Blanketeers" in 1817, the Peterloo massacres two years later, the revolt of the agricultural workers in 1830, the meteoric rise and precipitous decline of the Grand National Consolidated Trade Unions, Owenite socialism, the Ten Hours Movement, and Chartism—concrete manifestations of the rebellious adolescence of the growing industrial labor force—made the half-century prior to the Great Exhibition in 1852 a period of unrest and discontent unparalleled in the history of Britain.

This, then, was the respose of the vast majority of people caught up in the process of industrialization to the welfare problem. However one evaluates the course of real wages during the industrial revolution, it is difficult to deny the undercurrent of unrest, intermittently erupting in overt violence, which accompanied Britain's passage over the hump of industrial growth. There were, to be sure, special circumstances one may adduce to explain it. Twenty-three years of war broken only by a short armistice imposed a regime of austerity on British society in the midst of the industrial revolution which, though stimulating the accumulation of industrial capital, undoubtedly bore more heavily on working-class groups than others. The price of subsistence rose more than money wages as resources were diverted to the production of war materials. Moreover, civil liberties were repressed and the activities of workers circumscribed, because the ruling classes feared that the democratic message of the French Revolution might evoke disloyal conduct on the part of those who already were suffering from the strains of the industrial transition. With its ever-present danger of impressment into the service of the royal navy, wartime was never a pleasant period for the lower classes. Thus in the midst of the industrial revolution many British citizens, particularly those who did not possess political rights, were deprived of civil liberties which they regarded as theirs by virtue of their national status. They therefore had reason to be bitter when many of the repressions enacted during wartime continued into the peace that followed. While war unfortunately appears to be an all-too-normal way for human beings to conduct their affairs, it can hardly be attributed to economic growth or industrialization. It therefore was a special circumstance during the period with which we are concerned that exacerbated the discontent and unrest accompanying industrialization.

Perhaps the most important thing to observe about the labor unrest during the second part of the industrial revolution is that it took shape in overt demonstrations and attempts at organization, yet did not interfere with the process of economic growth. In part, this reflects factors which we have already discussed. Though by the second quarter of the nineteenth century the industrial labor force had become a significant proportion of the total labor force, the typical Englishman was still not a factory worker or urban resident. Those who were in the industrial labor force had not necessarily discarded the attitudes characteristic of the older world out of which industrial capitalism emerged. Further, with low wages, even if they were higher than those earned in agricultural labor, and long hours, workers had neither the energy nor income to support an effective trade union movement. There were, in short, resistances to organization within the ranks of labor that were all the greater because of Britain's advance position in the industrialization process.

Trade unions thus appeared spasmodically during this period, occasionally registering local successes, but seldom attaining sustained organization. Sometimes, as in the case of the Grand National Consolidated Trades Union, this was because the ambitions of the organizers were far ahead of the aspirations and capabilities of the rank and file. But usually it was because workers did not have financial or moral resources to support and sustain a trade union. An unsuccessful strike would at once destroy its treasury and support among partially committed workers. And with all the will in the world, workers could not easily find funds for union dues when recession and depression periodically depleted their savings.

While the growth of trade unions was inhibited by their susceptibility to economic adversity, it was further restrained by what might be called an ambivalent legal environment. The labor movement in Britain dated from enactment of the Combination Acts in 1799 and 1800, formalizing the common law prohibitions against combinations in restraint of trade. Though they applied to both workers and masters, these laws had a greater impact on the former. Until their repeal in 1824, overt union activity was illegal and attempts at organization had to be carried on in surreptitious ways. With repeal and the emergence of trade unions into the light of day the intensity of labor activity became entirely too great for Parliament and in 1825 the Combination Laws were partially reimposed. Thereafter unions had a quasi-legal status; they lived within the law so long as they did not attempt to make too much of their collective strength in campaigns against employers.

Not only were trade unions harried by their uncertain legal position, but labor leaders themselves were hard pressed by prevailing standards of justice. The Home Secretary could sentence men to Australia for seven years, fourteen years, or even life for crimes against property. And there were occasions, not frequent to be sure, but often enough to restrain all but the most intrepid, when capital punishment was meted out to working-class leaders who had been too active in demonstrations of rebellious workers.[28] In its formative stages, when the habits of discipline had not yet been firmly implanted in workers and when their collective strength was still quite amorphous, the labor movement was especially vulnerable at the leadership level. Lacking the bureaucracies characteristic of contemporary labor organizations with their vice-presidents and second and third in command, trade unions suffered irreparable damage when an indispensable man fell afoul of the law.

§   *Civil Disorder and the Reform Bill of 1832*

While the union phase of the labor movement was inhibited by its ambivalent legal status and successful only in establishing a tradition of organization, the political phase, though no more productive of concrete gains for labor, brought on the first break in the hold of the aristocratic oligarchy on the machinery of government since the political settlement of the Revolution of 1688. We refer, of course, to the passage of the first Reform Bill in 1832. The industrial revolution played hob with the old system of political representation in Britain by inducing both an increase and a shift in the location of population. The growth in the industrial strength of the Midlands and northern counties increased the number of people living in unincorporated towns without representation in Parliament and conversely increased the representation of older areas in England which lost population. These inequities combined with a limited franchise to create an unstable political milieu. The entrepreneurial classes who felt strongly entitled to the rights of political citizenship did not possess voting privileges by virtue of their industrial status. Still less was there a place for workers within the constitution. Yet the former was responsible for changing the face of England and increasing its wealth many times, and the latter bore the brunt of the contingent welfare problem. There was then a community of political interest between these social groups which in other respects were antagonistic. Forced into tacit alliance by the discriminations they mutually suffered, they sought to change the existing constitutional order. Where, however, entrepreneurial groups had the persuasive power of wealth behind them and representatives in Parliament working for them, the working classes had to rely on cruder methods of demonstration which not infrequently degenerated into riots and violent clashes between the demonstrators and the forces of law and order.

It was this threat to the stability of the social order that prompted the oligarchy to extend itself and bring new groups into the councils of government. When the Duke of Wellington broke the impasse in the House of Lords by throwing his support to Lord Grey's Reform Bill, he did not do it out of dedication to democratic ideology or devotion to the middle classes. He acted to save parliamentary institutions which he thought threatened by a revolutionary virus. He preferred to see greater representation in parliament than to risk the loss of that hallowed institution in a democratic rebellion. In this respect he reflected the prevailing view of the ruling classes, none of whom looked upon the Reform Bill as the first installment of Britain's gradual move to democracy. The first Reform Bill was designed to be a once-and-for-all measure to still the voices of protest of the most influential opponents of the oligarchy and to provide broader government support for meeting the grievances of the others.

The labor movement's threat to the stability of the British social order was real enough. The increasing concentration of population in the towns and cities took place before the establishment of a regular urban police force. Weapons and the other kinds of technology relevant to the wielding of police power were not so advanced that government had a pronounced advantage vis-à-vis citizens. And because the British economy's omnivorous demands for capital limited the resources available for utility and welfare purposes and the means for placating unrest, it was all the more important that the police power of government be organized effectively. Prior to 1835 magistrates had to rely on the yeomanry or the army when civil disorder threatened. In view of their "irregular" status, it is perhaps understandable that the urban mob made magistrates nervous, for even when assembled for peaceful purposes it could play curious tricks on the imagination. The massacre at St. Peter's Field outside Manchester in 1819 on the occasion of a mass meeting of the unemployed was apparently set off by magistrates who were apprehensive about their ability to control the crowd if it became aroused by the fulminations of orator Hunt. The creation of the first police force in London by act of Parliament in 1835 was therefore an important measure in strengthening the ability of government to control unrest, not least of all because it regularized the police service and made it easier to forestall the outbreak of violence.[29]

If growing urban population gave the discontent of the day massive and popular proportions, the exclusion of the middle classes from the rights of political citizenship created a potentially dangerous group of leaders for directing the unrest into revolutionary channels. At least Francis Place, the radical tailor of Charing Cross, was not unmindful of the possible need to resort to arms in order to achieve political reform. His reports of military preparations in the north of England during the second Reform Campaign in 1832 spoke volumes for the determination of the more active members of the middle classes to force the oligarchy to accept changes in the constitution.[30]

§   *The Poor Law Amendment Act of 1834*

The Reform Bill of 1832 was a stroke of political genius in a country that had long since established parliamentary government. By modifying the franchise laws so that the members of the upper middle classes in the cities could vote, by redrawing parliamentary districts so that the rotten boroughs were obliterated and the newer cities given greater representation, England managed to avoid the revolutionary violence that subsequently afflicted the capitals of Europe in 1848. Yet in yielding to the forces demanding reform England did not go so far that she interfered with the conditions essential for stimulating economic growth. On the contrary, she brought into government the representatives of entrepreneurial interests who wanted to reform government in a manner consistent with their economic objectives and commitments. Labor after 1832 was, as it were, still on the outside looking in.

Consider, for example, the Poor Law Amendment Act of 1834, one of the most important legislative enactments of the Reform

Parliament. Prior to 1832 the unemployed and able-bodied poor had received outside relief from the parishes in the form of grants in aid of wages based on schedules drawn up by the Berkshire magistrates at Speenhamland in 1795. Originally intended to provide workers, whose real income had been eroded by the rise of prices during the first years of the Napoleonic Wars, a subsistence wage, these schedules had led to the pauperization of labor in the southern agricultural districts. In the expanding industrial areas of England Speenhamland had worked as a rough and ready system of unemployment compensation, but employers of agricultural workers forced down wages with the full knowledge that they would be supplemented from the local poor rates. Agricultural workers consequently became wards of the parish.

Though the Poor Law needed revision, the act of 1834 did not command widespread popular support. Rather it became a hated symbol among the working classes of the ascendancy of the newly enfranchised middle classes. The reason for this is not hard to come by. Guided by Utilitarian principles, the Royal Commission which investigated the old, and made recommendations for the new, Poor Law formulated a proposal which was intended to cope both with unemployment and with the growing burden of an unemployable population. These objectives were to be achieved by abolishing outdoor relief, building union poor houses for the administering of indoor relief, and making the terms for granting it so odious and onerous that unemployed workers would only turn to it as a last resort. The principle of less eligibility was thus laid down as the guide to the administration of relief in the new industrial society that was evolving in England.

Though compliance with the terms of the Poor Law Amendment Act undoubtedly had a salutary effect on the pauperized labor in the south of England, in the Midlands and northern counties where it was imposed more slowly and complied with even more reluctantly, its effect was harder to evaluate. One thing was certain, however: workers believed that they had been deprived of a right and that the condition of labor had been stigmatized by the withdrawal of outdoor relief from workers who through no fault of their own had become unemployed. It was an ignoble and mean act, made no more palatable by the frequent refusal of parish officials to conduct the poor house in the crudely utilitarian spirit demanded by the Poor Law Commissioners.

Whatever one may think of the new Poor Law, which became the foundation of Britain's nineteenth-century social security system, it was an answer to the welfare problem eminently consistent with the requirements for industrial growth under capitalism. It reduced the burden of the poor rates by imposing the responsibility for unemployment on the individual worker rather than on the society. If the deterrent effect of the workhouse did not solve the problem of poverty—and the level of income was still too low and the fluctuations of income too violent to allow such a simple solution—it certainly strengthened the disciplinary impact of unemployment. The bargaining position of the worker vis-à-vis the employer, always weak because of the distribution of both material and nonmaterial assets in favor of the latter, was further weakened by the uncertainty of job tenure and the imminence of the workhouse. A job acquired such importance that the worker could not always afford to bargain over the terms of employment; he had then to adjust to the demands of the employer, thus allowing the accumulation objectives of the latter to take precedence over the goals of labor.

§   *Unemployment as the Responsibility of the Individual*

How was it possible for the government of this period to take the views that it did on the responsibility of the individual for unemployment and poverty, especially in view of the fact that subsequently almost all societies, irrespective of their ideological commitment, have come to accept these problems as a corporate responsibility? First of all, as we noted earlier, the attitude toward labor of a society taking the lead in emerging from subsistence conditions was much harsher than in societies whose normative views of labor were formed on the basis of fuller empirical knowledge of the industrialization process. Second, entrepreneurial and individualistic values, as we have also noted, were widely disseminated in Britain, not just confined to entrepreneurs and capitalists in a narrow sense. The gap between employer and worker in the new industrial enterprises was still small enough to permit the spread of the values of the former among some of the latter. Moreover, the industrial revolution created many new skilled positions to which workers might aspire as a solution to their present discontents. The notions of self-help and individual improvement were assiduously cultivated by mechanics' institutes and the movement for workers' education.[31] Third, the relationship between increases in output and increases in population was such that mass unemployment was a cyclical rather than a chronic problem. Though it is difficult to determine the direction of causative influence in the change of these variables, they reacted with one another in such a way as to allow per capita income to rise before the end of the industrial revolution. Population growth stimulated the demand for output, and output growth permitted a sustaining of a larger population. Secular unemployment was therefore minimized and the long-run burden on the poor rates held down. The resilience of the expanding British economy, its ability to bounce back from crisis and depression, periodically restored the opportunities for earning wage income in the private sector of the economy.

Fourth, a factor which was probably more important than any others, Britain industrialized at a time when the chances for migrating to another society were still extremely good. The North American continent, located in the middle latitudes, needing manpower to develop its manifest economic potential, was a powerful attraction for anyone who was frustrated by economic conditions in nineteenth-century England. Because of its location on the sea, the transportation barriers to migration were not so great as they were in landlocked countries. Because of the common language in Britain and the United States, the cultural impediments to migration were minimal. And if the prospective migrant was disturbed about leaving British territory, he could try his luck in Canada or Australia. In short, the frontier in the west was open to persons who wished to migrate.

By creating new employment opportunities and destroying

old ones, industrialization was a powerful stimulant to population movements. In England the indigenous population moved
into the expanding manufacturing and industrial centers from
the surrounding counties. At the same time Irish workers came
across the Irish Sea and Scotchmen across the Tweed to the
northern manufacturing centers. The rate at which the cities
grew, however, was held back by the simultaneous emigration of
population from Britain to the United States, Canada, and
Australia.[32] Thus the increasing output of industrial Britain did
not have to bear the full burden of the concomitant population
increase. It was therefore feasible, though perhaps not charitable,
for Britain to impose the responsibility for unemployment and
economic distress on the individual when he could, if hard
pressed, seek relief in another country.

If the frontier acted as a safety-valve for the discontent engendered by the industrialization process, it did not do so in the
sense that it drew off from Britain the poorest workers and those
who suffered the most severely from the dislocations of accelerated growth. In the first half of the nineteenth century, before
the steam and steel age had effected a revolution in ocean transport, the cost of migrating to America precluded passage for the
very poor unless they were subsidized. While there was considerable interest in Britain in the subsidizing of migration as a solution to the welfare problem, quantitatively it never proved to be
a significant program. The people migrating were yeomen, mechanics, semiskilled workers, and those who had sufficient resources, energy, and initiative to undertake the responsibilities
and undergo the difficulties which life in a new country inevitably raised. But these were precisely the people who, if they had
remained in England, might have made the labor movement too
effective an instrument in the pursuit of consumptionist objectives for the maintenance of a high rate of growth.[33] Frustrated
and discouraged by the obstacles confronting them in industrial
Britain, they migrated to the new world. Had they not had this
release, they would have swelled the ranks of the unions and
political action groups which were trying to bring the industrial
community to terms with the aspirations and needs of the working man.

§　*Some Early Measures to Mitigate the Welfare Problem*

Thus Great Britain, her industrial revolution engineered by private, autonomous entrepreneurs, could afford to leave the welfare problem to the autonomous responses of individuals, partly for reasons associated with the early appearance of industrialization. This did not, of course, mean that the British government did nothing to allay the severity of the welfare problem. The conscience of England was too much disturbed by the new industrialism to pass it by without some corporate expression of concern. From very early in the nineteenth century the Parliament passed legislation affecting the hours of labor. This culminated in the Ten Hour Bill of 1847.[34] But for the greater part of the industrial revolution the effectiveness of this kind of legislation had been attenuated by insufficient provision for inspection and enforcement. Moreover, the whole debate over the corn laws was couched very largely in terms of the urgency of the welfare problem. However much men like Richard Cobden and John Bright were dedicated individualists and propagandists for capitalistic enterprise, they cannot be accused of lacking concern for human welfare. Rather one might say they had a surfeit of it. Believing wholeheartedly in Ricardian economic prescription, they had no doubt but that the lifting of the corn laws would both preserve the conditions for accumulation and improve the standard of subsistence of the working classes. But unlike hours legislation, the rescinding of the corn laws reduced the role of government in economic life and its welfare effect therefore depended upon the performance of the private economy.

The autonomous response of individuals to the welfare problem took essentially two forms: one, the wealthier classes and those aligned with them used private resources to try to improve the moral and/or economic status of the poorer classes; two, the poorer classes continued the attempts we have already discussed to organize their collective strength in the labor movement. The first response manifested itself in a number of different ways. Wealthy individuals contributed to and supported hospitals. Contributions to church and chapel defrayed the expense of religious charities. But much more enthusiasm was evoked over those activities which were designed to improve the character of the deserving poor so that they could either rise above their mean status or, hopefully, learn to live with it contentedly. The industrial revolution, perhaps not fortuitously, coincided with the great religious revival in England which, in attempting to reform the established church, swelled the ranks of dissenters. Reacting against the irreverence of the eighteenth century and the high living of the Anglican gentry and clergy, the Wesleys injected into the conscience of England a fervor and piety which left a marked impression on nineteenth-century reform movements, whatever their avowed objectives happened to be. William Wilburforce was the great evangelical humanitarian of the age. His monumental efforts for the abolition of slavery in the colonies were matched by equally fervent crusades for workers' education, temperance, educational reform, Sunday school attendance, and other purposes, all designed to fortify and strengthen the moral resources of the British population so that they would be the better able to take advantage of the manifold opportunities for individual enrichment opened up by industrialization. Indeed, the union movement itself did not escape the wide spell cast by the Wesleyan revival. Where labor leaders springing from the Marxian tradition were agnostic and scoffed at all scriptures except that of their own secular deity, as often as not the English labor leader carried into the economic struggle a set of fundamental beliefs acquired in the church or chapel whose realization, he felt, depended on the successful conclusion of his effort.

§　Chartism

While an individual, autonomous response to the welfare problem permeated Britain, the more dramatic response, if not the more successful, was the repeated efforts of the Chartists to wrest from Parliament further reforms in the franchise and the organization of the Commons. Inspired by the success of the

middle classes in the Reform Bill of 1832 and disillusioned by
the failure of the union movement to sustain itself in the 30's,
the Chartist leaders mounted a massive campaign for parliamentary reform which drew into its ranks a heterogeneous following, united in little else but its desire for an extension of the
reforms of 1832. Skilled London artisans, stockingers and the
ever-distressed handloom weavers, Birmingham monetary reformers, poor law reformers, and unemployed workers all came to the
support of the six points of the Charter. Three times the Chartists
petitioned the Parliament for reform at periods in the trade
cycle when recession had increased the number of unemployed
supporting them—1839, 1842, and 1848—and three times the
Parliament rejected the petition.

The Parliament's refusal to act upon the petition of the
Chartists was facilitated by the splits and the differences among
the latter with respect to tactics and objectives. Not being a
cohesive mass movement it did not pose the threat to the maintenance of social order that it otherwise would have. When certain groups within the movement advocated physical force as
the appropriate means of achieving its objectives, the advocates
of moral force shied away and became hesitant to identify themselves too much with a program that might jeopardize their long-
run chances of achieving their particular nostrum. A man like
the artisan William Lovett, who composed the first charter, was
not likely to follow the lead of Feargus O'Connor and his fustian
jackets. No more were monetary reformers like Thomas Attwood
or opponents of the Poor Law like William Oastler likely to feel
comfortable in step with James Bronterre O'Brien or George
Julian Harney. Chartism thus fell of its own weight and with
each successive petition became less of a mass movement.

Though Chartism must be accounted a failure in terms of
the immediate objectives it set for itself, it was not a failure in
terms of the long-run development of a democratic labor movement. On the one hand, it dramatized the demand of the working classes for political emancipation and demonstrated forcefully to the politically privileged classes that they were not satisfied with the status quo of 1832. On the other hand, the experience gained in supporting the Charter showed labor leaders that

the Parliament, based as it was after 1832 on wider representation, would not be intimidated into a wholesale extension of political rights by demagogues and demonstrations of unemployed workers. The path to a more satisfactory solution to the welfare problem appeared to lie, not through direct political action, but through painstaking organization of workers in trade unions that would be able to sustain themselves over time and therefore press employers consistently for improvement in wages, hours, and working conditions. In other words, failure of the Chartist Movement induced labor leaders to concentrate their main effort on that part of the economic front where they were most likely to attain success—among the skilled workers.

Industrial capitalism thus gained a breathing spell in which the conditions for economic growth were not jeopardized too much by the consumptionist demands of the working population, while workers themselves remained free to struggle with the problems and difficulties of organizing their collective strength. If the Chartist Movement had been more militant and more effectively organized it might have brought about one of the following mutually exclusive results. One, it might have been successful in democratizing political rights and electing a Parliament which could have imposed constraints on the entrepreneurs too severe for a continued high rate of economic growth. Alternatively, in anticipation of such an eventuality, the labor movement might have been more severely repressed than it was, limiting its opportunity for future growth.

§   *Summary*

The development of the British economy and political community after 1850 lies outside our purview since the industrial revolution drew to a close toward the middle of the century. Yet the purport of our analysis for the growth of the democratic process in that period is clear. As the first nation to industrialize, Britain had no example of a more developed economy to emulate. Economic growth during the industrial revolution, therefore, was first and foremost the creative handiwork of private entrepreneurs who made the innovations in productive tech-niques and organization that eventually resulted in a rise in per capita income. Because of the availability of resources of good quality in Britain, a favorable location, and a technology rudi-mentary enough to be fairly easily learned and disseminated, entrepreneurial activity, and perhaps more important, entrepre-neurial values, were widespread. One response to the welfare problem—a problem exacerbated by the shortage of capital and the inability of the British economy to meet the social needs of the growing urban population—was the seeking out by individ-uals of better positions where they could minimize its effects. This they could do either by trying to rise to a higher economic status in Britain or by migrating to another country. For those who had neither the inclination nor the ability to resolve the welfare problem by their own individual efforts, the collective response was inhibited by the inertia of traditional patterns of thought and action carried over from rural communities and by the delay in the appearance of a proletarian ideology which could serve as a guide to action. But because of these deterrents, associated with the early position of Britain in the industrializa-tion process, other kinds of controls which might have forestalled the growth of an independent labor movement were unnecessary. Controls there were, to be sure; but, as we have pointed out, these tended to be permissive in the sense that they allowed workers to form labor organizations though attenuating their effectiveness. If the Chartist campaigns were unsuccessful, the legal environment of Britain was at least permissive enough to permit them to be mounted. Having been rebuffed by the politi-cal order which had but recently brought into its councils the members of the upper middle class, labor leaders turned their main effort to the organization of skilled workers. With the ris-ing tide of Victorian prosperity in the second half of the nine-teenth century the trade unions had an economic basis on which they could acquire permanency and respectability. Because skilled workers were the first to be organized, their demands for first-class political citizenship could be the more easily acceded to. Having shed the incubus of the oppressed handloom weavers and unemployed Irish navvies and having come to appreciate the benefits of the Victorian virtue of thrift, they no longer seemed to threaten the consensus on which a constitutional political system must be based. While, therefore, the British political system was necessarily nondemocratic during the industrial revolution, the conditions for the subsequent piecemeal installation of democracy did not have to be sacrificed on the altar of economic growth.

Chapter 6

The United States:
The Natural Haven of
Industrialization and Democracy

INDUSTRIALIZATION IN THE nineteenth century spread to the European continent and America on the strength of many of the factors which had initially set off the industrial revolution in Britain. Both the United States and Germany, for example, were located in the middle latitudes with favorable climates and consequently long growing seasons. Similarly, they both possessed natural transport systems which, as the commercial revolution opened the oceans to trade, brought them into the world economy. Moreover, they either possessed industrial resources of high quality or had access to them. On the side of the intangible subjective factors, Germany and the United States grew out of the European scientific tradition which fostered both a belief in experimentation, change, and progress and a desire for the material goods of this world. When, therefore, the forces making for autonomous growth in Britain were transmitted to the western world by the exportation of British capital, techniques, and labor skills, they induced a similar, though by no means identical, kind of economic growth. Private entrepreneurs, with more or less aid from government, took the initiative in investing resources in the expansion of productive capacity which yielded external economies to the society. With the development of the factory system and the concentration of population in urban centers the welfare problem created tensions and conflicts. The character of and response to those conflicts had a marked impact on the evolution of political systems. In this and the following chapter we shall discuss both the United States and Germany. They illustrate, each in its own way, the democratizing influence of industrialization where conditions are suitable for autonomous growth.

§   *The Significance of America's Natural Environment*

That the political and economic development of the United States was unique is among the most commonplace of observations. But hackneyed truths are so familiar that people accept them as self-evident and seldom ask themselves why they are true. Unlike Britain where the forces of industrialization went far to break up the old order and make room for the evolution of democratic political institutions, the United States had no old order to break up. The feudal tradition with its hierarchy of statuses and invidious distinctions which compelled the lower orders to defer to, and humble themselves before, their superiors never took root in America. Its transfer was aborted by the vastness and virginal character of the new world. In Tocqueville's felicitous phrase, America was born free.[1]

It is appropriate to start our analysis of American economic development with a consideration of the natural background in which it took place, for the freedom of which Tocqueville spoke was clearly related to the fortuitous circumstances of space, climate, and natural resources. Where the typical underdeveloped economy of today is burdened with far too large a population for its meager supply of resources, America was held back by too meager a supply of labor for its tremendous storehouse of natural wealth. In the colorless jargon of economics, America was favored by high land-labor ratios.

From every point of view America's natural setting was ideal for growth. The Atlantic Ocean protected it from hostile incursions of the European powers, while giving it access to the main routes of world commerce. A system of inland waterways and a benign topography rendered the penetration of the continent from the eastern coastal plain a practicable, if not easy, task at a time when the technology of transportation was not highly developed. Though the climate varied from the subtropical desert climate of the southwest to the continental forest climate of the northeast, there were many parts of the country with near optimal conditions of precipitation and temperature. In the eastern half of the North American continent rainfall was abundant, well-distributed, and predictable, and it was neither so hot nor so cold that human beings were debilitated or prevented from energetically developing the natural wealth of the land. The natural wealth of America was fabled and almost seemed to belie the concept of scarcity and diminishing returns which was so important to the outlook of classical economists. Timber, fur, fish, coal, iron ore, oil, and a soil that had been for centuries accumulating the organic and inorganic substances essential for plant life, were ready for exploitation. All that was needed was a population with sufficient initiative and capital to work these resources into consumable output.

So obviously important was this natural inheritance that it has often been singled out as the factor responsible for stamping America with its unique characteristics. Frederick Jackson Turner formulated a frontier thesis which appealed very strongly to those people who conceived of the American way of life and the American outlook as fundamentally different from the European social order.[2] By dramatizing the democratic influence of the frontier he minimized the influence of European society in the emergence of America. According to the thesis, America was not simply a product of European aspirations seeking fulfillment in the climate of the new world. Rather, the democratic experiment flourished precisely because the values forged in the crucible of the frontier flowed eastward and subordinated European values to the rugged individualism of the indigenous American.

The Turner thesis has provided grist for the mill of many a social historian and critic, and we have no intention here of repeating the many difficulties and problems it raises. The point is that however loose Turner's formulation of the thesis, however questionable his interpretation of the evolution of the indigenous American character, it cannot be denied that he seized upon and analyzed circumstances which clearly differentiated American society from European society. We do not need to accept a literal version of the safety-valve thesis in order to recognize the premium that open and unpopulated space may place on individual initiative and self-sufficiency. If it did not *cause* the individualism which provided much of the energy for the development of America, it surely provided a milieu in which people with individualistic propensities could flourish. If Turner turned his back on Europe and faced west, we can look both ways and observe the interaction between European ideology and American environment.

By the time the industrial revolution took place in America in the latter half of the nineteenth century, this interaction had so far established a consensus with respect to fundamental values that matters of economic and political philosophy were not really at issue.[3] The early immigrants to America, whether dissenters seeking escape from the restrictions of an established religion or individuals searching for freedom from social and political oppressions, found a world in which the Lockean notions of natural law made great good sense. For in the wilderness it required little discussion to prove that what a man wrested from the soil belonged to him by virtue of his having mingled his labor with the bounty of nature. In a sparsely populated land it was evident to men who had little capital to work with that the income they earned, the output they produced, was attributed more to their own efforts than to the cooperation afforded them by the other members of society. Whether or not they had heard of Locke, pioneers acted instinctively on the premises of his philosophy.[4]

And surely it is not accidental that Thomas Jefferson, the most eloquent American philosopher of the Lockean view, was an upcountry farmer who was keenly aware of the problems and aspirations of the small landowner. His model of agrarian democracy was based on the widespread ownership of the abundant supplies of land in America and, articulated before the industrial proletariat he distrusted had appeared on the American scene, remained the source of American ideological values long after the industrial revolution destroyed the primacy of agriculture. We shall return shortly to some problems that Jeffersonian philosophy raised for a growth-oriented American society at the formation of the United States. Here we wish to emphasize its individualism and the role it performed in establishing an American *weltanschauung* prior to the arrival of those waves of immigrants in the nineteenth century, immigrants who came from countries where the social and economic conditions were such that Lockean notions of individualism could not be expected to flourish. The remarkable thing about the industrial revolution in America was the persistence of the individualistic response to the welfare problem it raised even among those who suffered severely from it. If this cannot be explained in terms of the ease with which immigrants could escape the discontents of the city by moving to the frontier, it can be partially explained in terms of the predominance of individualistic values formed prior to the dawn of the industrial age, and sustained in the industrial era by the omnipresence of an exploitable public domain. In short, Jeffersonian philosophy muted the effect of collectivist notions that may have been carried by immigrants from the old to the new world.

Not only did natural conditions in America stimulate the spread of Lockean individualism, but they fostered the growth of representative institutions as well. Since the new world was devoid of traditional social organization at the time it was opened to colonization by immigrants from Europe, a new social order had to be made. The model, naturally enough, which guided the creation of society in America was the institutions of the old world. The British transplanted British institutions; the French, French institutions. But, as we indicated, not all European institutions flourished equally well in the American habitat. Feudalism, for example, with its complex system of land tenure, of mutual rights and obligations, could not be maintained where there was an abundant supply of land and a shortage of labor. Labor either had to be enticed to such a world by the prospects of reward or purchased as a piece of capital equipment. A slave labor force or a free labor force survived, but not one that was neither slave nor free. If feudalism was defeated by space, representative institutions thrived on it. The English especially brought to the new world the assemblies or legislatures that they looked upon as the rightful means for articulating their interests in the political order. In a world in which there was little tradition to guide conduct and no well-established estates to which one had to defer, the assemblies became the custodians of the popular consensus and the place in which grievances could be aired and demands imposed on the governor-general or the representative of the crown. Because the colonies were so far removed from metropolitan England and confronted by problems so different, the assemblies as political units acquired a status that could never be accorded to the crown. Respect for a representative political order grew along with disrespect for the Hanoverian English monarchs.

Thus even before the industrial revolution took place in America the circumstances of its world location, its position relative to the mature societies of Europe, and its great supply of natural resources made it receptive to an ideology of individualism and to representative political institutions. Indeed, the image of America that held such a strong attraction to the population of Europe in the nineteenth century was compounded from these elements. It was precisely because of this image that the vested interests of the aristocratic and authoritarian societies of Europe feared the subversive influence of the American experiment.[5] And rightly so. The French Revolution may not have been caused by the American Revolution, but the latter certainly had a hand in inspiring it. When the French middle classes and the Parisian mob brought down the *Ancien Régime,* they were seeking a way of life that many thought had already been attained in America.

§   *The Subordination of Democratic Impulses to the Requirements of Growth*

We have not used the word democratic to describe the political order that evolved in colonial America, because it was not democratic as we have defined the term. The typical colonial assembly was neither fully sovereign nor was it elected on the basis of manhood suffrage. The crown could countermand the decisions of the assemblies through the governor-general of the colony. The assemblies themselves were in the main representative of propertied interests, though there was considerable variation in this among the colonies. The American Revolution, however, stimulated democratic development, because in order to ensure maximum participation in the revolt against Britain it was necessary to make its appeal as universal as possible. The Declaration of Independence significantly enough extolled life, liberty, and the pursuit of happiness—but not property. In his patriotic manifesto Jefferson stood to the left of John Locke. Moreover, the assemblies of the rebellious colonies in the exigencies of war tended to become increasingly representative of a wider public. So far did the new nation move in the direction of democracy that it posed some difficult problems for those groups in the United States who were chiefly responsible for its economic development and destiny. In short, at the formation of the United States there was a conflict between the onrushing forces of democracy and the prerequisites of economic growth. Since the resolution of this conflict was crucial to the development of both the economic and political systems, we now turn to an examination of it.

The American Revolution, in the language of the Marxists, was a bourgeois revolution. Though rationalized in the universal categories of natural law, it was led by men of substance, lawyers and merchants, who were mainly interested in protecting the autonomy of their own political institutions and their own lives from what they considered the unwarranted and arbitrary actions of the British monarch. The revolution was conservative. Englishmen in the colonies were asserting what they understood to be their constitutional and traditional rights vis-à-vis the crown, just as in the previous century Englishmen in the Commons had asserted their rights in the rebellion against Charles I. Where the French Revolution contained a strong utopian dynamic in its drive to create a new world by destroying the effete feudal institutions of the *Ancien Régime,* the American Revolution had objectives limited to the reestablishment of the relatively free institutions which had been evolving in America for the greater part of colonial history. To be sure, there were democratic and radical voices raised during the Revolution, but these did not represent men of substance, the men of economic standing. Tom Paine, Samuel Adams, Patrick Henry, and even Thomas Jefferson were a mixed blessing to these men of standing, essential perhaps for establishing popular support for the revolution, but a decided nuisance when the job of reconstructing the political order was at hand.

If the men of substance were made uneasy by the democratic ideologues of the Revolution, their worst fears were confirmed by the chaotic performance of American society during the Confederation. Victorious in their struggle against the centralized power symbolized by the British Crown and jealous of the newly won prerogatives of the state assemblies, the men of the Continental Congress were loath to cede to a central authority of their own making the same kind of authority from which they had recently rebelled. In consequence, the Confederation lacked the power to create a political framework stable enough for the effective maintenance of domestic order and for the stimulation of economic activity. Its ability to govern was aborted by the requirement of unanimous consent by the delegates to the Congress from the various states. The Confederation could not raise adequate revenues to meet the common needs of the several states, nor could it enact tariff legislation which would have reduced the barriers to trade among the states. Faced with the need for funds which could not be obtained through taxation, the Congress as well as the states resorted to borrowing and the emission of paper money. Inevitably both bonds and currency depreciated, further weakening the financial strength of government.

The printing of paper money was not an innovation of the Congress or the states. As early as 1690 the colonial assembly in Massachusetts had authorized the issuing of paper money, and from time to time thereafter other colonies had attempted to solve their financial problems in the same way.[6] Without exception, however, Britain had always declared such issues illegal.

Jealous of its creditor position in relation to the colonies, Britain would not tolerate any actions on the part of the colonists which threatened to depreciate the value of their obligations to it. Cheap money and rising prices were such a threat. With the successful conclusion of the Revolutionary War, the states broke out of the Mercantilist system and their dependence on Britain, but did not lose their need for money. The pressure for paper emissions on the state assemblies was too strong to resist in circumstances where there was a chronic shortage of money. Now, however, the shoe was on the other foot, for the creditors who stood to lose by an easy money policy no longer were the benefactors of British crown policy; they were local patriots of economic substance whose creditor position made them especially sensitive to financial profligacy.

The men who gathered in Philadelphia in 1787 in response to the call for a constitutional convention were not simply motivated by a desire to protect their economic interests. There was a good deal more at stake than this. But neither were they interested in creating a democratic political order. For most of them democracy was an epithet of disdain, a synonym for the mob. The radicals of the Revolution were conspicuously absent from the Constitutional Convention. In fact, the delegates took great pains to conduct the proceedings in isolation from the pressures of public opinion. The document which this remarkable group of men contrived was a masterpiece of compromise of the conflicting interests and concerns represented at the convention: north and south; large state and small state; aristocracy and popular rule; security and liberty; state autonomy and federal authority. However much some of these compromises may have raised difficulties for government in the modern era, in 1789 they made it possible for the states to cede to the federal government enough power to deal with the problems on which the Confederation had foundered. The price of creating effective federal government, however, was the attenuation of popular controls over it. If the founding fathers gave voice to democracy in the House of Representatives, they intended to muffle it in the Senate, the Presidency and the Supreme Court.

§   *Jefferson vs. Hamilton: Democracy vs. Growth*

Even more than the drawing up of the Constitution, the first administration under it dramatized the dilemma that democratic forces may raise at early stages of economic development. While the Constitutional Convention had been composed of a selected group of men who were united in their concern over the ineffectualness of the Confederation, George Washington's Administration contained representatives of more widely divergent points of view. Away in Paris during the Constitutional Convention as the Confederation's ambassador to France, Jefferson had returned and taken office as Washington's first Secretary of State. The first Secretary of the Treasury was Alexander Hamilton. Perhaps no administration since then contained two men with such conflicting philosophies. In his effort to stand above factional dispute, Washington had brought into his cabinet representatives of those conflicting views, which subsequently formed the basis of the extra-constitutional institutions so important to democratic government, political parties. From our standpoint, Jefferson and Hamilton epitomized the conflict between democracy and growth.

We have already had occasion to refer to Jefferson's belief in the virtues of the small agrarian community and the wide dispersion of property ownership. A philosopher of the eighteenth-century Enlightenment, Jefferson believed that "man was a rational animal, endowed by nature with rights and with an innate sense of justice, and that he could be restrained from wrong and protected in right by moderate powers confided to persons of his own choice and held to their duties by dependence on his own will."[7] These rational qualities, however, could best be realized in an agrarian community; the city breeded ignorance and tyranny and compelled people to live under institutions which corrupted their inherent rationality. The lesson of the Parisian mob during the French Revolution had not been lost on Jefferson.

In contrast, Alexander Hamilton had little confidence in the rationality of the common man and a deep distrust of democracy. If he had had his way at the Constitutional Convention, the president would have held office for life and would have been armed with an absolute veto power over the Congress and with authority to appoint state governors with similar powers over the state legislatures. Not having a strong attachment to any particular state, it was all the easier for Hamilton to advocate a strong federal government as the prerequisite for maximizing the national strength, wealth, orderliness, and security of the new state. As Secretary of the Treasury, he went far to achieve these goals by establishing a system in which the moneyed classes were induced to support the federal government through self-interest. If Hamilton distrusted the common man, he had an uncommon faith in the role that the entrepreneurial classes were to play in the development of America's economic potential. His Report on Manufacturers, presented to the Congress in December, 1791, was one of the most prophetic documents ever written by an American statesman. The profound significance of Hamilton lay precisely in the creation of a stable economic and political milieu. In this milieu the entrepreneurial and moneyed classes, in pursuit of individual gain, brought forth the manufacturing and industrial order foreshadowed in his Report on Manufacturers.

Hamilton's Reports on Public Credit and on a National Bank embodied the essence of his plans for establishing the financial framework appropriate to capitalist economic development. On the one hand, he advocated the assumption by the Federal Government of the obligations of the Continental Congress, the Confederation, and the revolutionary state governments. This was to be done by issuing new Federal securities in exchange for the older governmental debts at the original value of the latter. On the other hand, he urged the creation of a United States bank whose operation would insure the circulation of the money supply at par. The creation of a Federal national debt was intended to focus the loyalties of wealthy creditors on the new Federal Government, thereby weakening their parochial state loyalties, while a sound currency was designed to establish the monetary stability necessary for stimulating capitalistic economic activity. Moreover, the two proposals would raise the value of American obligations in foreign money markets and stimulate the flow of capital to governments and business firms.

There is little doubt that the acceptance of these reports by the Congress had a salutary economic effect on the growth of the economy. Had the Federal Government repudiated the debts of its revolutionary predecessors, particularly that part of the debt held by foreign creditors, it would have cut itself off from the mainstream of the economic forces which then were transforming the western world. Hamilton, as it were, minimized the diseconomies of the Revolution by giving its creditors, whoever they might be, their pound of flesh. The young American economy maintained its standing in the world economy even though it had chosen to break with the world's dominant economic power. There is, however, reason to doubt that the Hamiltonian measures had wide popular support. And certainly a man of Jefferson's persuasion, with his concern for the problems of the small farmer who constituted the majority of the population at the formation of the Republic, had misgivings about the equity of the measures. Hamilton's great strength, born of his aristocratic disdain for the little man, lay in his lack of concern with such questions. If assumption feathered the nest of speculators who had bought up depreciated state and continental bonds from the original owners, if sound money imposed currency stringencies on hard-pressed frontier farmers, or if the newly created national debt necessitated the imposition of regressive taxation to raise the revenue for interest payments, Hamilton was not the man to hold back because of a commitment to distributive justice. His belief that mankind in general was vicious precluded such a commitment.[8] Nor did the Whiskey Rebellion, clearly the consequence of Hamilton's economic policies, give him pause. He "advised Washington that severe measures were imperative to teach the masses respect for law and order"[9] and was angered by the President's unwillingness to hang the leaders when the rebellion was put down.

It was on the occasion of Shays' Rebellion, some six years prior to the Whiskey Rebellion, that Jefferson observed, "God forbid we should ever be 20 years without such a rebellion."[10] Though one may admire Jefferson's democratic theory and libertarian impulses, one may have serious reservations about their appropriateness to the conditions confronting the United States at the time. Jefferson was to have his opportunity to administer the new society in due time, but at the outset the hardheadedness of Hamilton, manifested in the policies of the Federalists, was essential for establishing a political and economic framework in which growth could proceed unhampered. The natural conditions of America and the absence of a traditional social order stimulated the development of a vibrant individualism. The revolution against Britain, brought on in part by this same individualism, released and articulated democratic forces prior to the creation of a society in which they could be sustained. The problem of the men at the constitutional convention in Philadelphia and the members of Washington's Administrations was to construct a government which would acknowledge the existence of these forces and yet contain them to the extent necessary for creating a stable political and economic environment. It was the genius of these statesmen that their creation was equal both to the immediate task of establishing domestic order and to the longrun task of accommodating democratic pressures when it became appropriate to do so. However much democrats may dislike Hamilton and men of his persuasion, they should recognize the necessary part they played in constructing the foundations of American democracy.

§   *British and American Political and Economic*
    Development Contrasted

At this point it will be useful by way of contrast to call to mind the characteristics of British political and economic development, discussed in the previous chapter. The British political system had evolved through centuries of constitutional practice. By the eighteenth century parliamentary institutions had been perfected to such an extent that they would have been easily recognizable to a visitor from the twentieth century. It was not democratic, but this we argued was essential for preserving the conditions appropriate for accelerating the rate of economic growth during the industrial revolution. As that revolution gathered momentum various groups of individuals were jarred loose from their traditional commitments and values by the demands growth imposed on labor and entrepreneurs and by the aspirations it fostered. Autonomous groups seeking to reconcile these demands and aspirations gradually formed and eventually acquired enough strength and influence to compel the ruling political elite to extend political privileges to a more representative sample of the population. First the middle classes and then the workers were brought into the electorate. Economic growth had so restructured society and shifted the centers of population that the maintenance of political stability required the democratization of the political process. That this was accomplished without a breakdown in the British political order was attributable to the resilience and viability of parliamentary institutions, to their capacity for accommodating social and economic change.

The contrast, then, between Britain and America is clear. In the former, economic growth compelled the democratization of the political process, given prevailing governmental institutions. In the latter, governmental institutions had to be created which would restrain democratic forces so that the forces making for economic growth could be given free rein. In Britain, economic growth transformed an oligarchy into a democracy; in the United States, an adolescent democracy had to be disciplined in order to prepare the way for the mature democracy made possible by economic growth.

We have devoted a considerable amount of space to a discussion of the historical background of political and economic development in the United States because it is so unique and yet so taken for granted. It is the only country in the western world which may make a legitimate claim to democratic credentials prior to its passage over the hump of economic development.[11] That this was so is most certainly attributable to the circumstances of geography and to the fact that it recruited its population initially from a country with the most highly developed constitutional institutions and liberties in the world. In stressing the background of American development, therefore, we are stressing circumstances that are historical in the sense that they will not recur. It is well to bear in mind as we continue our discussion of American political and economic development that its significance lies not so much in its universality, or its potential universality, as in its particularity.

§ *The Autonomous Character of American Economic Growth*

In the light of America's unique background, it is hardly surprising that its industrial development was preeminently the product of autonomous forces. Economic growth was initiated and carried forward by individuals acting through business firms as much as, and even more than, was the case in Britain. Certainly the ideology of autonomous growth seized hold of American society with greater tenacity than it did in England. As pointed out earlier, the philosophy of John Locke found a congenial home in the immense reaches of America, the citizens of whom, at least those who mattered most, found little reason to quarrel with his *laissez-faire* progeny. It was not just the natural background of America, however, that brought forth autonomous growth and the dedication to *laissez-faire* ideology. America was part of British-centered industrialization and received its own impulse for development from many of the same factors affecting Britain. Not only was ideology transmitted from Britain to America, but skills and capital as well. To realize the integral dependence of American growth on British development, one only need recall that cotton manufacturing in the United States was established by Samuel Slater, born in England in 1768, who studied the Arkwright machinery and system of production during his apprenticeship in the land of his birth. The United States was part of the world economy at a time when the margins of growth in Britain were being pushed out by men whose drives and ambitions were very much oriented toward individual accomplishment. Government was viewed, if not with hostility, at least with some suspicion. Associated with mercantilist prescriptions interfering with the freedom of action of entrepreneurs, and with privileges discriminating in favor of the aristocracy and the wealthy landed interests, government did not seem to comprehend as well as it might the requirements of the new industrial order.

The antipathy to government of the industrial entrepreneurs changing the face of England was even more pronounced and had a stronger longrun impact when brought to the United States. In the first place, having revolted from British rule, the States were generally hostile and suspicious of strong centralized governmental authority. In the second place, since America lacked an effective indigenous aristocratic tradition of *noblesse oblige,* there was not a very effective philosophy of positive government to oppose the prevailing philosophy of negative government. The latter point, perhaps, requires further explanation.

However much the entrepreneurial classes in the northern industrial districts in England may have thought the government unnecessary, in Britain the government never totally abdicated its control of the social-economic process. Almost from the very start of the industrial revolution, Parliament formulated policies which constrained the freedom of action of employers. In part this was attributable to a kind of paternalism born of the aristocratic responsibility upper classes sometimes felt for lower classes. As far as industrial processes were concerned, this manifested itself in a belief that employers should have some concern for the total condition of their workers, that they should not look upon them simply as objects of trade to be purchased at the lowest price. Moreover, those who held such views were not loath to use the power of government to compel employers to live up to their social responsibility. Hence the peculiarly English phenomenon of Tory Radicalism and the relatively early promulgation of factory legislation. In the United States, the only segment of society that might pass for an aristocracy in the old world sense was the southern slavocracy, and in the event the conflict between south and north prevented aristocratic paternalism from being transmuted into some kind of positive governmental concern for welfare. When the south was defeated in the Civil War, there was nothing to restrain or modify the impact of *laissez-faire* and the negative concept of government.

It should be clear that this attitude towards government was the reverse side of the assertive and confident belief in man's individual capacity to control and manipulate his environment. Men like Samuel Slater, able to comprehend mechanical processes, migrate to a new society, and reproduce them in industry, did not view government from a dependent and subservient status. Conscious of their own strength and resourcefulness, they were inclined to look upon government as a means to their own ends rather than as an agency whose function it was to set the purpose of society. In a word, government was thought to be servant, not master. When the Constitution was written, the statesmen at Philadelphia were not trying to erect a purposeful government; they were trying to establish a governmental structure which would allow purposeful men to pursue their interests without fear either of popular disorders or arbitrary and repressive actions by public officials.

We have stressed the attitude towards government because this was especially consistent with the autonomous character of economic development in the United States. On the objective grounds of economic policy, government contributed more to American industrialization than the ideologues of *laissez-faire* care to admit.[12] In the construction of the transportation network which brought east, west, north, and south together in national markets both state and Federal Government played a crucial role. The opening up of the Erie Canal in 1825 set off an orgy of canal building subsidized by states anxious lest they lose the expanding commerce of the west to New York.[13] Similarly, the construction of railroads, which brought an end to the great period of canal building, was subsidized by state governments with their eye on the main economic chance. Moreover, after the Civil War generous land grants by the Federal Government to railroad interests provided them with the resources essential for completing the transcontinental rail system. Whenever the expansion of output was expected to yield external economies, as in a program of improving internal transportation and communication facilities, government was willing to grant business some kind of reward to compensate it for the delay in the payoff on private investment.

Nor should it be overlooked that as the owner of the tremendous unexploited public domain, the Federal Government, whether it wanted to or not, inescapably had a hand in the course of the American economy's development. We have mentioned the land grants to the western railroads. In addition, the land grants to the states and to various groups interested in exploiting the natural resources of the public domain, as well as the evolution of a policy for distributing land to individuals, were manifestations of the Federal Government's impact on growth. Furthermore, one may point to the rise of the tariff after the Civil War as evidence of the willingness of government to participate in economic life.

Though government undeniably played its part in the industrialization of the American economy, its role, in a sense, was more significant for what it did not do than for what it did do. As landowner, the Federal Government did not supervise and control the use to which resources were put. Government firms did not take responsibility for the mining of copper, iron ore, and coal or for the cutting of timber. Nor did it build and then operate the railroads. It disposed of its wealth as quickly as practicable in order to allow individuals to exploit the commercial and industrial potential of the nation's resources. Its policies, in other words, were not inconsistent with autonomous growth. Indeed, they were very largely a reflection of the demand of autonomous individuals for assistance when the price calculations of the market did not yield a suitable or safe guide to private investment.

§ *The Industrial Revolution*

The industrial revolution in the United States transformed the structure of the American economy in the fifty years following the Civil War. During the first half of the century the preconditions for industrialization were met. The construction of a national transportation network knit the economy together, the tide of population began to move more strongly to the west, the agricultural surplus expanded enough to support a proportionately larger urban population, and entrepreneurial values were widely disseminated among a class of people anxious and willing to develop the manufacturing and industrial potential of America's bounty. The Civil War itself was a stimulus to industrialization. Already expanding in the decade prior to the war, manufacturing activity was accelerated by the inexhaustible demands of the armies for food, clothing, and armament. In the ebullient period of growth following the war, all the classical indices of industrialization revealed the marked extent to which the structure of the economy had changed. From 1860 to 1910 total population grew from 31½ million to 92 million,[14] the proportion of the population in urban areas jumped from 19 per cent to 45 per cent,[15] the size of the labor force more than tripled, from 10½ million to some 37 million,[16] the proportion of the labor force in agriculture fell from 59 per cent to 31 per cent,[17] the value added by manufacturing increased from about $860 million to $6.3 billion,[18] and per capita gross national product almost tripled.[19]

During this period the iron and steel industry assumed its modern position of central importance in the economy. Technical changes affecting supply—the shift from charcoal to coke and the adaptation of the Bessemer process, for example—and the demands of the railroad and construction industries for finished steel products combined to bring forth an unparalleled growth in output. The expansion of steel output and the growth of traffic on the railroads created demand for greatly increased output of coal. As machine processes were adapted throughout industry a persistent demand for lubricating agents provided the market to which Drake's strike at Titusville was such an appropriate response. Still later in the period the beginnings of the electrical and automotive industries produced the kind of output which subsequently was to become the foundations of the "affluent society" in America. Thus innovation and technological factors affecting supply, input and output complementarities, and markets expanding under high price and income elasticities brought America a many-sided growth which permanently withdrew it from the ranks of the underdeveloped and catapulted it to the position of number one industrial power of the world. By World War I America had fulfilled the promise contained in its large and variegated supply of natural resources.

§   *Factors Minimizing the Welfare Problems*

As indicated earlier in this chapter, the political and economic relationships of the industrialization process in America were unique because of the establishment of many of the conditions of democracy in advance of the period of accelerated economic growth. Though the democratic forces released in the Revolutionary War were disciplined and constrained in the writing and enforcement of the Constitution of the United States, the westward expansion of population and the settling of new territories brought new states into the Union which more fully represented the turbulent and popular forces of the frontier. Since each state controlled its own franchise requirements, the new states generally were more democratic than the original seaboard states. The extensive growth of the country overwhelmed the predominantly eastern strength of the Federalists and set the stage first for Jeffersonian democracy and then for Jacksonian democracy. If, then, Jefferson and Jackson opened the door further to popular forces than the original Constitution-makers thought advisable, how was it subsequently possible during the industrial revolution for the Rockefellers, Carnegies, Vanderbilts, and Fricks to pursue their interests with so little concern for the public at large? Why did the welfare problem, the inevitable outgrowth of the industrialization process in its early stages, not lead to the imposition of stronger constraints on the operation of the economic forces tranforming American society?

In suggesting answers to these queries, one must immediately recognize that the welfare problem in the United States was not so serious as it was in Britain. In the first place, the objective circumstances in which workers found themselves in America were, with little doubt, superior to those in England. The great attraction which America exerted on European citizens in the nineteenth century was not simply a matter of an ideological longing for freedom and release from the more rigid restrictions of a class society. Real wages were higher in America than in England and Europe; American workers ate more and better food and lived in less squalid quarters than their English peers.

Moreover, during the course of the industrial revolution the standard of living of American workers rose more rapidly. As we have seen, there is considerable doubt as to what happened to the standard of living of English workers in the period from 1780 to 1840. If Marx's immiserization hypothesis is not borne out by the extant price and wage data, neither do they reveal a marked improvement in the condition of workers. The price and wage data covering the period from the Civil War to World War I in the United States are far from complete, but they would appear to indicate that real wages rose approximately 30 per cent.[20] And certainly there is no suggestion in these data that the standard of living of the working population fell.

In the second place, a large proportion of the population increase during the industrial revolution was attributable to immigration. Some 22 million persons immigrated to the United States between 1860 and 1910.[21] Until the turn of the century most of them came from central and western Europe, thereafter from eastern Europe. These large population movements westward across the Atlantic had an important effect on the welfare problem from at least two different points of view. On the one hand, those immigrants who became part of the labor force, whether as unskilled or skilled workers, came from countries in which their economic circumstances were more straitened than they turned out to be in the United States. Thus the standards they applied in evaluating their well-being were not necessarily the same as those which might have been applied by indigenous American workers. While they retained memories and impressions of the low absolute level of wages in rural and urban employment in Europe, the higher wages in America appeared to be a propitious omen. In short, for the immigrant who had survived the hazards of passage to America and established himself in employment, the welfare problem might not have seemed so discouraging.

On the other hand, and perhaps more significantly, the recruitment of a large number of unskilled and semiskilled workers from the ranks of the immigrants increased the heterogeneity of the labor force, widening social and ethnic divisions and making the articulation of discontent more difficult.[22] The differentiation of the labor force with respect to wages and skills was closely paralleled by differentiation with respect to national origin. Skilled workers were more likely to be native born or of British origin than unskilled workers who, particularly in the later period of immigration, typically came from Italy, Poland, Russia, and eastern Europe. Many of the latter were peasants whose ingrained conservatism became even stronger in the face of an alien and unfamiliar culture. Lacking the pioneering skills and the capital required for farming in the expanding west, they gravitated to the urban ghettos where they could at least find a semblance of the traditional values and institutions with which they were familiar.[23] Moreover, national animosities among the immigrants themselves inhibited the formation of a labor movement around their mutual interests as workers. Further, because their manner was often strange and because in their desperate need for employment they frequently took jobs as strikebreakers, they earned the enmity of native-born workers.[24] Indeed, one may conjecture that many American workers maintained a stronger identity with the capitalist system precisely because of feeling a greater gulf separating them from foreign workers than from their employers.

However conjectural that may be, there is no doubt that immigration was partly responsible for stunting an effective radical labor movement. In addition to its divisive influence on the labor force, it pretty well demolished the popular appeal of socialism. Socialism was most viable and posed its greatest threat to the major parties when it drew its strength from the native populism of the midwest, from the small shopkeepers, farmers, and workers who felt threatened by the growing power of industrial and financial capitalists. Eugene Debs, for example, came to socialism through his intense feeling for the problems of these people rather than from any appreciation of Marxian dogma.[25] When, however, immigrants from central and eastern Europe, who had been schooled in the doctrinal disputes of European socialism, became active in the American socialist movement in the early part of the present century, they alienated much local support. Too often they seemed more interested in dogma than in the adaptation of socialism to American conditions and consequently socialism came to be viewed as a foreign ideology and program. Its indigenous populist support was diverted to the major parties and it became increasingly introverted, concerned more with heresy and schism than with a program which could rally the support of American workers. To this very day socialism has not really been able to recover from the un-American incubus with which its immigrant adherents invested it.

In the third place, the welfare problem was minimized in the United States by the belief in individualism and the relatively high degree of social mobility. Throughout the discussion of American development we have stressed its autonomous character. Private entrepreneurs rather than the state were primarily responsible for bringing about the acceleration in the rate of economic growth. Social mobility is, in a sense, a sociological analogue of autonomous growth, for it is essential in broadening the sources from which entrepreneurial ability is drawn. We have already touched upon the absence of a feudal class system in America. This, of course, was a stimulus to social mobility, for to the extent that status was not ascribed to the individual on the basis of his position in the class structure, it was possible for him to achieve status through his own efforts. Moreover, the rewards for achievement were all the greater because, lacking a feudal aristocracy, those who gained high economic status became, in effect, the indigenous American aristocrats. Men like Rockefeller and Carnegie attained a position in American society quite beyond their peers in Britain. Rockefellers or Carnegies, of course, were no more common than log-cabin presidents. Yet the demands of an extensively developing society for professional, technical, and managerial skills were so great that the possibility of achievement was a reality to which many individuals could aspire. Even the meanest immigrant could harbor expectations for improvements in his own status. While he himself might not be able to rise far above his station, he could not unreasonably anticipate that his sons and daughters, freed from the stigma of foreign accent and customs, might succeed in advancing up the social ladder through greater affluence. Entrepreneurial values and the belief in individualism trickled far enough down into the ranks of society that the potential collective response to the welfare problem of industrialization was weakened. Many men who otherwise might have turned to political action or trade unions sought release from their problems in individual achievement.

Finally, the very size of the continental land mass tended to dissipate the welfare problem. Regional differences between north and south and east and west and the distances separating them made it difficult for workers to make common cause over their mutual problems. Even after the transportation revolution had created national markets and railroads spanned the continent, the task of bringing together New England textile workers, Pennsylvania steel workers, Chicago meat packers, and Colorado silver miners in order to formulate a program or a plan of action for labor placed too great a strain on the meager resources of the developing labor force. Moreover, just as ethnic antagonisms rendered a group of workers less amenable to organization and systematic political or trade union activity, so did regional differences in belief and attitudes.

§   *The Labor Movement During the Industrial Revolution*

Notwithstanding the modifying influence of these factors, there was a welfare problem and a pronounced response to it. The heavy demands on investment for building the structural capital of an industrial economy did not leave enough resources for meeting the social (welfare) needs of the laboring population crowding into the centers of employment. The tenements in the cities teemed with people and disease, the cities themselves offered little in the way of recreation to the workers and low income groups, the workers toiled ten to twelve hours for six or seven days a week in factories and mines that were not adequately safeguarded against accident, and frequently their children were forced to work before they had had the opportunity to acquire an education or even to appreciate the need for one. In short, income had not yet risen high enough to afford workers the amenities of high consumption. Most of the workers' budget, perhaps as much as 80 per cent or more, was necessarily allocated to the bare necessities of food, clothing, and shelter. The communities in which they lived afforded them few collective goods which could be accounted positive contributions to their standard of living. And on top of this the cyclical course of the growth of income in the capitalist market periodically caused unemployment which often dissipated the savings that workers had managed to accumulate. Between the Civil War and World War I crises interrupted the development of the economy in 1873, 1885, 1893, 1903, and 1907. No matter how resilient the economy in surmounting them and returning to the growth path, they imposed hardships on these people whose welfare and standard of living depended upon the continuous receipt of wage income.

Long hours of labor, the rewards of which were often sacrificed to unemployment, did not breed contentment, especially when the undeniable evidence of the growing industrial wealth of the economy created expectations of a higher standard of living. We have already noted that conditions of economic growth in the United States permitted many people to rise above their dependent status through individual achievement and entrepreneurial activity. Others disillusioned by their American experiences returned to the Europe from which they had recently emigrated, the counter migrations tending to be especially high following economic crises and periods of unemployment. But for those who lacked the interest, means, or ability to move up or away from the welfare problem, collective action through trade unions or political organization offered a possible solution. Thus the foundations of the labor movement were laid as workers gradually and painfully groped for the kind of organization most suited to the special conditions of American life.[26] In 1869 the Knights of Labor was formed by Uriah S. Stephens as a ritualistic fraternal organization for all workers regardless of craft, creed, or color in order to combat the parochialism of the then existing craft unions. Stephens was replaced by Terence V. Powderly in 1879 and the Knights entered upon its period of greatest growth, culminating in 1886 in a membership of some 700,000. A mass organization, but with little control exerted by its national executive over its constituent local assemblies, the Knights grew on the basis of a more or less spontaneous reaction to the deflation of the late 70's and early 80's. Not only workers suffering from depressed wages, but farmers and small business men plagued by declining prices were attracted to its ranks by its message of solidarity. Moreover, a series of railroad strikes in the early 80's and agitation for the eight-hour day brought the question of labor organization to public attention, giving the Knights a kind of notoriety which, however unwanted by Powderly, increased the appeal of its local assemblies. Though the Knights grew rapidly in the 80's, it collapsed just as quickly. The Haymarket bombing in Chicago in the spring of 1886 did much to hasten its decline. The incident caused dissension within the organization between Powderly and those who wanted to protest the injustices of the Haymarket trials more strongly and impugned the Knights' reputation outside the organization among those who saw it as an anarchistic and leftist threat to the stability of middle-class America.

If the Knights of Labor had passed its peak in the middle 80's, the Amalgamated Association of Iron and Steel Workers, the most powerful craft union in the country, came to grief in the early 90's. The battle between the Pinkerton agents and the workers at Homestead, Pennsylvania in 1892 is fabled in American labor lore, but whoever won that particular skirmish, the union not only lost the strike against Carnegie but the capacity to carry forward its organizing activity. Carnegie and his lieutenant Frick had successfully carried out their intention of breaking the union. Two years later in 1894 Eugene V. Debs' American Railway Union, which he had organized in opposition to the craft exclusiveness of the Brotherhood of Locomotive Firemen, led workers in a strike against the Pullman Company with disastrous results. The intervention of national troops sent by President Cleveland to Chicago and the use of an injunction obtained in Federal Court against the officers of the union defeated the strike and destroyed the union. The nadir of the fortunes of the labor movement had been reached.

But even as the unionism of the 80's and 90's was being destroyed by a combination of stout employer opposition and governmental intervention, the American Federation of Labor was building the organization which has become a permanent part of the American economic landscape. Founded in 1886, the policies of the A.F. of L. were based on Samuel Gompers' understanding of the mistakes committed by the labor movement in its struggle for recognition in the years after the Civil War. Foremost among these, he thought, was the attempt to incorporate political action and radical ideology in the drive to improve the economic status of labor. Gompers dedicated the A.F. of L. to the achievement of economic ends by economic means. He eschewed political programs and concentrated his energies on the organization of economic power that workers could bring to bear on employers. He looked to skilled and craft workers for support, both because their limited numbers made them easier to organize than unskilled workers and the nature of the service they supplied industry made them more important to the operations of the firm. Moreover, since skilled labor represented a small proportion of total labor cost, employers were less reluctant to accede to the wage demands of a craft union than to the wage demands of an industrial union. Conscious of the dissipation of the potential economic power of skilled workers in industrial and political unionism, Gompers set for himself the task of organizing labor at the top. Thus was born the American version of business unionism which fully accepted the institutions of the capitalistic economy and attempted to secure for skilled workers the maximum possible share of the increments to output that these institutions brought about. Disillusioned by radical and messianic plans to change capitalism, business unionism devoted itself to the pragmatic and mundane issues of wages and hours.

§ *Limitations on Union Activities*

In the light of the discussion in Chapter 4, there are several observations to be made about the development of the American labor movement in the second half of the nineteenth century. Since the conditions of economic growth minimized the seriousness of the welfare problem, the labor reaction to it could be held within limits appropriate to continued growth through a policy of permissive controls. Unions did, in fact, appear during the industrial revolution as working-class institutions of protest trying to improve the status of labor. Autonomous organizations in the sense that they arose on the strength of the social needs of the workers and did not seek sanction for their activity from governmental authority, unions pointed up the separateness of state and society while serving as training grounds for the dissemination of the values and understanding essential for a representative and democratic society. Yet unions did not have a steady and uninterrupted growth. Indeed, the number of union members in the middle 90's was not much greater than it had been at the end of the decade of the Civil War. This was partly attributable to the restraints imposed on the conduct of unions by government. The sending of federal troops to Chicago on the occasion of the Pullman Strike in 1894 was but the most dramatic instance of governmental interference with the activity of unions. Persistently throughout the period the "criminal conspiracy" doctrine of the common law, as interpreted by federal and state courts, armed those with a vested interest in debilitating the strength of organized labor with legal sanction to resist the growth of unions. Unions might seek members among workers, but their leaders could be legally enjoined from taking action which threatened irreparable loss to private property. Harried by legal discrimination, the union movement did not catch hold and acquire permanent stature until it accepted standards of conduct which were consistent with the operations of the capitalistic market. In being suspicious of political action and radical ideology, the A.F. of L. was really registering its suspicion of any forces external to capitalism which might prevent it from generating the increments to income on which the bargaining strategy of the A.F. of L. was based.

Thus the United States passed through the early stages of industrialization relatively unhampered by the restrictions that a labor movement might have imposed on those responsible for accumulation. To answer the question previously raised, the Rockefellers, Carnegies, Vanderbilts, and Fricks were able to pursue their interests with so little concern for the preferences of the public at large because of the limited effectiveness of the groups opposing them. The labor movement was one such group. Yet in time it became an autonomous and independent force which performed a crucial function in restraining the interests of capital and in establishing those institutions through which the conflicts of labor and capital are adjudicated. We are not concerned in this book with the development of the labor movement and rise of industrial unionism in the twentieth century. Our chief concern has been to explain the lag between the onset of industrialization around the Civil War and the establishment of the labor movement towards the end of the century as it affected the emergence of American democracy. We emphasized throughout this chapter that the experience of the United States was unique in that it had moved a long way toward democracy even before it entered upon the industrial revolution. We have examined the factors which nonetheless allowed accelerated economic growth to take place following the Civil War without destroying the autonomy of a group which subsequently became important in fulfilling the conditions of a democratic society.

Chapter 7

German Industrialization: The Weakening of the Democratic Impulse

IN A FAMOUS PASSAGE Karl Marx once observed that "Man makes his own history, but he does not make it out of the whole cloth; he does not make it out of conditions chosen by himself, but out of such as he finds close at hand."[1] Where "America was born free" in the sense that it created its institutions and traditions out of the whole cloth, Germany had little cloth to work with. Its history hung over it like a pall and so shaped the growth of modern Germany that, however beneficent or democratic the influence of autonomous growth, it could not easily offset its past. Germany had been, first of all, a politically diversified and amorphous congeries of states, principalities, kingdoms, and free cities which never spontaneously or readily grew into a coherent nation. Though its central location in Europe ultimately was to have great advantages for its industrial development, politically it was disadvantageous as long as Germany was surrounded by more powerful nations reluctant to permit the growth of a unified political community in their midst. Thus the Treaty of Westphalia (1648), concluding the disastrous and

[158]

enervating Thirty Years' War, divided Germany into more than three hundred political units in order to satisfy the security objectives of Cardinal Richelieu and France. Less than two centuries later, when Europe had curbed the expansionist impulse of revolutionary France, the settlement reached at the Congress of Vienna sharply reduced the number of German states, but still left thirty-nine. By 1815 England had been a nation whose citizens possessed a consciousness of themselves as Englishmen for perhaps some four centuries. France had been a nation in the modern sense at least from the reign of Louis XIV. And the United States, young though it was, already had behind it the glories and triumphant history that create the tradition and purpose of a nation. Germany, however, was still steeped in the parochialism and localism of its many political units, though its contact with France during the Napoleonic Wars had done much to awaken a German national consciousness.

The diversity of political units in Germany meant that unification, when it was finally achieved during the second half of the nineteenth century, had to be the work of one state powerful enough to overcome the many obstacles that prevented Germans from joining forces in an effective national union. This task devolved upon Prussia. The largest of the German states, with noncontiguous territories straddling the whole of Germany from the Russian border in the east to the Rhine in the west, Prussia in 1815 was strategically placed to pressure and cajole reluctant princes and kings into a union which was finally consummated at Versailles in 1871 following the Franco-Prussian War.

The predominance of Prussia in Germany's march to unification, particularly as manifested in the brilliant and devious use of power politics by Bismarck, revealed characteristics of German society important to an understanding of the impediments which stood in the way of the democratization of political processes as industrialization transformed the economy. In the United States and Britain political institutions evolved in response to rebellion against central authority, but in Germany central authority created the political institutions which articulated the German nation. And because national consciousness was awakened relatively late, the German people were all the more willing to support a centralizing state power. Catholic and Protestant, Prussians and Rhinelanders, workers and merchants, however divergent on religious and social issues, could yet attain consensus on the desirability of unification. Thus the way was open to Prussia to achieve the German national purpose.

That Germans in their political capacity were not more assertive and hence were submissive to the authoritarian Prussian state cannot, however, be explained solely in terms of their overriding dedication to national unification. Germans were more compliant than their peers in Britain or the United States. The hierarchical nature of the German family, guild, and class structure stressed the subordination of individuals to their superiors. In the decades following the Thirty Years' War these institutions became more firmly fixed even as they were declining in the other nations of western Europe. Moreover, at least, for the Protestants, in northern and eastern Germany, Lutheranism disseminated the belief in submission to civil authority as a fundamental value. Luther himself had left no doubt as to his position when, during the Peasants' Revolts in 1525, he sided with the princes and excoriated the peasants for civil disobedience. There was no great religious tradition of dissent to focus on the limiting of governmental powers as a means of protecting religious belief. Furthermore, German ideology was strongly romantic and idealistic and preached the fulfillment of the individual in association and identification with some entity larger than himself. For Hegel it was the state, for Marx class, but whatever the specific content of their system of thought German philosophers and ideologues tended to return to the classical Platonic tradition and place the individual in a social context which took precedence over any aspirations he might have had as an individual. Nothing is more un-German than the philosophy of John Locke and the atomistic notions of individual welfare based on it.

The German social structure, religion, and ideology do not necessarily explain the greater submissiveness of Germans to authority, because these factors themselves may merely be effects of more fundamental causes.[2] We cite them, however, as evidence which is consistent with the alleged German characteristic, if it is not ultimately explanatory. To the extent that the historical circumstances from which Germany emerged in the nineteenth century debilitated the capacity of individuals to assert themselves or their rights against the state, they weakened the mechanism by which industrialization might have been expected to lead to the democratization of the political process. In Chapter 4 we argued that democracy is not likely to develop because of the democratic values and pretensions of the holders of political power. Rather it comes about because political leaders must extend political privileges to larger groups in the population as the necessary price of maximizing their opportunity for maintaining the prerogatives of power. If as in the case of Germany the population seemed predisposed to the acceptance of authoritarian rule, then those pressures and acts of civil disobedience which might jeopardize an existing political order would not so easily become manifest. It is indelibly part of Germany's history that there has never been a successful instance of rebellion or revolution against constituted state authority. Germany cannot look back to a Declaration of Independence, a Magna Carta, or a Declaration of the Rights of Man which embodied the aspirations of individuals in the presence of arbitrary rule and which memorialized their success in curbing it. Its past did not condone the revolutionary conduct which might impugn the legitimacy of authoritarian political regimes.

If the indigenous German population was subjected to influence which stifled their individualism, the non-German population attracted to Germany by the economic opportunities opened up by industrialization was not notably more individualistic. The prevailing direction of the movement of population during the nineteenth century was from Europe to America. This necessarily meant that the latter was constantly being infused with people who had had to assert their individuality enough to leave one world and take on the problems of a new one. The political system that grew in America was a product of the wedding of British political institutions imported by immigrants and the seemingly unlimited land of a vast continent. Germany contributed to the migration of America in the nineteenth century and to that extent, perhaps, lost the type of person who might have invigorated the democratization of political processes in Germany. But certainly the peasants from Poland, Russia, and the marche lands of Eastern Europe who entered Germany, frequently as seasonal laborers, added little democratic ferment to the German scene. Coming from societies which in the main were more rigidly structured than German society, they had had no opportunity to acquire the individualistic ways of the Anglo-American world. They were an exploited, downtrodden group which admirably served the purposes of the farming Junkers in the eastern Prussian provinces.

§   *Germany on the Eve of the Industrial Revolution*

Thus far we have been discussing the factors in the historical background of Germany which tended to limit the democratizing influence of industrialization. These have been stressed because we shall have occasion to notice in the next chapter the impact of similar factors in the development of Russia, and they therefore lend some historical substance to the generalizations we have previously made. We do not, however, want to stress these factors so much that we lose sight of the effect that the industrial revolution in Germany did have on the political process.

On the eve of the industrial revolution Germany was still in some respects a medieval society. The population was predominantly rural and during the first half of the nineteenth century remained so. In Prussia, for example, 73.5 per cent of the population was classed as rural in 1816, and by 1846 the figure had only fallen to 72.0.[3] Rural conditions varied between west and east Germany. In the wake of the revolutionary reforms in France, the former was creating individual peasant proprietorships by commuting and extinguishing the feudal dues and obligations of the peasants. The latter was extending the sway of the Junker economy, the large estates of which were operated as commercial ventures and manned by a rural and largely landless peasantry. In both east and west, however, the influence of the manorial system with its complex set of mutual rights and obligations was being undermined; peasants were beginning to acquire the freedom of movement which was essential for a growing and changing economy.

In the cities and towns the guild was the most important form of economic organization. Prior to 1840 there were almost no factories employing an industrial proletariat. The typical shop consisted of a master and a journeyman or apprentice who were bound by the regulations of their guild. So stringent were these that even as late as 1843 masters outnumbered workmen.[4] If the guilds controlled the tanners, shoemakers, hatters, tailors, and other crafts which catered to the needs of the urban population, additional output was produced under domestic conditions by peasants whose agricultural pursuits did not employ them full time. The iron industry, the woolen and linen industries, the toy industry originated as by-employment for peasants. In order to supplement their income they processed local materials for merchant entrepreneurs. At a time when the cotton textile industry in England was fully mechanized and had created drab northern mill towns such as Manchester, Germany was barely entering the stage of incipient industrialization. The old forms of economic organization still dominated the scene, though conditions for the appearance of the new forms of enterprise were gradually being established.

Among these conditions was the creation of an internal market large enough to support the specialized functions of an industrial economy, and free enough to stimulate the movement of goods and resources. So long as Germany was divided into numerous states, each of which could impose duties and taxes on the transit of goods across its territory, manmade barriers to trade prevented the development of a free German market. Because of its peculiar geography, with non-contiguous territories in both east and west, and because of a commitment to the principle of free trade, Prussia was in a strategic position for, and had an interest in, inducing the non-Prussian German states to enter a customs union. The Prussian tariff of 1818, designed to maximize trade and revenue under the special circumstances of a country with noncontinuous territories, provided the foundation for the building of the Zollverein. In 1834 this opened the greater part of Germany outside of Austria to the free movement of goods internally while imposing a moderate tariff on the importation of goods from outside the union. Though it no doubt antagonized those smaller states and principalities which could not withstand the pressure it could bring to bear upon them, Prussia was thus the principal architect of a policy which overcame the economic disadvantages inherent in political particularism.

Not only did Prussia take the lead in the creation of a free trade area in Germany, but in the construction of railroads. Goaded by the indefatigable efforts and propaganda of Friedrich List on behalf of a German railway network, conscious of the great military advantages of an efficient transportation system, especially in the light of the poor roads in Prussia, and favored by relatively low construction costs, the Prussian state in the middle years of the century subsidized and encouraged the building of railroads. In 1844 there were about 500 miles of track in Prussia, but by 1860 there were about 3500 miles.[5]

§   *The State in German and American Growth*

It is appropriate at this point to make some observations about the role of government in German development in contrast to the role of government in American development. We noted in Part One that to the extent there were important external economies associated with the production of particular types of output, one could expect government to subsidize them. This proposition was abundantly illustrated in both the United States and Germany. Through various means—surveying assistance, land grants, guaranteeing interest on loans, owning shares, planning construction—the state assisted in the building and operation of railroads. The circumstances in the United States were such, however, that it was expedient for government to subsidize the first units of output and then withdraw from active participation, leaving the railroads in private hands and to the autonomous forces of the market. In Germany, on the other hand, the state was never prepared to abdicate that far to the market because the state's role in fashioning the conditions essential for the development of German society continued to be paramount. In 1789 the United States laid down the ground rules to govern the conduct of autonomous individuals whose energies were bent to the task of developing the potential of a virgin continent. But German governments, particularly Prussia, had to be continually concerned about the circumstances anterior and prerequisite to autonomous development. Unification, of course, was extremely important in this regard, and since its success depended on the union of many independent, sovereign states, located in the complex political order of central Europe, the power of Prussian government had to be great enough to overcome the force of local particularism. Thus the railroads were not simply instruments of economic unification, as in the case of the United States; they were instruments of political unification as well. Inextricably bound up in the power struggles of the European continent, Prussia could not afford so casual and easy-going an attitude towards the railroad as the United States.[6]

Furthermore, governments in Germany had to decree or legislate what more or less existed naturally in the United States. The systems of feudal land tenure and rights and obligations affecting the organization of agriculture had to be revised in order to permit that agricultural progress without which industrial development is almost impossible. But the emancipation of the peasant, carried forward so vigorously by Prussian reforms in the first part of the nineteenth century, was totally unnecessary in the United States. Feudal institutions had been excluded in that country by the abundance of land and the lack of a feudal class hierarchy. The point is that both in the positive task of creating the structural foundations of an industrial order and the negative task of clearing away the obstructions to change, mobility, and experimentation inherited from previous social orders, the state in Germany played a larger role than it did in the United States. While German economic growth may be characterized as autonomous, the functions of the German state never became so limited that they could be thought to stand outside of the process of growth. In Germany the state had to do much that nature had done for the United States.

§   *The Industrial Revolution*

The industrialization process which was visibly stirring in the decade of the 50's moved into high gear during the last three decades of the century. All indices of change revealed the same thing, that Germany was undergoing a most rapid industrial transformation. Total population increased from 41 million in 1871 to almost 65 million in 1910. The proportion of population living in rural areas dropped from 63.9 per cent in 1871 to 40.0 per cent in 1910.[7] This increase and change in the location of population took place against the background of heavy migrations to foreign countries, especially the United States. Until emigration fell off sharply in the 1890's, it had been as high as 200,000 in the middle 50's and 221,000 in 1881. For the period from 1886 to 1890 the annual average was just under 100,000.[8] The railroads, knitting the German economy together, facilitated the movement of peasants from the countryside to the cities and the seaports. Industrial and manufacturing opportunities offered the lure to movement. How great these were may be inferred from the dramatic increases in the output of basic industrial resources. In 1871 Germany produced 29.4 million metric tons of coal and 8.5 million metric tons of lignite. By 1913 these figures had risen respectively to 191.5 and 87.5. Pig iron production which had been 529 thousand metric tons in 1860 was 14,794 thousand metric tons in 1910. By way of contrast, the United Kingdom produced 3,888 thousand metric tons in 1860 and 10,171 thousand metric tons in 1910.[9] While the United Kingdom was increasing its output of pig iron somewhat less than three times, Germany was increasing its output more than twenty-five times. Not surprisingly, by 1910 Germany was the leading steel producer of Europe, producing more than the combined outputs of Britain, France, and Belgium.

Meanwhile, the woolen textile industry made the transition from the old system of domestic production to the factory system; by the eve of World War I it had become one of the great export industries of the empire, even though it only raised a fractional portion of its raw material requirements at home. The cotton textile industry also passed into the factory during this same period, but in the face of the more established industry in Britain it did not achieve the position in foreign markets of the woolen textile industry. Perhaps the most rapidly developing industries in Germany during the industrial revolution were the chemical and the electrical trades. The output of potassium salts, for example, increased from 2 thousand tons in 1861 to 9.6 million tons in 1910.[10] The world output of sulphuric acid was alleged to have been somewhat more than a million tons in 1878, but by 1907 Germany's output alone was more than 1.4 million tons. Used for fertilizers, dyes, and explosives, the expansion of chemicals increased the productivity of agriculture and the marketability of German goods in foreign and domestic markets. In the last two decades of the nineteenth century, the electrical industry expanded rapidly, leading to the extensive use of electric lighting and the electrification of urban railways and bringing Germany to the threshold of the age of electrical appliances. By World War I it could truly be said that Germany was the number one industrial power of Europe, having outstripped Britain, the country from which the industrialization impulse originally came.

§ *The Welfare Problem*

So rapid was the pace of German industrialization that it was hardly surprising that it was accompanied by the welfare problem characteristic of periods of early industrial growth. With the lion's share of the economy's investment surplus allocated to the building of railroads and the expansion of the metallurgical, mining, and electrical trades, there was little enough left over for the construction of the urban facilities necessary for providing the rapidly expanding industrial population with the basic amenities of life. As in Britain and the United States, housing for workers was particularly crowded and squalid and the cities themselves did not provide the recreational facilities which might have made these conditions bearable. Moreover, as the German economy became increasingly industrialized, it became more dependent on the state of the world economy and thus was subject to the fluctuations in economic activity which periodically raised the specter of unemployment. If the factory workers were better off than the domestic workers they were displacing, the former could not escape the depression of trade which affected all forms of economic organization. The German workers were helpless before the capricious conduct of markets, especially during the worldwide deflation of the last quarter of the nineteenth century. Yet with the greater uncertainty of existence in a capitalistic economy, there also were greater expectations created with regard to what the economy held in store for workers. In a remarkably short time Germany had been transformed from a localized feudal economy to a nationwide capitalistic economy. As recently as 1850 the guild mentality, with its commitment to a relatively fixed and changeless life, dominated German economic life. The essence of industrialization was the breaking down of old parochial attitudes and their replacement with the forward-looking drives of the market mentality. Insofar as workers became more mobile during industrialization, they could not help but acquire new views about their role in life. They could no longer feel that their lot and status in the economy were inalterably fixed when there was so much evidence of change around them. Thus, industrialization in Germany, as was the case in most countries, held out many opportunities to workers, but for many of them frustrated their realization in the squalor of the city and the uncertainty of employment.

It is our thesis that during the nineteenth century the nature of the welfare problem was such that it could be contained by permissive labor controls, at once allowing the continued growth of per capita income and the emergence of autonomous groups in society strategically placed for demanding the extension of democratic rights. As in the United States, there were certain factors contingent upon its position in the world industrialization movement which tended to reduce the magnitude of the welfare problem in Germany. In the first place, while Germany was industrializing there were open lands to the west to which the workers could migrate. The German economy did not have to bear the full burden of the population increases brought on by expanding output. We have already noted the German emigration in the latter part of the nineteenth century. Coming largely from the rural sector where low wages, continuing feudal relationships, and the absence of civil rights drove workers to seek out a new life either in German industry or in the new world, the emigrants divested the German economy of a potential source of discontent. Had they remained at home in the German industrial areas, they might have made the welfare problem more serious by increasing the average size of the unemployed labor force in industry.

In the second place, though industrialization in Germany followed that in Britain it was still part of the same technological era. And Germany probably found it somewhat easier to adjust to the industrial age by virtue of being so close to the pioneer and yet not being first. On the one hand, Germany responded to essentially the same set of wants as the British economy earlier in the century. The technology of rail transport, steam, and textile manufacturing did not create any new wants as much as it improved the efficiency with which the historically given wants of food, clothing, and shelter were satisfied. When, therefore, Germany set out upon the road of industrialization, it was not emulating an economy whose labor force had already achieved a qualitatively different standard of living. Indeed, there is room for dispute about the relative status of German and British workers in 1848. Certainly it is not abundantly clear that the British worker, having passed through the take-off into economic growth, was very much better off than the German worker who was about to take off. The strength of the British metallurgical industry may have inspired German industrialists;

the consumption standards of British workers were hardly a goad to German workers.[11]

On the other hand, the technology of the nineteenth-century industrial era did not unduly restrain the resources of the economy or the skills of the labor force. It was not possible for Germany to contemplate adapting a power or transport technology other than that developed in Britain. There was nothing else it could do, given the development of the arts and science in the nineteenth century. Later in historical time, in the twentieth century, the number of technological choices confronting the economy embarking on industrialization became much greater and gave rise, accordingly, to different consequences for the rate of growth of income and consumption. Since it did not have to bear the development costs of industrial technology, as did Britain, Germany could adapt it to local conditions with greater confidence in its commercial feasibility. We do not mean to give the impression that industrialization in Germany was merely a passive adaptation of techniques whose advantages were abundantly clear to all concerned. One has only to call to mind the incessant struggle and peregrinations of Friedrich List on behalf of a German national railroad network to realize the strength of resistance to the technology of the new age. The point is, however, that once this resistance was overcome Germany could draw upon the stock of technical knowledge that had been accumulated in England during the pioneering railroad era of the 20's and 30's. Similarly, the textile industry did not have to repeat the discontinuous growth of mechanical invention in spinning and weaving that was characteristic of its development in the eighteenth century in England. It merely had to adapt techniques that had already been perfected in England and France. In consequence, the factory system, especially in the production of woolen cloth, spread very rapidly towards the end of the nineteenth century.[12]

The first point we made with respect to the historical timing of German industrialization suggests that Germany was able to minimize the welfare problem by shedding dissidents to the United States. The second point suggests that the welfare problem was further minimized by a more predictable growth in consumable output in response to the growth of the structural capital of the economy. The rise in the standard of living of workers was not so inhibited by the technical problems of discovering or inventing optimal equipment as was the case in Great Britain.

§ *The Influence of Ideology in the Formation of the Labor Movement*

Notwithstanding these factors which may have modified its severity, the welfare problem nonetheless persisted throughout the industrial revolution in Germany. If it was not so blatant or ugly as the welfare problem in Britain, it still called forth a movement of protest which if anything was more of a threat to the process of industrialization than similar movements in Britain. Here one may note disadvantages of being a latecomer in industrialization to offset the advantages previously discussed. Just as industrialization led to the accumulation of productive techniques of wide applicability, so it led to the accumulation of a literature of protest. However advantageous it was to follow close upon the heels of the pioneer of industrial techniques, it was not equally clear that it was similarly advantageous with respect to the literature of protest. We observed in Chapter 4 that there is nothing natural about the organization of movements of protest. Workers have to learn the techniques of trade unionism and political action just as they have to learn the skills of industrial employment. The inertia that labor organizations must overcome provides a breathing spell in which capital may be accumulated free of the hampering restrictions and demands of labor. The literature of protest served the function of articulating the complaints of workers suffering injustices from the social-economic system and directing their attention to possible solutions. The literature provided the slogans and catchwords by which labor leaders attempted to appeal to the relatively inert masses and so may be conceived of as a catalyst, reducing the lag between the start of industrialization and the effective organization of workers in response to the welfare problem.

Unlike Britain, Germany entered upon the industrial revolution with an extant ideology that not only identified the source of labor's difficulties in the industrial world, but suggested the way out of them. Karl Marx had fully formulated his theory of historical materialism prior to Germany's take-off into economic growth, but the model which inspired it was the British industrial experience of the first half of the nineteenth century. Had Marx lived fifty years earlier and had he been a more benign personality with a greater tolerance for human foibles, Marxism might have had a greater impact on the organization of protest movements in England. As it was, he was an irascible man who lived too late. The industrial revolution ran its course in England without the "benefit" of a Marxist labor movement. In Germany, however, Marxism blossomed into the biggest mass movement that the European continent witnessed in the nineteenth century. When the Communist Manifesto first saw the light of day in 1848, there was scant attention paid to the exhortations of Marx, except by the Prussian censor, but by the end of the third quarter of the century, the structure of the German economy had industrialized enough to have created the proletariat to whom Marx made his chief appeal. We turn now to a consideration of the German labor movement with two problems in mind: One, why did it not interfere more with the growth of income in German capitalist development, and two, in what sense could it be considered a democratizing influence in the development of German political institutions.

§   *The Legacy of 1848*

The year 1848 provides an appropriate departure for an examination of the German labor movement. At this mid-century point the revolutionary hopes of the opponents of authoritarianism were raised high only to be dashed in a reaction that set the stage on which the labor movement emerged in the following half century. The revolutions of 1848 were without exception a failure throughout Europe, except as far as they indicated the limits of the tolerance of ordinary citizens for the arbitrary and authoritarian actions of political authorities. In a sense they marked the end of an era, for, after 1848, with the advance of the technology of war and destruction and the development of transportation and communication facilities, it became increasingly difficult for citizens *qua* citizens to raise the banner of revolt.[13] Without the connivance of the military or without the intervention of some catastrophic external event, it no longer was possible for citizens to bring down the government of the day by throwing up the barricades and sounding the tocsin.

In Germany the revolution arose from the frustrations of the middle classes, who did not have political rights commensurate with their economic power, and the economic hardships of handicraft workers and guildsmen, who were beginning to feel the competition of the new forms of economic enterprise. In Cologne and Aachen, for example, the middle classes numbered some 100,000 but sent only three delegates to the Diet of the Rhine Province, while the nobility, numbering less than 7,000, sent twenty-five.[14] As for the working classes, the Hungry Forties were as voracious in Germany as elsewhere on the continent. High prices, particularly of the food typically consumed by the working man, and unemployment lowered urban living standards and the resistance to insurrection. Yet when the revolution came, moving eastward from its indigenous French habitat, it lacked the substance to sustain itself. Too afraid of the unbridled fury of the working classes to align themselves with them, the middle classes did not possess enough strength in their own right to stand up against the power of king and aristocracy. The workers themselves were split between the artisans and guildsmen, whose revolutionary energies sprang from their desire to restore the privileges of the old economic order, and the many fewer factory workers whose interests lay in the extension of industrial freedom. In short, the revolution lacked mass support and resolute leadership. The Frankfurt Parliament, the institution symbolic of the aspirations of the middle classes for constitutional rule, was grounded in ambiguous franchise requirements which limited the participation of the working classes, and in any event turned out to be a brilliant and vacillating debating society which was quite unable, and unwilling, to prevent the reassertion of authoritarian rule. By the end of the year the Prussian monarch had reoccupied Berlin with the troops forced to flee in the spring uprisings, and by decree promulgated the constitution which reestablished an authoritarian political order.

The failure of the revolution of 1848 in Germany points up some contrasts with the industrializing countries which we have examined thus far. Britain escaped the revolutions of 1848 in large part because its political institutions were so resilient that they were able to accommodate the new alignment of economic forces thrown up by the industrial revolution. While the working classes did not actually secure political privileges, they were instrumental in the attainment of political reforms that subsequently could be extended. If the Chartists, for example, were not immediately successful, they at least articulated goals which thereafter could not be lost sight of by any aspiring political figure. But the political reforms in Britain and the Chartist campaigns following them came in the late stages of the industrial revolution when the mass basis of British society with its peculiar problems necessarily compelled the attention of responsible leaders. In Germany, however, the revolution of 1848 took place before the structural features of an industrial society had been established. In consequence the mass support for constitutional rule was lacking and it was not possible to create political institutions which could readily serve as the basis for a gradual extension of political rights among the working classes. The legacy of 1848 was unfortunate in every respect. The confidence of the middle classes in their political perspicacity was shattered and many of their leaders were forced into exile. The enmity of the working classes toward the middle classes was exacerbated, thus rendering more difficult the cooperation of those groups who might be expected to look upon democratic political institutions as a means of furthering their class aspirations. With the middle classes thus demoralized and alienated from the working classes, it was all the easier for Prussian authoritarianism to claim the legitimacy of its scepter.

As Britain slowly moved toward full democracy by extending the pale of the constitution and Germany dashed the political expectations of an unprepared and premature middle class, the United States embarked upon industrialization within the context of a political system which, because of its free and non-feudal heritage, was undisturbed by the European revolutions of 1848. The middle classes were firmly in command because there was no feudal aristocracy from which they had to wrest authority and as yet no proletarian working class which could challenge the prerogatives of their rule. As we saw in Chapter 6, when the working class began to grow it did not become proletarian so much as individualistic in its outlook, since the conditions of development in the United States fostered the widespread dissemination of entrepreneurial values.

The German labor movement was inevitably affected by the reaction following 1848. Up to that time the predominance of the guilds and domestic employment precluded the growth of trade unions in the modern sense, and though there were some abortive attempts to organize labor in Frankfurt and Berlin during the revolution, these did not outlast the year. The repression of radical political activity and the proscribing of trade unions by Prussia and the other German states meant that for a time the only legal organization which made any appeal to the working classes was the Progressive Party of Herman Schulze-Delitzsch. But since it was predominantly middle class in orientation and approached labor with a program stressing the policy of *laissez-faire* and the virtues of thrift and self-help, the Progressive Party did not meet the problems of the gathering industrial labor force whose capacity to solve its problems alone and unaided was limited by subsistence income. It remained for Ferdinand Lassalle to sound the call for a class-conscious labor movement independent of the middle classes and the liberal economic policies of Schulze-Delitzsch. Employing the Ricardian "iron law of wages" to demonstrate the futility of ameliorating the condition of labor through the capitalistic market, Lassalle demanded that the state cooperate with labor in the establishment of producer cooperatives which, by making workers their own employers, he thought, would allow them to rise above subsistence. The Lassallean movement in its early phase, therefore, tended to be somewhat antitrade-union; the doctrine it espoused denied the possibility of raising wages in a capitalistic economy. In England the trade union wing of the labor movement developed prior to the socialist wing, but in Germany it was the reverse. Lassalle emphasized initially the need for political action and the extension of the franchise among the workers so that the state could be compelled to interfere with the market and set up producers' cooperatives.

The socialist impact of Lassalle on the German labor movement was, of course, reinforced by the influence of August Bebel and Wilhelm Liebknecht, Marx's chief lieutenants in Germany. Hostile to and jealous of Lassalle's success in the organization of the General German Workers' Association, they looked for support to the trade unions which the Lassalleans at first scorned. So rapid was the growth of trade unions in the 1860's that the latter could no longer ignore the challenge of the Marxian strategy. The Lassalleans therefore set up a number of trade unions with which it hoped to corral and organize the support of the working classes. Thus by the end of the decade there were two branches of the socialist movement competing for the allegiance of German workers, the party of Lassalle and the party of Marx, the latter officially organized as the Social Democratic Labor Party at Eisenach in 1869.[15]

The dual socialism in the German labor movement lasted until 1875, when the Lassalleans and Marxists came together at the Gotha Congress and formulated a common program. Though Marx himself was highly displeased and wrote a polemic against the program of the Congress addressed to Wilhelm Liebknecht, the German socialist and trade union leaders in Germany were well pleased to have done with the internecine rivalry which had debilitated the effectiveness of the working-class movement. However much Marx may have felt that his party sold out to the Lassalleans, the program of the newly constituted Socialist Workers' Party was firmly socialist in outlook. If it countenanced too much trifling with the capitalist state to please Marx, it at least looked forward to "the promotion of the instruments of labour to the common property of society."[16]

§ Repression and Growth of the Labor Movement

The organization of the modern German Socialist Party at Gotha came in the decade in which the German economy entered upon its most rapid stage of development. One must therefore ask how it was that a movement whose economic objectives were so hostile to the conditions of capitalist accumulation did not interfere more with the growth of the German economy. For if these had been attained, the distribution of income might have been altered, leaving less disposable income to the investing entrepreneurial classes. The chief reason the program of the socialist party did not impede the progress of the German economy was that the working classes lacked the power to carry it out. Prussia as reconstituted after the Revolution of 1848 was hardly a constitutional order in the British sense. Ministers were responsible to the hereditary king and not to the *Landtag*, whose lower house was elected on the basis of a three-class voting system that underrepresented the urban working classes. Moreover, in the federal German government established following the Franco-Prussian War, Prussia was the dominant state with almost a third of the votes in the upper house, the *Bundesrat*. While there was universal manhood suffrage in the election of the lower house, the *Reichstag*, the upper house possessed a suspensory power which allowed Prussia to veto any legislation initiated in the lower house which it considered ill advised. And just as Prussian ministers were responsible to the king, so the Imperial Chancellor was responsible to the Emperor who indeed was the same person as the Prussian king. In other words, Germany as finally unified in 1871 was the creation of Prussia and the opportunities for the working classes to press for the enactment of their program were as limited in the one as in the other.

Having little power or influence in the structure of Prussian

or German government, the labor movement was unable to prevent the enactment of measures which were designed to curb the
growing strength of the socialists and trade unionists. The most
notorious of these, passed by the *Reichstag* in 1878, was the
*Gesetz gegen die gemeingefahrlichen Bestrebungen der Social-
demokratie,* the so-called Anti-Socialist Law, which made the activities of the Socialist Party illegal. Such attention by the Imperial Government was, no doubt, a measure of the success of
the socialist movement, but for the time being it greatly inhibited socialists and trade unionists alike. The leaders of the labor
movement were driven underground or forced into exile and the
only remaining legal base for its agitation was the floor of the
Reichstag whose socialist contingent was at first reduced by the
negative impact of the Anti-Socialist Law on the socialist vote.
Thus where Britain and the United States used common law
interpretations against combinations in restraint of trade to limit
the power of labor, Germany used the statutory power of government.

The willingness of the German state to repress the socialists
did not reflect a lack of concern for the conditions of the workers.
On the contrary, it was much concerned. In its brief for the 1878
law it contended that "this [social-democratic] agitation seeks to
disseminate amongst the poor and less educated classes of the
population, discontent with their lot as well as the conviction
that under the present regime their condition is hopeless and to
excite them as the 'disinherited' to envy and hatred of the upper
classes."[17] If the Anti-Socialist Law was designed to still the agitation, the social legislation enacted by the state in the 80's was
intended to assuage the conditions which gave substance to the
agitation. The insurance laws for sickness (1883), for accidents
(1884), and for old age (1889) and invalidity made Bismarck's
Germany the prototype of the modern welfare state.

Though more paternalistic and more willing to use the
coercive instruments of government in limiting the activity of the
labor movement than either the British or American state, the
German state nonetheless relied on what we have previously called
permissive policy for controlling labor. As an independent autonomous response to the problems of industrialization the labor

movement therefore continued to gain strength and support in German society, even while it was being harassed and repressed. The Bismarckian regime did not attempt to impose total controls on labor any more than it attempted to impose total controls on industry. If the separation of state and society was not so clear in Germany as in the Anglo-American world, it still had meaning and indeed was manifest in the manner in which the labor movement overcame the impediments placed in the way of its development.

It was a reflection of Germany's European origins and the period of its industrialization that even under the aegis of Bismarck it could never completely suppress the socialist movement, however much it wanted to. At the height of the socialist repression, as we noted previously, the only refuge for the movement was in the *Reichstag,* whose members were unwilling to limit their own freedom in order to excise the party from their midst. While Germany was not a democracy, its political institutions, though far from representative of the popular interest, exerted limits on the freedom of action of the German government. Bismarck had to place the Anti-Socialist Law before the *Reichstag* twice before it was passed, and when it did become law it did not prohibit socialists from running for the *Reichstag* and conducting electoral campaigns. In consequence, the party gained voting strength though the police vigorously persecuted its leaders. In the election of 1881 its vote fell to 312,000 from a previous high of 493,000. Thereafter it rose to 550,000 in 1884 and 763,000 in 1887. By this measure Bismarck's Anti-Socialist Law was a failure, and all the more so because the movement gained an international reputation by refusing to yield before the persecution and intimidation of the state. When, therefore, Bismarck was dropped as chancellor by Wilhelm II, one of the first acts of the new regime was to rescind the Law. With greater freedom to carry their case to the public, the socialists received 1,427,000 votes in the election of 1890, or almost 20 per cent of the votes cast. The socialist movement had come of age.

That the socialist movement had a democratizing influence on German society cannot be gainsaid. However far the German political system may have been from democracy as an ideal type, the industrialization process in the circumstances of the nine-teenth century created a group sufficiently independent to persist in its demands for the privileges of political participation. When it was persecuted it grew stronger rather than weaker. Its elec-toral successes did not bring labor into the councils of govern-ment, for the complex machinery of government in Prussia and Germany was designed to forestall the popular preferences rep-resented in the *Reichstag* and prevent them from controlling the behavior of the ministers of the emperor. Yet the success at the polls by groups antagonistic to the government made it more difficult for authoritarian Prussian rulers to manipulate the machinery of control. So long as the Kaiser and his chancellor felt compelled to observe the formal governmental procedures provided for in the constitution of the German state, opposition in the *Reichstag* was a base for potential democratic growth. For though they might dissolve the *Reichstag* if they were at an im-passe, Kaiser and chancellor had no guarantee that the election would return representatives more amenable to their wishes. With open elections and competing parties, the government could not repress issues that it might otherwise prefer to ignore. Having allowed some vague semblance of democratic procedure and unwilling or unable to repress totally the forces hostile to its rule, the leaders of the German Reich could not discount these forces when from the floor of the *Reichstag* their repre-sentatives articulated the aspirations of the working classes.

§   *German Social Democracy and the Development of Political Consensus*

Thus autonomous growth in Germany threw up groups ex-ternal to the government with demands for political and social reform which arose out of the problems of industrializa-tion. Moreover, as the economy matured in the late nineteenth century these demands tended to become more consistent with the requirements of democratic society, increasing the pos-sibility of continued modification of Prussian autocracy in the period prior to World War I. It will be recalled from the discussion in Part One that the formation of a consensus, permitting participants in the political process to accept an adverse decision, is fundamental to the emergence of democracy. Lacking such consensus, the costs to the contending parties or persons of losing the electoral decision may be so high that they prefer to subvert the process of choice. In Germany industrialization created the strongest Marxist movement the world had yet seen. In a society already divided among a Junker aristocracy, a landowning peasantry, and an industrial and financial bourgeoisie, it was not at all clear that the appearance of a movement which demanded the expropriation of the property of all three classes in the interest of the proletariat could be said to have created a more profound consensus in German society. For the man who stood the chance of losing both an election and his property was not likely to look kindly upon the extension of political privileges to those who threatened him with such grievous losses.

The German Social Democratic Party was undeniably hostile to the bourgeoisie, the Junkers, and the state and all those institutions which Marxian ideology taught were but a reflection of the underlying capitalistic mode of production. For the Marxist there could be no consensus in society until the means of production were so fully developed that property and class relationships were no longer essential to the carrying on of productive activity. So far did these beliefs prevail among German Marxists that the development of social democracy in Germany was in a sense a movement which emphasized its uniqueness and separateness from the rest of German society.[18] Rather than seeking integration and participation with the bourgeois community, the socialists created a world of their own replete with athletic clubs, cultural societies, and social groups. German Social Democracy was a way of life. If Marx was disappointed with the program of the party formulated at Gotha, he would have been highly pleased, had he lived to see it, with the program the party adopted at Erfurt in 1891, the first legal congress of the Social Democratic Party after the rescinding of the Anti-Socialist Law. Twelve years of repression seemingly had not made the party any less revolutionary and on the face of it, it came out boldly for the necessity of revolution in the creation of socialist society. How, then, is it possible to hold that the socialist movement fostered a consensus in German society that might have permitted the growth of a democratic political community?

The answer to the question depends in large part upon the effect that continued industrialization had on the evolution of the labor movement towards the end of the nineteenth century. For even as the Socialist Party was declaring at Erfurt its allegiance to the revolutionary principles of Marx, the rank and file of the party were revealing their willingness to make peace with the institutions of Imperial Germany and to seek their objectives within the limits that these institutions imposed. It was at this time that the Revisionist controversy broke out in Marxist circles and caused so much soul-searching both in the German Social Democratic Party and in the Second International. Influenced by the pragmatic and empirical viewpoint of the Fabian socialists while living in exile in England, Eduard Bernstein took a long hard look at Marx's predictions in the light of the development of industrial capitalism in the late nineteenth century and concluded that many of them were wide of the mark.[19] Most significant of all, he denied the validity of the immiserization hypothesis. Real wages were not falling; rather they were rising. On the basis of his reevaluation of Marx, Bernstein urged upon the party a revision of its tactics, suggesting that the traditional goals of socialism could be attained through evolutionary, nonviolent means.

The rejection of the revisionist argument by Bebel, W. Liebknecht, Karl Kautsky, and the leaders of the German Social Democratic Party belied what had come to be a strong view within the party. While in its early history the socialists dominated the labor movement, trade union leaders became increasingly important as the rise in real income brought about by industrialization in its later stages gave the movement an important function to perform in labor markets. Always to the right of the socialists, trade union leaders tend to be impatient with their longrun ideological views. Concerned with improving the wages, hours, and working conditions of workers, trade union leaders necessarily think in terms of negotiation and compromise. Though the socialist may measure his performance in terms of the purity of the doctrine he espouses, the trade unionist measures his in terms of the increased wages he has obtained for the workers or the number of hours he has reduced the average work week. All this was true of the German trade union leaders around the turn of the nineteenth century, and it was from this wing of the labor movement that the revisionism within the Social Democratic Party won so much support.

At the Erfurt Congress of the party in 1891 the trade unions from a doctrinal point of view were held to be subordinate to the party and concern was expressed lest the growing strength of trade unions lead to the separation of the skilled workers, where organization was first successful, from the mass of unskilled, industrial workers. But at the Party Congress in 1906 the co-equal status of the unions was fully recognized as a resolution was adopted which declared that in matters of mutual concern the Party and the trade unions in consultation should formulate a common policy. The increasing strength of the trade unions in the labor movement meant that in matters of policy affecting labor the left wing socialists were disarmed. Thus the general strike, for example, an important tactical weapon in the arsenal of the latter, was impugned by the former on the grounds that it was typically called by men who had no interest in the day-to-day problems of the workers and usually accomplished nothing but the weakening of the unions. The rise of the trade unions, therefore, must be accounted propitious for the creation of that consensus on which the democratic political community must depend, for in moderating the ideological and messianic views of the Social Democratic Party and raising the pragmatic problem of the welfare of workers in their conditions of work, they focused the labor movement on issues which could be compromised and moved it away from issues which in their very nature could not be compromised.

Moreover, the electoral success of the Party in the *Reichstag* predisposed many of its politically oriented members to accept nonrevolutionary political action as a means of achieving their ends. Projecting the trend of past elections into the future, many socialists could envisage the gaining of a majority position in the

Reichstag, from which they could further envisage the bringing of irresponsible imperial ministers to heel. Whether or not they ever asked themselves what might happen if the electorate did not see its way clear to giving them the backing needed for securing control of the *Reichstag,* the longer they adhered to evolutionary political tactics, the less palatable the violent, revolutionary tactics of left-wing Marxism appeared. Revolution is hardly a natural phenomenon and most people are pleased to exchange it for shortrun gains, either real or imagined. The German socialists were no exception, and though the Party did not disavow revolution, its members were in the main willing to make peace with the institutions of industrial capitalism.

§   *Impediments to the Growth of German Democracy.*

On the eve of World War I Germany had not yet become a democratic political community, and the grim series of events following the war, leading to the totalitarian regime of Hitler, would appear to confound our hypothesis about the democratizing influence of autonomous industrial growth. Though we are not concerned here with developments in Germany beyond World War I, a few observations are in order. First of all, one should note that at a comparable stage of its industrial development Britain also was not yet a democratic society. But following the midpoint of the nineteenth century, Britain had more than fifty years of uninterrupted peace in which the democratizing influence of autonomous industrial growth could work itself out in franchise reform. The relative isolation of Britain from the affairs of the European continent meant, in effect, that foreign disturbances which might have interfered with the gradual extension of voting privileges to the working man were minimized. If, as we have just implied, democratic reforms are least likely to be instituted when there are foreign threats to the security of the state, then Germany's opportunities for realizing the democratic potential of industrialization were limited by World War I and the events subsequent to it. However one may explain the origins of the World War, it subordinated the issues on which democracy might have evolved to the necessity of the state in fighting the war. Moreover, defeat by the allied nations, the abortive revolution of 1919, Versailles and the occupation, the disastrous inflation of the 1920's hardly fashioned a secure environment in which democratic traditions could gain a firm foothold in German society.

Secondly, as we observed at the outset of this chapter, Germany's historical legacy made the barriers to democratic evolution more formidable than in Britain. It arrived on the world scene as a nation relatively late. In the process of its formation the state acquired a greater hegemony over the individual than was the case in the Anglo-American world. The German as an individual was singularly unsuccessful in asserting his rights vis-à-vis the state, partly because of the pallid tradition for doing so. All the more reason, then, that time was an essential ingredient for the development of those beliefs, attitudes, and convictions which could sustain a people in the struggle for the freedoms and rights out of which democratic society historically has evolved. The industrialization of Germany broke the feudal mold and created the autonomous groups of individuals with the problems and aspirations which were consistent with democratic evolution. The end of the hundred years' peace, however, in the holocaust of world war and its aftermath destroyed the environment in which aspirations for democracy could evolve into a strong commitment to democracy.

In our discussion of Germany another factor has come out which has some bearing on our hypothesis about the historical sequence of industrialization and the emergence of political democracy. Up to World War I Germany seems to bear out the hypothesis. Industrializing in the nineteenth century on the heels of Britain at a time when North America still welcomed immigrants, Germany was not beset by a welfare problem which generated labor discontent beyond the capacity of permissive policies to control it. Some workers migrated to new lands, others succeeded in rising to higher status in the industrial hierarchy, and still others formed the basis of the parties and unions in the labor movement which became an independent force seeking the

extension of political rights and privileges in German society.
That the German government was not more responsive to this
force was attributable to what we may call, for lack of a better
phrase, the web of involvement in world affairs. External circumstances rationalized the status quo in political relationships to
rulers and ruled alike. Generally at times of war or in crises
which threaten war rulers do not like to change the constitutional rules of political conduct and the ruled are less likely to
press for change. External problems take precedence over internal problems. This, of course, is often of great convenience to
rulers, and in the contemporary world we have long since become
familiar with the phenomenon of the crisis manufactured in
foreign affairs to divert the attention of a restive population from
domestic affairs. One suspects, however, that the web of involvement in foreign affairs has become an increasingly important
factor as the impact of industrialization has spread throughout
the world. No longer is it possible for nations to enjoy the splen-
did isolation of nineteenth-century America. Whether nations
like it or not, they are caught up in complex interdependent relationships for technological and economic reasons, if for no
other. We shall examine this factor at greater length in a later
chapter. Here, in conclusion, we shall merely point out the obvious—to the extent that foreign problems, issues, and crises
plague a country in its development, it is that much easier for
political leaders to forestall the granting of political rights to
citizens. For the necessity of safeguarding the security of the
state has throughout history been the petard on which individual
freedoms have been hoisted.

Chapter 8

The Twentieth Century Against Democracy: Russia and Totalitarian Industrialization

THE INDUSTRIALIZATION IMPULSE to which the United States and Germany responded with such vigor in the nineteenth century affected Russia very little. While these nations were confronting and surmounting the problems of the transition from an agrarian to an industrial economy, Russia lay dormant, its rich resources and large population immured by an autocracy whose arbitrary and capricious conduct compared favorably to oriental despotism. In the nineteenth century Russia was a colossus of economic and political underdevelopedness.

The historical circumstances which accounted for this primitive condition set Russia apart from western Europe, and even more from North America. First of all its size and world location inhibited its development at the time the forces stimulating change were affecting Europe. Comprising some eight million square miles, or one-sixth of the earth's surface, Russia was a continental land mass most of which was located north of the forty-ninth parallel in arctic tundra that could not support human life. Moreover, its northern location limited its access to the sea. When the voyages of discovery opened up the oceans to world commerce, Russia became an outpost in the world market far removed from the main channels of trade. So long as Europe had been confined to interior trade routes, Russia had provided one of the bridges between Europe and Asia and had prospered. The commercial revolution, however, which created the conditions out of which industrialization emerged in Europe circumvented the Russian economy.

Furthermore, the size of Russia inhibited the spontaneous or autonomous development of its resources. There was no natural system of internal waterways, such as there was in the United States, to facilitate the domestic movement of resources and population. The rivers in Russia ran north and south and flowed out to the frozen arctic. Though resources were abundant, they were not located in close enough juxtaposition for effective utilization under the conditions of nineteenth-century technology.

Unlike another great continental nation, the United States, Russia was not protected by natural barriers at its borders. It was open to invasion from the east, south, and west, and over the centuries it had been beset countless times by Tatars, Turks, Germans, Swedes, and other hostile nations and people. Conversely, its geographical defenselessness compelled Russia itself to be expansionist as it attempted to substitute land and space for the absence of oceans and mountain ranges. From the very outset, therefore, for geographical if for no other reasons, Russia was caught up in the web of involvement in international affairs, a circumstance which increased the autocratic nature of its rulers. Obsessed with the problem of external security, as they had to be, and bedeviled by the Herculean task of maintaining domestic order among the different ethnic and religious peoples in their far-flung lands, the tsars of Russia did not leave the fortunes of state to spontaneous and autonomous individual behavior. They were authoritarian and more often than not despotic.

The autocracy of the Russian tsars was all the more severe because of the attenuated state of the middle classes who otherwise might have imposed some limits to their rule. This, too, partially reflected geographical circumstances. Had the commercial revolutions proceeded apace in Russia, a commercial middle class might have grown along with it, but, as we have seen, the movement of commerce to the oceans left Russia behind. And even before the commercial revolution, Russia was cut off from western Europe by the Tatar invaders with incalculable consequences for the growth of the social system. From about the middle of the thirteenth to the middle of the fifteenth centuries Russia was held in bondage to eastern tyrants who made the Russian princes their minions in order to facilitate the exacting of tribute from the people. It was during this period that the Renaissance and the beginnings of the Protestant Reformation in Europe did so much to shake up received systems of ecclesiastical and secular authority and to create individuals and groups who conceived of themselves as having an existence in their own right apart from monarchs and popes. These cosmic forces which stimulated the development of individual and middle-class consciousness passed Russia by just as did the commercial revolution. There was no Russian Renaissance nor Protestant Reformation. As Europe was emerging from the medieval period with an outburst of artistic, intellectual, and cultural creativity, Russia was throwing off the Tatar yoke and reaffirming its own monolithic rule, a distinguishing feature of which was the subservience of the Russian Orthodox Church to the tsars.

While the growth of the middle classes was aborted in Tsarist Russia, the mass of the population was being enslaved in the system of serfdom. Here again the contrast with western Europe is striking, for at a time when many of the burdens of feudalism were being lightened on the continent, and in Britain had all but disappeared, serfdom was being imposed on the Russian peasant. The territorial expansion of Russia in the sixteenth and seventeeth centuries required the support and maintenance of great armies whose leaders were paid off in landed estates and the bound labor to work them. The price of obtaining hegemony over empire and security against invasion from the east was the enslavement of the peasants who, whether owned by the state or private landowners, lost the right to make their own life and control their own destiny.

Given these oppressive historical and geographical circumstances, it is hardly surprising that when the influences of industrialization spread out from Britain in the nineteenth century, it made little impression on Russia. Russia had neither the skilled labor, the entrepreneurial class, nor the capital to adapt the new industrial technology to the economy. Moreover, the very progress of industrialization in the west seemed to make the problems of Russia more difficult, for it highlighted the backwardness of Russia and evoked throughout the whole century a soul-searching examination by the intelligentsia of the morbid state of the Russian mind and society. Between the Decembrists at the beginning and the Marxists at the end of the century, Russia was rent by the controversies of the Slavophils and westernizers, populists, anarchists, terrorists, and other nihilists, all of which reflected a society with so inarticulate a purpose and so poorly integrated that the incentives and rewards for entrepreneurial and industrial activity had little social depth or support. In short, Russia was too obsessed with first principles to be able to provide a secure environment for entrepreneurship.

§ *Russia as a New Center of Industrialization*

Notwithstanding the ideological and social deterrents to growth in autocratic Russia, there was in the last decades of the nineteenth century an acceleration in the rate of economic activity. Since midcentury, the state had been encouraging the construction of railroads and eventually assumed ownership of them. Their utility for the movement of troops to the far reaches of the Russian empire had not been lost upon military leaders, but the convenience of the state in this respect brought benefits to the economy. With wider markets from which to draw resources and sell output, the number of manufacturing and industrial concerns increased in the 1890's. The output of coal, pig iron, oil, and cotton textiles rose steadily. It was in this period that the metallurgical center in the Donbas became the greatest producer of iron and steel in Russia, surpassing the output of the older center in the Urals. It was also the period in which the oil industry in the Caucasus became the second largest producer in the world.

Though there is no blinking the evidence of accelerated growth in Russia at the end of the nineteenth century, we shall not take this period as the point of departure for our discussion. The rate of growth attained then was aborted by the Revolution in the twentieth century which destroyed the institutions of Tsarist Russia. The nascent capitalism of Russia, nurtured by foreign capital, foreign technicians, and an autocratic state, never had the opportunity to reach maturity. Instead it was replaced by a system of economic organization contrived by men whose goals and objectives in life were very largely fashioned out of their hatred of capitalism. Central planning did not spring full-grown from the mind of Lenin. We know from a reading of *State and Revolution,* published on the eve of the October Revolution, that he had the most naïve notions about the problems of consciously directing economic activity. Moreover, we know that his whole energies were focused on the struggle to seize control of the state and that in the tradition of Marx he had devoted little time to speculating about the dimensions of the socialist state. The planning system evolved from the harsh experiences of the civil war and the period of recovery following it, and it was not until 1928 with the inauguration of the first five-year plan that the Soviet economy assumed its modern guise. In that period in which the Soviet leaders sought out the economic system which could reconcile their ideological demands and national needs, the Russian economy grew little, if at all. In 1928 Russia was hardly better off than it was in 1913, and it would not be difficult to adduce indices which would reveal that it was worse off.[1] In other words, there was a hiatus in Russian economic development occasioned by World War I, the Revolution, and their aftermath. It is therefore not unreasonable to place the effective start of the industrialization process in Russia in the late 1920's.

Because of the timing of Russia's industrialization and the system of economic organization evolved in the process, it is appropriate to conceive of Russia as a new center of development, in contrast to Britain as a center of development in the late eighteenth and early nineteenth centuries. Where the latter stimulated the development and transmission of forces which fostered autonomous growth, the former has fostered state growth. By the end of the nineteenth and the early part of the twentieth centuries, the growth centered on Britain had more or less reached its extensive limits. The English-speaking nations in the British Commonwealth, the United States, and the nations of Europe north and west of the Oder had established the structural economic basis for steady growth, and the rest of the world —the nations of Asia, Africa, Latin America, and eastern Europe—had accommodated itself as best it could to the raw material and food demands of the industrialized and industrializing economies. In the twentieth century Russia broke out of the pattern of economic dependency and interrelatedness that evolved with nineteenth-century industrial growth and through the state initiated a new pattern of industrial growth. It is, of course, too soon to say how far the Russian model of industrialization will be adopted by the countries which remained underdeveloped in the old system, but undeniably it is an alternative that some countries already have emulated, and still others would like to emulate.

Soviet economic development, then, represents a break with the past. It is especially important, therefore, to comprehend the circumstances affecting the organization of the Soviet economy. Without such understanding it will be difficult to assess the impact of industrialization on the evolution of the political order. We must know the magnitude of the obstacles to democratization in order to evaluate the part, if any, that industrialization may play in overcoming them.

§   *The Ideological Influence of Marxism*

No analysis of the origins of the Soviet political and economic system can be undertaken without explicit consideration of the role that ideology has played in the motivation of the leaders of Soviet society. For the October Revolution was instigated by Lenin ostensibly for the purpose of achieving those goals that Marx had assumed were the ultimate destiny of the working population. To ignore the influence of Marx in the formation of the Soviet state would be no less negligent than overlooking the influence of Locke in the foundation of the United States. There are, however, two senses in which ideology may affect behavior: one, through the written word, mandate, or doctrine of the master, as manifested, say, in the Ten Commandments which Moses was alleged to have received on the top of Mt. Sinai; or two, through the attitudes and values that the doctrine inculcates in its adherents. The distinction being drawn here is somewhat tenuous because one cannot acquire the values of an ideology without having been at some point subjected to the doctrine. Nonetheless, the distinction is important, especially in the case of the Soviet Union, for there was nothing in the literary outpouring of Karl Marx that provided the slightest assistance to men dedicated to administering the socialist state according to Marxian principles; what it did do, however, was create a will to collective action that became extremely formidable when the state was the agency for carrying it out.

Let us expatiate a little further on this point. Marx's system of historical materialism posited a functional relationship between economic and noneconomic forces such that changes in the former induced changes in the latter. He then argued that in the development of the forces of production, society passed through a series of stages with different institutional characteristics, each one of which was better than the one preceding it, until the process culminated and presumably ceased in communism. The creative force which propelled society through feudalism, capitalism, and socialism to communism was the class struggle that centered on existing property relationships. Marx contended that revolution could only take place in the fullness of time in the sense that the productive possibilities of the property relationships of a stage of economic development had to be fully exploited before these could be changed by radical political action.[2] That is to say, the socialist revolution could not hope to succeed until capitalism had matured and created a working class so large and so hostile to the interests of capital that it could no longer be controlled by the repressive instruments of the capitalist state. Before the arrival of the strategic period the working class was neither large enough nor enough conscious of its long-run interests to be able to act with the resolve and strength necessary for taking over the power of the state. Premature revolution was bound to fail.[3]

According to this analysis, it could hardly be said that Russia in the early twentieth century was ripe for the socialist revolution. Barely entered upon the first stages of capitalist development and populated by a mass of ignorant and superstitious peasants, Russia contained only the most rudimentary traces of that class in whose name the revolution was supposed to take place. Lenin, of course, was not put off by the inappropriateness of the economic conditions in Russia to the Marxian prescription for revolution. Indeed, his most important doctrinal contribution to Marxism was his explanation and justification of premature revolution. Lenin projected capitalism on to a world stage and related the conflicts among the capitalist states to the internal problems with which they were confronted.[4] Among these the most pressing, which threatened to subvert the very essence and rationale of capitalist existence, was the declining rate of profit. To forestall this, capitalists entered into combination and attempted to monopolize trade and industry. Failing through this means to stay the inexorable decline of profits, they sought colonies overseas where their investment could bring a higher rate of return. Inevitably, the turn to imperialism brought the capitalist nations into conflict with one another, especially when there no longer was unexploited territory for them to seize. In this, the highest stage of capitalist development, the rivalry among nations made them highly susceptible to the revolution. The internal contradictions of capitalism led to external conflicts and war and the breakdown of the international system of capitalist domination. All that was needed to destroy the system in these moribund circumstances was a group sufficiently bold to grasp the nettle and take over the state in some nation, for revolution in one part of the capitalist world order would necessarily spread to other parts. What better place to ignite the fire of world revolution than in Russia? In its inchoate economic condition, Russia experiencing all the trials of early capitalism had not yet reaped any of the benefits. Russia was the weakest link in the chain binding the capitalist world system and it was here that it could be broken most easily. Thus Lenin.

Lenin's *Imperialism* showed scant respect for the doctrines of Marx, and the October Revolution showed even less respect. Yet the influence of Marx on the attitudes and values of Lenin was profound and this can easily be seen by recalling briefly the welfare implications of Marx's system. Where the liberal-utilitarian tradition conceived of individuals as utility-maximizing entities, Marx viewed them as members of classes whose welfare was bound up with the aggregate conditions affecting the destiny of classes. In capitalism, according to this view, the choices of workers were not really freely made, but were determined by the necessity under which they constantly lived to sell their labor-power to capitalists. To use contemporary jargon—which Marx, no doubt, would have thought highly inappropriate—the externalities and interdependencies of choice were so pervasive in the capitalist system that it was quite impossible to make any sense of welfare that was derived from the summation of individual utilities. Freedom of choice only had meaning when workers were relieved from the compulsions of economic necessity, that is, when society had passed through the stages of development and reached communism, at which point the economic problem presumably would have been solved.

The contrast of Marxism and liberalism as welfare systems, then, was (and is) marked. Where the latter saw social welfare arising from individual choice and values whatever they might be, the former saw welfare devolving upon individuals in an anticipated state of development whose characteristics were at best highly amorphous even to those fully initiated into the intricacies of the doctrine, and at worst totally unrelated to the preferences of the presumed beneficiaries. The Marxian welfare system was a species of idealism which denied the existence of the individual apart from the collectivity and therefore was extremely attractive to anyone who was inclined to conceive of the salvation of the individual in terms of the progress of the collectivity, whether it be state or class. Lenin, of course, was such a person. While one perhaps should not attempt to explain his extraordinary will to power as a manifestation simply of his devotion to the welfare values of Marx, one should not discount this influence. Lenin was extremely sensitive to doctrinal issues and always tried to base his actions in "sound" Marxian precedent. This suggests that he attached great importance to the goals and objectives which he understood Marx to be striving for. In fact, his strength as a leader derived in no small part from the integrity of purpose with which the mantle of Marx cloaked him.

§   *Totalitarianism and the Absence of Legitimate Opposition*

The implications of Marxian ideology for the organization of Soviet society were far reaching. Its teleological premises made Lenin and his colleagues implacably ruthless in their opposition to those differing with them. Because opponents stood in the way of history's progress towards the fulfillment of Marx's welfare aspirations in communism, of which the Communist Party was the sole custodian, they had to be destroyed.

The Soviet political system derived its outstanding characteristics from the Communist Party's custodial demands and its claim to the monopoly of truth. Though we do not need to enter here upon a detailed description of this system, we must point out a striking difference between it and the political systems of the industrializing countries of the nineteenth century, namely the institution of one-party rule and the absence of a legitimate opposition. Even in the authoritarian Prussian regime of the nineteenth century there were competing political parties, some opposed to the policies of the king. However much a Prussian Prime Minister such as Bismarck may have attempted to manipulate the parties in the *Landtag,* he did not proscribe them. And when the *Reichstag* of Imperial Germany finally passed the Anti-Socialist Law at the insistence of Bismarck, the Social Democratic Party was still permitted to run candidates for the lower house and carry on their campaign against the regime from its floor. As for Britain, the party system had been in the ascendancy since the Glorious Revolution, and in the United States competing parties appeared following the Washington Administration. In Russia, however, as the Communist Party secured its control of the revolution, other parties lost out and eventually became illegal. If the Communist leaders (or leader as the case may be) genuinely believed that they possessed a special insight into the laws of society and its development which gave them a monopoly of the truth, then, of course, by their standards, there was no need for official opposition and competing parties. Once the Communist Party had determined the correct course of conduct, there was nothing to be done but to implement it by policy.

Further, the monolithic bent of Marxian ideology as far as party organization was concerned was aided and abetted by the absence of a tradition of representative political parties, a reflection of the pervasive influence of the Tsarist autocracy. Feudal estates never developed as representative institutions in the manner of feudalism in western Europe. When Nicholas II was induced by the Revolution of 1905 to call for the formation of a *Duma*, it was the first time in three centuries that a Russian ruler had done so. The rules laid down for its formation, however, assured its impotency in limiting the autocratic power of the Tsar, who could veto its enactments and was not dependent on it for revenues. Perhaps the most important representative institutions in Russia were the provincial *Zemstvos* created in 1864 during the early liberal period of the reign of Alexander II. But as they began to become effective instruments for limited types of economic and social reform, the central government asserted its authority and forestalled the aspirations that the *Zemstvos* were generating for constitutional rule. When therefore the Communist Party destroyed the legitimacy of opposition in the Russian political system, it was behaving very much in the tradition and manner of the tsars.

This fundamental characteristic of the Soviet political system raises a truly formidable obstacle to any democratizing influence industrialization may have. It may be useful at this point to discuss some of its implications. We have conceived of the extension of political rights to previously unenfranchised or unrepresented members of the community as the consequence of pressures brought to bear on governmental authority which strongly challenged or impugned its legitimacy and therefore constituted a threat to its existence. By changing the composition of the population in rural and urban areas and by exacerbating the welfare problem and creating expectations with regard to its solution, industrialization supplied the mass basis of this pressure. It had to manifest itself, however, in some form which would unmistakably reveal to political authorities its ineluctable and inexorable strength. Independent political action and trade union activity in the nineteenth century were a medium for such a manifestation. In the case of Britain the visible discontent engendered by industrialization led to the extension of the franchise to the upper middle classes in the later stages of the industrial revolution. Even in Germany the same phenomenon brought about some modification of the authoritarian German regimes.

In Soviet Russia, however, the circumstances of Marxian ideology, a tradition of autocracy, and the harsh reality of revolution combined to foster the development of a one-party political system which attempted to exert total controls over Russian citizens. How, then, can the discontent which industrialization breeds be transformed into effective forms of political pressure if there is no place in the Soviet system for opposition? If the prerogatives of nondemocratic Soviet political leaders cannot be challenged from outside "the establishment," what reason is there to believe that the leaders would ever be willing to devolve or decentralize their collective power on individual citizens? Especially in view of the fact that they presumably have come to believe that individual preferences and choice are nothing but a capitalistic chimera? Or is it possible that within the Communist Party different factions responding to various problems confronting Soviet citizens and contending for control of the Party will evolve "constitutional procedures" which will provide a more consistent link between the preferences of citizens and the policies of the leaders? Or, being even more speculative, will the day perhaps arrive when the Party at long last decides that output is high enough to allow individuals the free choice promised by the advent of communism? Though it would be presumptuous to allege that there are answers to these questions, they at least indicate the greater difficulties that stand in the way of democratization in the Soviet Union than those that stood in the way of the countries industrializing in the nineteenth century.

It is not enough, however, merely to point out that a totalitarian society places higher barriers in the path of democratization than an aristocracy (Britain in the late eighteenth century) or an authoritarian society (Germany in the late nineteenth century.) Nor is it adequate for our purposes to observe that the totalitarian regime in Soviet Russia emerged from the symbiosis of the historical Russian tradition and Marxian ideology. We want, further, to inquire whether the historical timing of Soviet industrialization has any bearing on its potential, or lack of potential, for democratization. This, after all, is the question of general interest which has a bearing on the problems of the currently underdeveloped economies. Is the Soviet Union unique or is there some ordering of the relevant variables brought about by late starts in industrialization which inhibit the release of democratic forces? In order to establish a better basis for answering this question we must look more closely at the imperatives of economic development in postrevolutionary Russia.

§   *The Dilemma of Russian Socialism in an Undeveloped Economic System*

At the time of the Russian Revolution, the process of industrialization in the western world had been going on for more than a century. The three countries with which we were concerned in the previous chapters had all passed through the industrial revolution proper and were beginning to experience a wider distribution among the working population of the benefits of rising income. If the factories and mines in Britain, Germany, and the United States were not yet earthly paradises, their harsher features were being modified. Conditions of employment were improving; the work week was tending to become shorter, and the arbitrary conduct of employers was being corrected by the combined effect of state legislation and the rules of trade unions. Having surmounted the "hump" of development, these countries had a large enough income to be able to look to some of the amenities of living for the masses of the population. Russia, therefore, by virtue of its late start in industrialization, had before it a whole century of experience from which it could glean both the goals of development and the conditions which it wished to avoid in achieving them. Marxian ideology, of course, was the purveyor of this experience, and however much Marx himself may have insisted upon the necessity of the capitalist stage of development in the progressive unfolding of man's destiny, he also protested with indignation and vehemence the hardships that capitalism imposed on man. In seizing control of the Russian state and forestalling the process of capitalist development in Russia, the communist leaders brought to the problems of economic organization and economic growth Marx's abiding and deeply-rooted dislike of the capitalistic market. Though they had few positive ideas about how they would go about achieving the ends of the socialist state, they certainly did not intend to rely upon the "anarchism" of the market.

Thus, where Britain, by contrast, created an industrial order on the strength of the autonomous and independent actions of many individuals seeking limited objectives outside the province of the state-directed system of mercantilism, Russia rejected the market mechanism in favor of conscious state planning in order to achieve longrun goals which it comprehended in the historical context of western industrialization. In Britain the capitalist market grew harum-scarum as individuals sought to maximize their own advantage; in Russia the capitalist market was not allowed to develop because the communist leaders' reading of history did not yield a favorable view of its performance.[5]

The decision to plan economic activity, however, was not taken lightly. An important part of the first ten years of the Soviet regime was taken up with the issues and problems involved in working out the form of economic organization both equal to the task of accelerating economic growth and consistent with the ideological imperatives of Marxism. Among the most difficult of these was the labor problem, or what in the previous century in Germany was called the *Arbeiterfrage*. Clearly Russia was faced by a dilemma after the Revolution which prior to 1917 tended to be obscured by the political machinations within the Russian Social Democratic Party and by the dramatic events of the Revolution itself. Tht dilemma was this: Having seized control of the Russian state and economy at an early stage of capitalist development, the Bolsheviks inherited the stigma and onus of the welfare problem which otherwise would have been borne by the capitalist class. Lenin had argued with great conviction that if the revolutionary spark were ignited, it would fire the revolution in the advanced countries in Europe which then could come to the aid of Russia as it struggled with the problems of development. If the abundant resources of the mature economies in Europe were thus made available to the immature Russian economy, the welfare problem could surely be alleviated. But as it turned out the world revolution never materialized and after World War I Russian was left high and dry, an island of socialism in a hostile capitalist sea. So the dilemma which was so conveniently out of sight before the Revolution showed its horns with a vengeance after the Revolution.

§   *The Organization of Economic Activity During the Preplan Years*

Lenin did not live to see the eventual resolution of the dilemma, but he set in motion the preplan system of economic organization which brought the issues to focus that the Communist Party had to deal with. Shortly after the October Revolution, Russia was torn by civil war and beleaguered by the intervention of the western allies and Japan. The exigencies of the situation were such that the Russian economy was quickly brought under central governmental direction in a phase of its development which came to be known as the period of War Communism. During this period, lasting from 1918 to 1921, industrial and manufacturing firms were nationalized and managed, in effect, as divisions of the government, labor was drafted both for industry and the army, and grain was forcibly requisitioned from the peasants. As one may well imagine, the period of War Communism was indescribably chaotic and one should not think of the economic system as being operative in any functional, integrative sense. The Bolsheviks themselves knew nothing about administration, public or private; they were first and foremost revolutionaries and not unnaturally they did not inspire the confidence of the technical and professional personnel that they inherited from the former regime. Both in the army and industry, however, the Bolsheviks had no choice but to rely on many persons who were hostile to their objectives. If they had difficulty in maintaining the support and loyalty of personnel in army and industry, they had even more trouble in maintaining the supply of grain and other agricultural produce from the country on which the army and industry depended.

One of Lenin's first acts after the October Revolution was the nationalization of land and its distribution to the peasants. This perhaps more than any other single action accounted for the eventual success of the Bolshevik Revolution, for the peasants had always felt entitled to the land which they had worked for the landlords and aristocracy and, here, in the first wave of revolutionary reform, the Bolsheviks lived up to their word and turned the land over to them. However, the stock of good will that the Bolsheviks had accumulated among the peasants was very largely dissipated in the series of the measures the former took to acquire the grain of the latter over and above subsistence needs. Having won title to the land, as they thought, the peasants were far from enthusiastic about parting with its product except on terms which they considered fair and reasonable. Thus when the new revolutionary regime employed the technique of the class war to obtain surplus grain and still later sent armed detachments of troops into the countryside to seize grain, the peasants struck back by concealing their stocks of grain, and, more devastatingly, reducing the amount that they planted. By 1921 the situation had so far deteriorated that the cities were not obtaining enough agricultural supplies to maintain the working population which in consequence was fleeing to the countryside. Output in large-scale and small-scale manufacturing concerns had fallen precipitously and with the breakdown of the exchange relationship between the agricultural and industrial sectors of the economy, money had depreciated beyond use in a galloping inflation.[6]

Though there were some Bolsheviks of peculiar ideological persuasion that thought the period of War Communism had a salutary effect for a socialist economy because it destroyed the value of money, Lenin had a more hardheaded view. Recognizing the collapse of the economy in the face of the peasants' resistance to the policy of grain requisitioning, he announced in the spring of 1921 a New Economic Policy. This had as its salient feature a partial return to the conditions of a market economy. Peasants were to be allowed to produce and sell for a market with freedom to purchase land and hire workers for wages. In the words of the imprudent Bukharin, they were told to enrich themselves, much as, ironically enough, Guizot had enjoined the middle classes in France during the reign of Louis Philippe. In the cities private enterprise was once again permitted in small shops and stores. Large-scale enterprise, earlier subsidized by subventions from the central government, was cut loose from such support and told to operate according to the cost accounting and profit calculations of capitalistic firms.

Surely, there has seldom been such an ironical twist in history as the New Economic Policy. Created, with high hopes, in the interests of the proletariat and in righteous opposition to the acquisitive capitalist spirit, the first Marxist state found itself turning to the very institution against which it rebelled: it had found that the direct methods of socialist administration did not yield the results essential to the state's continued existence. Capitalism had to bail out socialism, and no matter how gratifying to the adherents of the former, to many of the faithful it was a most egregious atavism.

Yet Lenin was not really betraying the social revolution as some people thought; in his famous phrase he was "taking one step backwards in order to take two steps forward." He had not intended that the New Economic Policy be a permanent form of economic organization, but only a palliative which would restore the Russian economy so that it could be reconstructed as a truly socialist order. Even before the announcement of the New Economic Policy a State Planning Commission had been established (February 1920) and a comprehensive plan had been drawn up for the electrification of Russia. Moreover, the state did not relinquish control of industry, but attempted to form a more stable environment in which state firms could function. In short, the market economy was not intended to open the door wide to capitalism, but rather to prepare the economy for the advent of socialism.

While the New Economic Policy induced a recovery of the Russian economy from the ravages of war and civil war, it did not resolve the dilemma occasioned by the premature timing of the socialist revolution. The economy did not grow during the 1920's beyond its 1913 level. Indeed, the New Economic Policy restored output at the cost of very substantial depreciation of the capital stock the new regime inherited from its predecessor. Gross output had recovered, but net output was down. The Russian economy still stood on the threshold of industrialization; the leaders of the Soviet state in the generation after Lenin had to devise means of accelerating the rate of growth and at the same time deal with the welfare problem which inevitably accompanies such a process.

§   *The Industrialization Debate of the 1920's*

There was by no means unanimity within the Communist Party about how these issues should be dealt with. In fact, divergent views on these matters were very much involved in the great struggle for the control of the Communist Party after the death of Lenin. On the one hand, a group on the right wing of the party, headed by Bukharin, Tomsky and Rykov, was well disposed to a continuation of some modified form of the New Economic Policy. This group drew its support from trade unionists within the Party as well as from those whose administrative duties during the New Economic Policy gave them some appreciation of the purpose and rationale of prices in a market mechanism. The right wing had learned the bitter lesson of the period of War Communism and was unwilling to coerce the peasants into providing the output necessary for the development of the industrial-urban sector of the economy. They wanted to set up price relationships in the market to provide the peasants with an incentive for supplying industry and the urban population with resources and food. For the right wing, planning consisted very largely of the coordination of the mixed economy that had grown up during the New Economic Policy and the gradual extension of socialism as economic growth permitted. The group's most significant argument, however, was that the rate of economic development depended ultimately on the size of the output the peasants were willing to trade to industry and that therefore it was necessary for the Party to cooperate with the main body of peasants and recognize their interests in the program of the new Economic Policy.[7]

The difficulty with the right-wing position was that the performance of the economy during the New Economic Policy revealed serious shortcomings to the market as a mechanism of exchange between town and country. When, for example, the terms of trade—the prices of agricultural commodities relative to the prices of industrial goods—moved in favor of agriculture, the peasants were most willing to exchange their output for the output of industry, because a given output of grain would yield an increasing real income. But from the point of view of a communist regime this was hardly a satisfactory solution. For one thing the real income of the peasant sector would grow relative to the real income of the proletarian sector, an anomalous circumstance for the first workers' state. For another, it strengthened the economic position of just those groups who could be expected to be hostile to the longrun objectives of the Party. Marxists tended to be suspicious of peasants with their stubborn and well-developed sense of private property; as recent revolutionists they were hypersensitive to the threat of counterrevolution from this source.[8]

When, however, the terms of trade moved against agriculture and created income relationships consistent with the ideological preferences of the Party, the peasant tended to reduce the amount of agricultural produce he offered for exchange against manufactured output. The agrarian reforms at the time of the revolution increased the proportion of land owned and worked by the middle and poor peasant, leading to a proportionate decrease in the exchangeable agricultural surplus and a proportionate increase in output consumed directly on the farm. Lower taxes and rents, as compared with the prewar years, reduced the peasant's need for cash and hence the pressure to sell produce in the markets. Thus when prices turned against the peasant, he was inclined to consume more of his own output, unlike his wealthier American counterpart who was more dependent on the exchange economy and often tried to compensate for lower prices with higher sales. The erratic movement of prices throughout the New Economic Policy pointed to the fact that the agricultural problem, already the Achilles' Heel of the Soviet economy, was not yet solved. Just as War Communism was brought to a disastrous end by the unwillingness of the peasants to supply grain to the city, so the New Economic Policy was threatened by the unwillingness of the peasants to supply an output through the market large enough to meet the needs of the economy for development.

The left wing of the Party, headed notably by Trotsky, took a hard position against agriculture. The members of this group believed that the pace of development set by the free disposition of agricultural output through markets would be too slow as long as the industrial sector was underdeveloped, and could not provide an adequate flow of goods for exchange. Rather than accepting market relationships as they evolved during the New Economic Policy, they advocated purposeful central planning in which the rate of capital accumulation in industry would be increased. This, they thought, would redound to the benefit of agriculture as well as industry, for it was necessary to build agricultural capital equipment such as tractors and combines in the industrial sector before the agricultural sector could be effectively modernized. The supporters of Trotsky, then, were advocates of forced industrialization and rapid proletarization of the labor force, achieved through the central planning and allocation of the economy's resources.

An issue was thus drawn between the left and right wings of the Communist Party, an issue crucially related to the subsequent development and organization of the Soviet economy, but which also has relevance for any economy which consciously has to deal with the problems of underdevelopedness—growth through industry or growth through agriculture. The Trotsky solution had implications which for some communists were as unpalatable as the right-wing deference to agriculture. If the state planned to accelerate the rate of capital accumulation in industry, what would happen to the standard of living and status of the workers? Would the state be playing the exploiting role that during the New Economic Policy had been played by the kulak and nepmen? If so, was there any reason to believe that the worker would be any better off? The left wing's answer to these questions, especially as formulated by Preobrazhenski, was forthright and in the light of Marxian doctrine magnificently bold. Preobrazhenski asserted that in order to prepare Soviet society for the advent of socialism it would have to pass through a period of "primitive socialist accumulation." During this period the satisfaction of present wants would have to be deferred to the more important task of constructing the capital equipment on which future growth depended. What shocked many a Bolshevik was the similarity, consciously and overtly pointed up by Preobrazhenski, between the requirements of growth in the socialist state and the capitalist state. Marx had used the phrase "primitive capitalist accumulation" to describe the process by which capital was initially made available to capitalists.[9] This turned out to be a long drawnout class struggle in which the workers lost their claim to property through enclosures, confiscations, inflation, and were placed in a position where they had no choice but to sell their labor-power to the exploiting accumulators. In short, Marx asserted that capitalism grew on the backs and lives of workers. Was Preobrazhenski suggesting that workers would have to put up with similar repressions in the socialist state?

§   *Factors Exacerbating the Welfare Problem*

This question brings us back to the problem of labor controls in a period of accelerated economic growth, for clearly, as Preobrazhenski suggested, growth cannot take place if the members of society consume the increments to aggregate output. How then should they be prevented from doing so? We have seen in the previous chapters how this problem was handled during the nineteenth century in the countries experiencing autonomous growth. In the twentieth century, however, the problem in many ways has become more difficult. The fact that Russia lagged behind the economic development of the western world gave its leaders an acute consciousness of the goals it was trying to maximize and, especially since these goals were enshrined in a welfare ideology, they tended to take precedence over the means of achieving them. In the classic manner of Rousseau, it was relatively easy for a Russian Marxist, observing his country's future in the past development of Europe, to rationalize a policy of forcing people to be free. Or to put it another way, it was more difficulty to leave people alone—to be permissive—when one thought one knew what their destiny was.

Not only did the latecomers' view of the past industrialization process support a totalitarian outlook, but the circumstances of lateness tended to make the control problem more urgent. First of all, consider the growth of population. In the late nineteenth century Russia was plagued by an excess rural population, and though in the early twentieth century the rate of growth of population was retarded by World War I, the civil war, and the famine of 1921, it soon was rising rapidly with the recovery that the New Economic Policy brought about. In other words, population in Russia was increasing ahead of output at the time the Soviet leaders were trying to resolve the many issues of economic growth and organization, creating aggregate unemployment with all its attendant difficulties. The increasing population reflected the impact on Russia of the advances in medical knowledge and of the growing output of the western industrial nations. To cite one example, the Hoover mission to Russia at the time of the famine was possible only because there was an advanced part of the world with a large enough output over and above its basic requirements to spare aid to the suffering nation. People were kept alive who would not have lived in a less economically developed period. At least in the case of Russia, the impulse from the industrialized west to increase population was greater than the impulse to increase output.

Second, the population of Russia was sequestered within the nation. By the time the Soviet leaders came to consider the means of accelerating the rate of industrial development, the opportunities for emigration were limited. In the nineteenth century the United States, Canada, and Australia were underpopulated areas of the world anxious to absorb the excess population of Europe, and as the technology of ocean transport improved and lowered the costs of travel, the migration to the new parts of the world reached deeper into Europe. But after World War I, the barriers to immigration were raised and foreign population was no longer welcome, especially in the United States. To be sure, Russia had an eastern domain which it had been colonizing even before the Revolution, but the natural conditions in Siberia were not propitious for making an individual livelihood and did not exert as strong a pull as did the American west. Thus when Russia came to accelerate the rate of economic growth, it was no longer possible to export surplus population.

Third, since Russia was industrializing in the wake of the more advanced western economies, the standard of living in the latter was a possible source of invidious comparison with the standard of living in the former. We refer, of course, to the demonstration effect which we discussed in Chapter 4. A necessary goad to stimulate the growth of an efficient labor force, the demonstration effect could be too much of a good thing if it generated wants too fast for the capacity of the economy to satisfy them. According to the Rostovian classificatory system, in the 1920's the United States and Canada entered the stage of high mass-consumption and in the next decade they were followed by Britain and Australia.[10] During these years Russia was struggling to build the growth sectors of its economy and in consequence the consumer standard of living advanced little, if any. Urban housing was squalid and cramped as the planners economized on residential construction, and the supply of food and clothing was sharply limited by the catastrophic events which engulfed the countryside during the collectivization drive.

The disparity in the standard of living between the western and Russian economies might not have exacerbated the problem of controlling labor except that by the 1920's the literature of protest and the tactics of labor organization and political action were so well developed that in the absence of strong controls the demands of labor for a greater share of the national product might have jeopardized the growth objectives of the regime. Unlike Britain, for example, Russia could not count on a long hiatus between the onset of accelerated growth in the industrialization process and the formation of effective movements of protest. Though Lenin himself had deprecated western trade unions and was suspicious of the opportunism of trade-union leaders, his party contained a trade union wing whose members were not so mesmerized by the longrun goals of socialism that they paid no attention to the immediate problems of the workers. Moreover, the trade unions themselves had had a hand in the administration of industry during the period of War Communism and from the very outset of the Revolution had been organized on a national basis. While the Trade Union Congress was dominated by the Bolshevik Party, for a time the Mensheviks and Left Social Revolutionaries participated in its proceedings and served as an opposition to the views of the former.[11]

Fourth, the program of industrialization first put forward by Trotsky and his supporters, which could only have been conceived in the light of the experience of more advanced economies, threatened, in the short run at least, to impose on the working population a greater strain and greater "abstinence" than an alternative proposal of development placing primary emphasis on the agrarian sector of the economy. For one thing the construction of hydroelectric power facilities, the expansion of heavy industry, and the development of new mineral resources tied up investment in projects which would not yield an increase in the real income of the working population as rapidly as if investment had been allocated to agriculture and light manufacturing. However important such investment might have been in changing the parameters of growth and creating new supplies of resources, its cost was high in terms of the satisfaction of present wants. This was all the more threatening to the stability of the regime in view of the fact that the Trotsky program called for the rapid proletarization of the population. Not only was the unemployment in the cities to be absorbed in the plans for capital construction, but the surplus population in the rural areas was to be brought into the industrial sector. Thus at a time when the scarce resources of the economy were to be allocated to investment in heavy industry, the population was to become increasingly concentrated in cities whose assets and utilities were not adequate to meet the need of urban residents. Circumstances such as these create discontent and potential sources of opposition to the policies of established governmental authority.

As it turned out, the solution of the Soviet regime to the labor problem in a period of accelerated economic growth was even more extreme than the program the Trotskyite left wing had envisaged. Stalin destroyed the opposition both left and right, but adopted the economic program of the former while adding a few characteristic features of his own. Starting in the year 1928, the era of the five-year plans inaugurated the system of central economic planning, or what may be better described as the command economy. The New Economic Policy was terminated and, except in peripheral occupations, private enterprise was no longer permitted. In rural Russia the transition to the planning system was as violent as the October Revolution, for it involved a fundamental change in the organization of agriculture which many peasants found deeeply repugnant. Collective farms were formed from individual homesteads and the peasants were forced to join and bring along any livestock and equipment they possessed. So strong was the resistance to collectivization that as much as one-half of the livestock herds were slaughtered in protest, a loss from which the Soviet Union did not recover for almost a generation. In the city the abandonment of the New Economic Policy was less disastrous, for the state already owned large-scale industry and the new economic program did not therefore call for massive changes in the ownership and control of resources.

§   *Soviet Planning and the Control of Labor*

The command economy as it took shape was essentially an
    organization designed to force a rapid rate of industriali-
zation, just as Trotsky had advocated during the struggle for
control of the party in the middle 20's. It consisted essentially of
planning authorities acting in a staff capacity in the formulation
of plans and administrative authorities acting in a line capacity
as they supervised the carrying out of the plans. The plans
drawn up by the State Planning Commission (Gosplan) embodied
the policy objectives of the Communist Party and took the form
of physical production objectives for the main industries and
sectors of the economy. Prices, wages, and costs were of importance, not as market instruments for articulating the preferences of consumers and workers for goods and services, but as
instruments for facilitating the allocation of resources, including
labor, and the distribution of output in accordance with the
directives of the plan. In other words, the preferences of the
Party leaders for the utilization of resources took precedence
over the preferences of individuals, and the gigantic administrative structure between the apex of supreme executive authority
and the base of operating firms, which cannot help but boggle
the imagination, performed the function of insuring the con-
sistency of the performance of the latter with the policies of the
former. In short, the top executives of the Soviet economy, starting in 1928, attempted first to plan the gross national product in
physical terms and second to supervise the execution of the
plan.[12]

Given this system of central planning, there were inescap-
able consequences for the organization of labor. If the plan
accounted for the division of output between investment goods
and consumer goods, and if, further, it specified the prices of
all goods and the wage rates to be paid different classes of labor,
then there remained nothing for workers to do about what had
traditionally been the concern of independent trade unionists
in the western world, wages and hours and the level of consumption and leisure. For these variables were all determined

by plan, and once having been set, could not be changed autonomously by the persons carrying out the plan. Clearly then central
planning of the Soviet variety was wholly inconsistent with the
bargaining function of western trade unionism. Only before
the plan was formulated could there be negotiations and bargaining about real wages. These would have to take place at
the center of the system where the decisions were made with
respect to the allocation of resources between investment goods
and consumer goods.

Not surprisingly, Soviet trade unions with the start of the
five-year plans became productionist organizations concerned
first with the achievement of the production norms established
by plan and only secondly with the income objectives of traditional unions. Strikes were prohibited as were wage negotiations.
This is not meant to imply that the unions lost their significance
in the Soviet Economy. On the contrary, they performed the
important tasks of facilitating the commitment of peasants and
inexperienced workers to industrial employment, helping them
to find housing, articulating their grievances about plant conditions, and administering the social security system. These functions, which seem so strange to anyone familiar with the history
of trade unionism in the western world, were not inconsistent
with the prior development of unions in Soviet Russia. Even
before the Revolution the union wing of the labor movement
had been dominated by the political wing; as early as 1902 in
his polemical *What Is To Be Done?* Lenin made the classic
statement about the appropriate relationship between the masses
in their trade unions and the socialist elite in the Bolshevik
Party. During War Communism, as we previously noted, the
unions played an important role in the nationalization of industry, and for a time during the New Economic Policy, the
trade unions negotiated collective wage agreements with employers. But for the most part the trade union leaders had little
independence in the years prior to the inauguration of the five-
year plans. With the state sector of the economy in the 1920's
growing relatively to the private sector, the scope for western-
type union activity was constantly diminishing. Thus when the
trade unions in 1928 became, as it were, a branch of Soviet gov-

ernment, this completed a trend which was foreshadowed in Lenin's ideology and carried forward during the New Economic Policy.

The contrast between Russia in 1928 and the western economies at a roughly comparable stage of development could not be sharper as far as the control of labor was concerned. In Britain, for example, permissive policy allowed workers to organize unions and engage in political activity to protest the injustices and hardships of early industrialization, but in Russia totalitarian policy emasculated the independence of working-class organization and sharply limited the capacity of workers to express dissatisfaction with the conditions of employment. In Britain, objective circumstances favoring an individual solution to the welfare problem, plus subjective views which inclined toward leaving people to their own devices, created a permissive milieu; in Russia, objective circumstances threatening too strong a collective reaction to the welfare problem for the attainment of an adequate rate of growth, plus subjective views overwhelmingly impregnated with concern for the future development of individuals, created a totalitarian milieu. In Britain, industrialization led to the formation of groups whose demands, pressures, and threats eventually caused the Establishment to increase the scope of constitutional rule; in Russia, the onset of industrialization bound individuals within the Establishment, rendering it difficult, if not impossible, for groups of individuals to work independently for its reform. The imperatives of economic development in the twentieth century had joined the ancient autocratic Russian tradition and Marxian eschatology to form the conditions for a totalitarian industrial order.

§ *The Growth of Soviet Income*

The transformation of the Soviet economy following 1928 bears witness to the success of the Soviet planning authorities in accelerating the rate of economic growth. Year after year the economy has attained the output goals on which it has placed the highest priority. Russia has become in the contemporary era the second industrial power of the world, in spite of the irrevocable output losses caused by the collectivization holocaust during the first five-year plan and World War II midway through the third five-year plan. Though Soviet statistics leave something to be desired and cannot be accepted without interpretation and reservation, there is little reason to doubt that the real national income of the Soviet Union for the past generation has been growing at an annual average rate of between 6 and 7 per cent.[13] This compares to an annual average rate of growth of the United States's net national product from the decade following the Civil War to the decade preceding World War I of perhaps 4.5 per cent. Aggregates such as national income and product are so large that they obscure as much as they reveal. One cannot easily use them for welfare comparisons, especially when the economies in question are so far removed in historical time and national values as the Soviet Union and pre-World War I United States. Whatever the composition of the aggregate output, however, the rate of increase obtained in the aggregate by the Soviet economy has been impressive.

The rapid growth of Soviet national income reflects the fact that the institutions which might have expressed the preferences of the population for an alternative allocation of resources have been attenuated. Investment, for example, was not inhibited by the pull that a market economy exerts on the utilization of resources for consumption. Not only could aggregate investment, then, be high, but it could be allocated among uses which stimulated the growth of the industrial sector of the economy. Thus industrial production, as distinct from agricultural output and the output of light manufacturing concerns, increased at an annual average rate of 8.9 per cent during the period 1928–50.[14] Moreover, as we have had occasion to mention before, resources could be reserved for investment in heavy industry by disinvesting in residential housing, i.e., by living off the social capital inherited from the Tsarist regime. Further, the absence of any sort of popular control over the planning and economic authorities meant that the inevitable mistakes committed in the formation of plans or in their execution could be sloughed off in the consumer goods sector. If it turned out that in a given planning period there was not enough structural steel on hand to complete the construction of both a steel mill and a shoe factory, the former could always be given a higher priority. What the western economies achieved by distributing income so unequally that the mass of consumers would have little disposable income left after meeting their basic wants, the Russian economy achieved by directing resources through plan and priority to the production of investment goods.

§   *The Failure of Industrialization to Create External*
    Pressure for Political Reform

We now return to the question asked earlier in this chapter about the democratizing influence of industrialization in the context of a totalitarian order. We have already noted that the nineteenth-century pattern of democratization is not likely in Russia because of the absence of opposition through which external pressure for political reform could be exerted on governmental authorities. The industrialization process itself would not appear to make opposition any more likely. For as the Soviet economy increases its industrial capacity, the strength of the Soviet government also grows, since it has at its disposal greater means for maintaining domestic order and controlling the population. Weapons can be produced in greater quantity, the improvement of communication systems enables central authorities to keep informed of the state of the public mind, and faster transportation facilities allow it to send key officials or even troops to trouble spots anywhere in the nation with great dispatch. Moreover, the spread of literacy and the growth of the mass media of communication have made it feasible for the Soviet government to train Soviet citizens into a mold formed by the aspirations and ambitions of Soviet leaders.[15] Educated in Soviet schools, informed of the state of the world by *Izvestia, Pravda, Trud,* and the government-controlled radio and television, entertained by government-produced movies, Russians have limited opportunity to acquire values and attitudes which can contravene official values and attitudes. Further, the continued industrialization of the Soviet economy has brought more than half of the population into the industrial sector where the various institutions and instruments of control can be imposed more readily. After thirty years of planned industrialization it is more difficult than ever to oppose the policies of the Party leaders from outside the Party. By now the Party has too much output at its disposal with which to control opponents of the policy it espouses.

If the industrialization of Russia is not leading to a democratization of the regime from the demands of groups external to the Communist Establishment, is it effecting any kind of internal reform which may contain the genesis of a democratic order? The answer to such a question must necessarily be speculative, because the machinations and the distribution of power and authority within the ruling group of a closed society are always obscure. One can guess at the alignment of forces in the presidium of the central committee of the Communist Party; but guesses are poor substitutes for confirmed knowledge. While in the western world there may for a time be similar obscurities about how cabinets, committees, or councils in government reach decisions and formulate policies, eventually these are cleared up as the participants retire from the political arena and devote their remaining years to the writing of memoirs, which frequently turn out to be rationalizations of the positions they took and the policies they represented in the crucial questions of state. In the Soviet Union political leaders have either died in disgrace or in office. If the former, they have not been allowed to write memoirs; if the latter, they hardly had the time. Since we lack a clear picture of the internal dynamics of the Soviet political system, we cannot go far in investigating the reform potential of industrialization. Indeed we can do little more than make inferences about the problems which are likely to confront the Party as real income continues to rise. Needless to say, our observations will be extremely tentative and at best only suggestive.

§   *Controls Occasioned by the Disorders of Planning*

The character of the Soviet economic system was determined largely by the decision of the Communist Party to accelerate the rate of growth through industrialization. Given the necessity to increase the rate of saving and investment faster than the ability or willingness of individuals to forego present consumption, the lack of an entrepreneurial tradition, the relative backwardness of the population, and obdurate natural conditions, this entailed the concentration of economic power in a command economy. Individuals were not free to dispute the decisions of central governmental planners, once these were embodied in a formal plan, but were bound to carry them out. We have noted that planning reinforced the totalitarian bent of the Soviet system by depriving the trade unions of independent status and making them an arm of the government. There also were conflicts constantly arising between central planners and operational personnel which tended to maximize the arbitrary and authoritarian conduct of Soviet government. The nature of these conflicts should be examined carefully because it is conceivable that rising income may modify them and hence prepare the way for more orderly political processes.

Were there no divergence between the social welfare function and individual preferences, there would be no need for a command economy. In the case of Soviet Russia, however, the social welfare function determined by the Communist Party is different from the preferences of Soviet citizens and so the Party acting through the government has to command assent to its economic plans. Planning, however, is an imperfect instrument. It is quite literally impossible for central planners to make the millions of decisions involved in allocating resources among thousands of competing uses. So interrelated are these decisions that no individual or collective mind can retain all the essential information for a consistent solution.[16] The gross national product simply cannot be planned in advance in such fine detail that, for example, the supply and demand of coking coal, tenpenny nails, eyeglasses, two and a half ton trucks, shoelaces, lu-

bricating oil, and structural steel will be equal at the prices set
by the central authority. Surpluses and shortages are bound to
appear. Even if one assumes that the preferences of individuals
remain constant, central planning is a formidable task. In fact,
planning in the Soviet Union is relatively crude in the sense
that it is aggregative and incomplete. Some sectors and industries
are planned more thoroughly than others but nowhere in the
economy is the planning so detailed that the plant directors are
relieved of the responsibility of making substantive decisions.
Though the latter receive through the administrative hierarchy
directives regarding physical output and the resources available
to them, they may have discretion not only about how to com-
bine resources to produce a given output, but also, in the case
of multiproduct firms, how to allocate resources among different
outputs.

Moreover, Soviet governmental authorities have found that
it is easier to command assent through positive acquiescence
than through mandate. They have therefore used prices in planning as a means of gearing individual drives and motives to the
purposes of the Communist party. Differential wages and the
pricing of consumers' goods provide a goal for workers to maximize output; profits and bonuses induce the directors of firms to
carry out the directives of the plan; and on the collective farm
the peasants are permitted to raise vegetables and poultry on
their own homesteads and sell them in markets at whatever
price they fetch.

It is because of the incompleteness of the planning process
and the use of prices to stimulate performance that conflict frequently arises between the central authorities and the personnel
responsible for directing production at the operational level of
the economy. The conflict may take a number of forms. In order
to facilitate the achievement of planned profits, the director of
a firm may select an output assortment different from that preferred by the planners, if it should be the case that the former
yields profit more readily than the latter. Because of the constant pressure brought to bear on plant directors for the fulfillment of physical production objectives, they may urge their immediate superiors to favor them with either lower output targets

or greater allocations of essential raw materials. Or, in the event of a particularly good productive period, they may be tempted to conceal output for fear of being "rewarded" with greater output targets. Further, since the greatest problem facing the plant director in Soviet Russia is the shortage of materials which he is responsible for obtaining—the plan merely assigns him priorities—he may find it useful to hoard materials, whether or not he can use them, in anticipation of barter arrangements by which he could get the materials he needs. He may even find it necessary to employ a pusher, a *tolkach*, who makes it his business to find out where surpluses of various materials are and to arrange the terms on which they can be procured. Again, plant directors may try to reduce their dependence on suppliers by producing for themselves what they are supposed to purchase from other firms. Nor is it only the shortage of materials that causes plant directors to circumvent the plan in order to achieve the goals set for them by plan. Faced by a shortage of skilled labor, they may try to pirate workers from other plants. Or, to protect themselves from pirating, they may have to upgrade workers to increase their wages so that other plants do not hire them away.[17]

If these and similar practices are widespread, they necessarily lead to a distortion of the plan. Output will not be produced in the planned quantities, and optimal specialization will not be attained. More resources will be used in the production of top priority commodities than originally planned, thus compelling a lowering of targets for the production of other commodities. Failure to conform to the money plan—for example, the wage bill—may bring about a condition of repressed inflation which distorts incentives and resource allocation throughout the economy.[18] To expand a bit on this last point, if more money wages are paid to workers to produce a planned level of output than was originally anticipated, then at the prices prevailing in the markets for consumers' goods, there will be redundant purchasing power. This may be used to purchase farm products in the collective farm markets, leading to a widening of the differential between free prices and state prices and to an accumulation of cash by peasants. The collective farm then may have increasing difficulty in keeping the peasants to their collective tasks, since the rate of return on productive activity on their own homestead will have increased. Or, in the face of the shortage of goods occasioned by the increase of the wage bill relative to the value of consumer goods workers may decrease their productive effort for the state. Finding that they are unable to spend the additional income in consumers' markets that they earn by working more intensively, they may fit their productive effort to the supply of goods available.

All these distortions at one time or another have occurred in the Soviet economy. While the planners have been able to maintain a high level of employment and achieve the output of those commodities and services on which the Soviet leaders place their highest priority—sputniks and steel, for instance—the detailed performance, the economy in microcosm, has been less satisfactory. Indeed, one might say that the Soviet economy is the supreme example of disequilibrium planning in the sense that the distortions of one period create the tasks for the next. Railroad capacity is not expanded at the rate required to move the planned output of grain, steel, coal and other commodities with optimal efficiency. Rather it is expanded when the growth of other sectors of the economy threatens the transportation sector with a physical breakdown. Though it might be argued that such a system has built into it a moral equivalent of war which permits the leaders to dramatize the productive effort they are calling upon citizens to make, such an argument sounds too much like making a virtue of necessity. In point of fact, the rate of increase of Soviet national income, great though it is, is inhibited by these micro-economic disorders.

Not surprisingly, then, the Soviet firm is enmeshed in a complex network of controls the purpose of which is to insure the compliance of the firm with the directives of the plan. Within the firm the chief accountant, the chief engineer, or the quality-control chief may try to prevent the plant director from deviating from prescribed practices by imposing, or at least raising issues of, budgetary discipline or technological standards. Trade union representatives or Party members may report to higher officials the names of executives who are guilty of malfeasance in the conduct of their duties. Rank-and-file workers in the plant may be encouraged by the leaders of the Party or the government to air their grievances about poor productive conditions and the persons responsible for them. Outside of the firm, the director is responsible to an economic council, but he also may be held to account by local governmental officials and local planning authorities. Moreover, he is subject to control by the representatives of the State Bank (Gosbank) where he must maintain an account and to whom he must turn if he needs short-term credit.[19] Further, agents of the Ministry of State Control may examine the records of the firm at any time they suspect that the orders of the Council of Ministers are not being properly carried out. And not to be overlooked is the Ministry of Internal Affairs (M.V.D.), always alert to threats to the state's security that may originate in economic sabotage.[20] Finally, over and above the controls which may be imposed on firms through governmental channels, there are those which may issue from the high councils of the Party itself.

Control is the very essence of systematic social organization and in an effective capitalistic economic system one will find institutional devices both within firms and outside of firms which compel conformance to the values society is attempting to maximize. Profits, for example, induce firms to produce at minimum cost and in competition bring about an optimum scale of output. However imperfect the functioning of the system in the real world, they do effect a more-or-less satisfactory adjustment of the allocation of resources to the preferences which consumers articulate in markets. Moreover, to the extent that the performance of the capitalistic market has been thought to be inefficient, governments in the western nations have not hesitated to intervene through tax and/or regulatory policies which modify the conduct of both firms and households. Widespread though these controls are, they do not destroy the autonomy of the economy. They reshape and redefine the nature of the constraints within which society wants the capitalistic market to operate.

In contrast to the western economies, the Soviet economy has almost no autonomy. Though households have freedom of consumer choice, firms are wedded to the government in the planning process. The controls imposed on them arise from the fact that the government, acting for the Party, insists that the collective goals of Soviet society, as represented in the plan, take precedence over the values and preferences of individuals. The latter, then, must be placed under constant surveillance to assure that they do not deviate from the social purpose of the community. Where in capitalism individual motivation is taken to be correct except when it leads to egregious violations of public morality, in Soviet Russia individual motivation is assumed to be wrong unless it conforms to the standards of the Party.

§   *Economic Controls as a Deterrent to Political Reform*

The complex of controls in which the Soviet firm is caught up does not create the kind of environment that stimulates the development of individual initiative and independence. Nor does it cultivate trust in one's colleagues. There are so many persons in a firm who may be reporting the director's conduct to higher officials through Party, government, or trade-union channels that suspicion inevitably poisons interpersonal relationships. And since the pressure for the fulfillment of the production objectives is so great, and the planning process so imperfect, most firm directors will at one time or another have been compelled to engage in illegal activities in order to meet their commitments. Thus the more vigorously one prosecutes the plan, the greater the likelihood that one will acquire in his dossier a record of law-breaking. Any such information, of course, may be overlooked as long as the firm in question meets its quota. In the event of failure, however, the record may be turned against those executives allegedly responsible. Suspicion, uncertainty, and fear are endemic, and such a system tends to bring forth a conservative and prudent type of behavior intended to maximize the chances of survival. To be conspicuously successful in one period may mark you for failure in the next.

Since Soviet society is totalitarian and allows little opportunity for an autonomous private existence, the nature of the

economic environment created by the planning system is clearly
relevant to the possibilities for internal changes in the political
order. If pressure for reform cannot manifest itself independently
of the state, it must be generated from within the "establishment." Initiative must come from the Party itself, the army, or
the professional managerial class, to name the most likely foci
of change. But the circumstances just discussed hardly provide
an optimal milieu for nurturing reform inclinations among plant
managers and administrative personnel. If they cannot trust the
reaction of their peers and carefully circumscribe those with
whom they maintain open and frank relationships, they cannot
engage in the kind of discussion and communication which gener-
ates politically cohesive groups in society. It is more difficult for
individuals of similar views and persuasions to find one another
because of the limited system of autonomous communication.[21]
The politically oriented members of the managerial class are
likely to settle down to an acceptance of the prevailing ortho-
doxy.

It does not seem unreasonable to suppose, therefore, that
the attempt to accelerate economic growth through central planning at low levels of national income had the effect of neutraliz-
ing the economy so far as the generation of political opposition
to the regime was concerned. In addition to the forces repressing
the political inclinations of the managerial class, it also may have
been the case that for a period of time many people accepted
the supremacy of the collective values articulated in the plans
and spontaneously subordinated their individual interests to it.
Or perhaps it would be more accurate to say that they identified
their individual interests with the objectives which the party
chose to maximize. We are familiar in democratic society with
the operations of a centrally administered economy during
periods of war when individuals defer to the overwhelming
values of sacrifice and victory and accept, more or less spontaneously, the priorities that central governments place on the utilization of resources. Similarly, in the early five-year plans the
element of idealism, the belief in the new society in the making,
was not an inconsiderable factor affecting individual responses
both to the sacrifices people were called upon to make and to

the machinations of the political organization. Unlike the market mechanism, a centrally administered economy expresses its collective purpose in terms that seem to be intelligible. The social function of the former is implicit in the self-seeking actions of individuals, whereas the production targets of the latter provide a set of criteria against which the social performance of the economy can be measured. Thus the idealism and hope disseminated initially by the planning process tended to make the charges preferred by the regime against economic wreckers and saboteurs appear as reasonable defenses of the desirable and hence legitimate collective purposes of society.

§ *The Democratizing Influence of Rising Income*

Suppose, now, that national income continues to rise in the Soviet Union. Can one expect any modification of these conditions? By way of initiating an answer to this question, the reader should be reminded that whenever a society has entered upon a period of accelerated economic growth during the industrial transformation, the conflict between social objectives and individual values has been intensified. While all societies have not resorted to the methods of the Soviet Union to resolve the conflict, they have in one way or another restrained individual conduct. In nineteenth-century industrialization permissive controls were used to restrain the activities of workers. But as income rose, there tended to be a widening of the consensus in society which permitted a democratization of the political process. The existence of constraints in the functioning of the Soviet economy is not so unusual as the forms they have taken. It is therefore important to consider the impact rising national income may have on the form of Soviet economic control, that is, on central planning.

As national income rises, the amount of output for which planning authorities have to account increases as does the qualitative complexity of the choices they must make. In early stages of development planners are aided by the rudimentary nature of the capital which must be constructed and the simplicity of the consumer wants which have to be satisfied. While plans will not integrate all conceivable quantities of input and output, they will provide for the expansion of the sectors and industries considered most important to the economy. In a sense it is difficult for planners to make mistakes when income is low, for the output from all feasible sectors is urgently needed. If the capacity of coal mines is expanded too rapidly relative to the demand for coal by the power, transportation, and steel industries, in subsequent periods appropriate adjustments can be made in the coal-using industries. But with the increase in the number of feasible industries and sectors for which output must be planned, the possibility of planning mistakes becomes greater. The problem for the planner is compounded if in addition to disposing of a larger amount of output, he must allocate it among uses which are subject to capricious changes of consumer tastes. If investment in coal, steel, or cement capacity will eventually be validated by the growth of the economy and its overall construction demands, investment in light manufacturing catering to a consumer market may not. The goods made for an unresponsive consumer market are a total loss. If the Soviet leaders decided to increase the output of consumers' goods in order to spread the benefits of previous years of capital accumulation among the Soviet population, they might well find that they were imposing an impossible task on their planners. For the decision to increase the output of consumers' goods, once per capita income rises above the subsistence level, is a decision to give greater weight to the preferences of consumers. While the leaders or planners may have very definite notions about what consumers *ought* to want, plans embodying these preferences will come to nought if the output produced does not move through the markets for which it was intended. The hegemony of the planners is greatest at the early stages of production, but as one moves forward towards final consumption, that hegemony is weakened. Accordingly, the decision to expand the consumer standard of living in Soviet Russia could conceivably compel some institutional change in the organization of the economy.[22] What comes to mind, of course, is the possibility of greater decentralization, of an increase in the autonomy of firms producing for the consumer market and to that extent a decrease of the control of planning and administrative authorities. Prices might then be used to facilitate production for a consumer market rather than to facilitate the achievement of physical production norms set by plan.

Since the decentralization of economic organization in the Soviet Union would mean a partial abdication of the power and authority of central planners and governmental officials to operating personnel at the firm and industry level, is there any reason to believe that the former would voluntarily choose this course? There is no assured answer to this question. We can merely suggest the aggregate influence that rising national income may have on their actions. It is possible to conceive of planners allocating just enough resources to the consumers' goods sector to maintain per capita consumption in order to maximize the resources available for investment. Consumption would then increase in the same proportion as population, and investment and the national income would grow at rates determined by the rate of growth of population and the capital-output ratio. Indeed, this is not merely a possibility. This is what has happened in the Soviet Union during the five-year plans. Consumption has been restricted in the interests of increasing the rate of growth and when there have been shortages of materials the consumers' goods sector has tended to receive lower priorities than the investment goods sector. The question here, however, is how planners can continue such an allocation of resources between investment and consumption in the face of continually rising income.

We have noted previously that in the administration of the Soviet economy it has been found prudent to obtain, wherever possible, positive acquiescence to the objectives of the plans in order to limit the use of overt coercion. Free consumer choice and free occupational choice, constrained by planned prices and differential wage-rates, have therefore been an important means for motivating Soviet citizens. Yet the effectiveness of such an incentive system bears some relationship to the quantity and quality of goods available for consumption. While there is evidence that national income can increase for a time without per capita consumption increasing, there is no reason to believe that this can go on indefinitely. With a rising national income and increasing evidence of the expanding capacity of the economy for all to see—stronger and better equipped army and navy, capital construction in industry and government, the growth of transportation facilities, bigger schools and universities—consumer expectations are likely to be revised upwards. One cannot expand income and urge individuals to work for a higher standard of living without creating a demand for one. If, however, consumer expectations do rise with rising income, then planners must seriously consider the demands of households for increased output of consumers' goods in order to maintain the productivity of labor as well as its positive acquiescence to the plans of the regime.

Once the output of consumers' goods is permitted to rise, internal dynamic forces may tend to work for further increases in consumption. Complementary relationships build up sets of interrelated demands for goods and services. The expansion of housing capacity creates demands for rugs, curtains, chairs, tables, beds, record players, records, stoves and so on. The growth of the output of automobiles increases the demand for garages and service stations, roads, restaurants, resorts, cameras, golf clubs. While these related outputs may be ignored by planners, they do so at the risk of aborting the gain the regime may obtain from allowing increases in particular kinds of consumers' goods. In short, a small increase in the output of consumers' goods may, by way of the demonstration effect, create a demand for a still larger increase in consumption.

Assuming that these pressures for consumption do exist in the Soviet Union and that the planners respond to them by increasing the degree of decentralization in the economy so that firms are better able to assess and produce for market demand then, conjecturing further, an environment may evolve which is more propitious for internal political reform than the environment of the command economy in the initial stages of industrialization. For to allow greater autonomy in the economic sphere to firms reduces the occasions of conflict between the center and the periphery of the system and prepares the way for a more rational and open type of conduct in which interpersonal expectations could be more stable. Moreover, if the governmental and Party leaders have less need to dominate and control performance at the periphery of the system, they may also become more amenable to suggestions and advice which emanate therefrom. In other words, decentralization made possible by rising national income may stimulate a kind of give-and-take in personal relationships which fosters the growth of a more widely shared consensus. We should not presume to conjecture still more and perhaps the purport of our discussion is clear, namely that while rising Soviet income in an industrialized economy may not be expected to have the same democratizing influence as industrial growth in the nineteenth century, it may create circumstances favorable to the regularization and stabilization of political procedures within the Communist Party so that a more open and less costly competition for power could take place than hitherto. The Party might evolve some kind of "constitutional opposition" which could serve as the basis for the orderly transference of political power.[23] Though one could hardly call such a development democratic by western standards, it would certainly be a democratizing influence on Soviet society.

§ Foreign Affairs—an External Rationale for Internal State Hegemony

This tenuous series of political consequences suggested by the secular rise of Soviet national income may strike the reader as both naïve and quite wrong. It should therefore be pointed out that they are not a prediction but rather the implications of rising income under the usual *ceteris paribus* conditions. Looking into these is like opening Pandora's Box, and only one ill shall be considered. In the chapter on Germany the web of involvement in foreign affairs was discussed as a deterrent to the further democratization of German society in the late nineteenth and early twentieth centuries. This factor applies to Soviet Russia with even greater force. If economic development is to have the benign influence on political organization conjectured about in the previous pages, time is of the essence. The future must seem secure enough that the state does not have external reasons for interfering with the painfully slow process by which aggregate conditions transfer to detailed reality. There are at least two counts on which one may be pessimistic about the Soviet Union in this respect. As mentioned earlier, it is more difficult in the twentieth century than in preceding centuries to remain aloof from world affairs because rising income and revolutionary changes in technology have brought the world into intimate interdependence. In the absence of a world consensus on first values, nations necessarily look to their external security since they feel threatened by societies representing antagonistic values. Moreover, the special circumstances of Soviet ideology project the Soviet state into international affairs because it leads Soviet leaders at once to expect hostile actions on the part of capitalistic societies and to anticipate the day when they will become socialist societies. With such a view of the world, it is hardly surprising that the positions Soviet leaders take in international politics help to perpetuate the crises which serve as a rationalization for the continued centralization of power at the apex of the Party and government. According to Soviet ideological writ the state will not wither away until Russia is safe in a conflictless socialist world.

We have thus come to a rather pessimistic position regarding the democratization potential of industrialization in Soviet Russia. Central economic planning, the Lenin variant of Marxian ideology, and the Russian autocratic tradition created after 1928 such a tightly closed society that it is difficult to imagine political reform taking place in response to the pressures and threats of groups external to the Establishment. The path of nineteenth-century democratization will not be followed by Russia. Yet the possibilities of internal reform in the wake of continually rising national income are jeopardized by the state's position in the world of international politics.

§   *The Regime of Nikita Khrushchev*

Is there any evidence that one might adduce in support of, or in contradiction to, the above conclusion? It has now been more than ten years since Stalin died, time enough for the battle for succession to have been fought and won by Nikita Khrushchev. Competent observers do not doubt that the present regime differs in significant respects from that of the old dictator, though it remains a totalitarian one-party system.[24] The rule of Khrushchev is not so harsh, and, with the exception of Beria, those who have opposed him seem to have survived, albeit in less auspicious circumstances. While central planning is still the basis of economic control, consumers have been repeatedly told, especially in the Third Party Program adopted by the Twenty-second Party Congress in October, 1961, that their day is at hand, that the Soviet economy is now in a position to surpass the production records of the United States. Workers have been promised a higher standard of living and a reduction in hours of labor. In the farm sector, peasants have been relieved of the obligation to sell grain to the state at prices below the cost of production. In some of its official policies and even more in its pronouncements the present government has been acting as if the economy had made the transition to self-sustained economic growth and entered upon a period in which consumers can be treated with greater indulgence. It remains to be seen how this attitude will affect the organization of the economy.

In 1957 Khrushchev did undertake a drastic reorganization of the economic administration, replacing many of the all-union ministries based in Moscow by regional economic councils.[25] It is not clear, however, that this apparent decentralization increased the autonomy of the operating firms, for the purpose of the change probably was to reduce the administrative inefficiencies which necessarily arose in a system so strongly anchored in the control of Moscow ministries. Firms with complementary outputs and inputs operating in the same region might well be unaware of one another because of the vertical nature of the command and communication systems. The regional councils were presumably intended to provide horizontal coordination of the activities of the firms in their jurisdiction. Moreover, the change may have been part of Khrushchev's efforts to secure his position in the party. By breaking up powerful ministries in Moscow, he had an opportunity to downgrade or remove from office men who had been unlucky enough to oppose him.

Such are the difficulties inherent in central economic planning that the reorganization of 1957 has already been superseded by a recentralization of the economic administration. The autarchy once centered in Moscow ministries became characteristic of the new economic regions. In the absence of a rational set of prices capable of communicating to the regional councils detailed instructions embodying the preferences of the central planners, the former, when they had discretion, placed regional above economy-wide goals. Regional self-sufficiency thus came into conflict with the optimal specialization of the economy and Khrushchev moved to reduce the more than one hundred regional councils to less than fifty.[26]

During this period of experimentation and change in the economic hierarchy, there has been continuing discussion among economists and planners about means of improving the efficiency of the planning process. Some favor the extensive use of linear programming, input-output techniques, and electronic computers to facilitate the formulation of consistent plans by the central planning authority. Others favor decentralization and an increase in the autonomy of firms with respect to the planning of, and contracting for, material supplies in order to relieve central authorities of much irksome, detailed planning. Clearly those who must plan are acutely aware of the increasing difficulties which will face them as income rises and the technological specifications of production become more varied and complex.[27]

Discussion and debate, however, are one thing; institutional change is quite another. While it is a measure of Khrushchev's Russia that the problems of planning have called forth views which in Stalin's Russia were considered too heretical to be expressed openly, it cannot be forgotten that Khrushchev is the leader of a party which is strongly addicted to the use of central authority in the maintenance of its hegemony. Soviet society has become less grim as national income has risen and there is reason to believe that the regime intends to pay more attention to the consumer. But, as yet, we cannot be sure what effect this will have on the organization of the economy, and still less on the organization of the political system. The problems of a rich society are not the same as the problems of a poor society. It remains to be seen how the Party will adapt Russian economic and political institutions to the dilemmas posed by affluence.

Chapter 9

Industrialization and the Prospects for Democracy in the Underdeveloped Economies

WHAT ARE THE PROSPECTS for democracy in the underdeveloped economies? Will India, Indonesia, Egypt, Ghana, Cuba, and other relatively poor societies in Asia, Africa, and Latin America become viable democratic states? Or are they bound by circumstances to evolve other forms of political organization? Were the constitutional democracies of western Europe and North America an accident of time whose historical evolution cannot be repeated in the conditions of the twentieth century? The analysis and discussion in the previous chapters have been directed to the problems that these questions raise and, though the political future of the underdeveloped economies cannot be predicted, it is possible to indicate the nature of the barriers to democratization which stand in their way.

§   *Natural Deterrents to Development*

In the nineteenth century the forces of autonomous growth centered in Great Britain spread to central and western Europe and North America but hardly anywhere else. The countries of eastern Europe, Asia, Africa, and Latin America did not pass through the industrial transition which had been made possible by the discoveries and inventions of the new scientific age and realized through the striving of countless private entrepreneurs. The great changes wrought in the western world following the industrial revolution in Britain left their mark on these countries but did not induce a similar process of self-sustaining growth. The agricultural and mineral resources of the east were developed in response to the voracious demands of the industrializing economies of the west for food and raw materials. More often than not the underdeveloped countries did not benefit from these exogenous stimuli because they were not acted upon by indigenous entrepreneurs. Rather they were the occasion for foreign owned and administered investment designed to construct the facilities essential for moving primary resources with maximum efficiency into the productive systems of the western economies. While the logistics of western industrialization opened up and developed new resources throughout the world, they did little to prepare the underdeveloped economies for utilizing their own natural wealth for their own ends. In consequence, the economic gap between east and west widened as industrialization raised per capita income in the countries of the latter.

The reasons why the western economies pulled further ahead of the underdeveloped economies in the nineteenth and twentieth centuries are many and vary from society to society. One thing is abundantly clear and needs to be heavily underscored: the social, political, and ideological backgrounds of the underdeveloped economies are much more diversified than those of the developed economies. The differences between Germany and the United States in these respects are much less than the differences between China, on the one hand, and India or Brazil, on the other. Indeed, the spread of industrialization in the nineteenth century among the economies of the western world was accelerated by the cultural homogeneity of countries related by a common European tradition. Thus in this discussion of the causes of underdevelopedness it is not intended to ascribe to all countries, regardless of their cultural background, the same reasons for their economic plight. The purpose of the

discussion is to bring forward the factors which in various combinations have inhibited the development of the non-industrial
economies.

Perhaps the most obvious deterrent to growth has been
the location and natural or geographical conditions of the underdeveloped economies. Industrialization in the 19th century
took place in a strikingly small portion of the earth's surface.
The countries that contrived industrial civilization were located
in the northern middle latitudes where a benign climate provided ample and well-distributed rainfall and temperatures
vigorous enough to stimulate energetic behavior but not so extreme as to preclude the cultivation of the earth's organic and
inorganic substances. Britain, the United States, and Germany
were principal benefactors of that long, gradual historical process, fostered by technological changes in transportation, agriculture, and industry, which shifted the center of economic
commerce and trade from the Tigris and Euphrates valley to
the Mediterranean sea to the Atlantic ocean. That the center
moved north and west rather than south and east was attributable in part to the type of geographical conditions with
which man could cope given the technological means he had at
hand. In an era when man was more controlled by than controlling of the environment, it was easier to push along water than
land routes. While Genghis Khan could rise deep in the interior of Asia with his mounted nomadic hordes and terrorize the
people of both Asia and Europe, he could not carry to them
the prerequisities of stable civilization. The Mongol tide rose
and fell, leaving destruction in its wake, but in the west
men followed the sea-routes first around Europe and then beyond, bringing with them the instruments for turning the rich
resources they discovered to their own advantage in stable economic organization. Thus did European civilization in the
modern era surpass the economic performance of the ancient
civilizations of China, India, and the Middle East.

Looking at these natural conditions from the perspective of
the underdeveloped economies, it is clear that they lacked either
the requisite resources or the juxtaposition of resources which
would have allowed them to participate in the industrialization

of the late eighteenth and nineteenth centuries, given the prevailing level of technology, tastes, and markets. The Middle East, for example, possessed few mineral resources with the obvious exception of oil which in the earlier period of industrialization was quite unequal to the task of creating a growth sector capable of inducing complementary responses in other sectors. Neither did it have a soil rich in organic substances which could have served as the basis for agricultural development. Sudden extremes in temperatures, little and unreliable rainfall, persistent pests and microorganisms which destroy plant life prevented the accumulation of the humus and other matter which build up soil fertility. These natural conditions were strong deterrents to the advance of economic civilization. It was not in Saudi Arabia, Persia, Iraq, or Syria that one could expect the development of a primary center of industrialization.

In contrast to the Middle East, China has little oil, but large coal resources which, however, are not complemented with good supplies of iron ore. Moreover, the distances which would have had to be overcome to set up an industrial complex capable of using these resources were beyond the techniques and skills which triggered industrialization in the west during the nineteenth century. It remained, therefore, an agrarian society, much as it was during the greatest periods of its dynastic supremacy, dominated by its topography and the monsoons which watered the southern coastal plains and river basins and made possible intensive rice cultivation.

In the western hemisphere, Brazil is an example of a country well endowed with resources. Coal, iron ore, tungsten, tantalite, quartz, nickel, oil, mica, manganese, and monazite exist in good supply and these minerals surely provide the raw materials of an industrial economy. Yet in the nineteenth century Brazil did not pass through the industrial transformation. For one reason, many of these resources were inaccessible and could not then be economically developed. Bigger than the United States with large parts of its northern territories covered by tropical rain forests, Brazil had first to construct extensive transportation facilities in unexploited and uninhabited areas before these resources could be mined and processed. For another, some of these resources did not become useful until a later technological era. Monazite, for example, is the main source of thorium, like uranium a fissionable material, but in the nineteenth century it had no use. What has been said here about the Middle East, China, and Brazil has in some particulars a counterpart in any underdeveloped economy. A victim of its location, climate, or resource endowment, the typical underdeveloped economy was not in a position to respond creatively to the impulse for autonomous growth which emanated from Britain in the nineteenth century. Instead it conformed to the demands and needs of the industrializing western economies, often becoming a single crop or single commodity export economy the very imbalance of which was essential to the maintenance of the stable growth of the former.

At the risk of belaboring the influence of natural conditions in development, we should like to emphasize an aspect of the geographical pattern of world economic development which is of incalculable importance. The fact that the center of world trade and commerce followed the course in which the natural environment raised the least resistance to man's efforts to make a living tended to create in the western world prior to the industrial revolution groups of individuals who believed that they could manipulate and use the environment for their own ends. Not being so brutal and harsh that they defeated man's every effort to control them, the natural conditions of Europe and North America called forth the active capacities of individuals. In the underdeveloped areas of the world, on the other hand, the natural environment was so ineluctable that man tended to become a passive agent whose life was spent in adapting himself willy-nilly to its cruel and frequently capricious demands. In the one situation, the notions of science, change, and development gradually came to the fore and affected the attitude of those individuals who pioneered the industrial revolution; in the other superstitions, magical rites, and religious and other worldly beliefs were perpetuated among people who felt the need for some rationalization of the mysterious world forces which so dominated their lives. In consequence of these divergent attitudes which reflected the relative impact of environmental conditions, the western world when it approached the threshold of industrial development was profoundly different from the underdeveloped economies as they contemplate industrialization today. Where the former already had before it evidence of man's ability to change the world—for example, in the voyages of discovery and the commercial revolution—the latter only has the evidence of the unchanging pattern of subsistence. In the western world, a growth psychology had been absorbed by at least enough men to make autonomous growth feasible; in the underdeveloped economies, the psychology of growth has first to be inculcated in people before they can become the controllers of their own destiny.

It is perhaps gratuitous to point out that these attitudes which are so intimately related to the prospects for economic growth also affect the prospects for democracy. If man is passive with respect to his environment and cannot really imagine the circumstances in which he might change and bend it to his needs, he also is likely to be passive with respect to the institutions which form his social and cultural life.[1] To use the suggestive category of David Riesman, he will be inclined to be tradition-directed, deriving his values and beliefs from the past and therefore being highly susceptible to the writ of authority, whether it be ecclesiastical or secular.[2] This type of person will not challenge the Establishment since he believes that his place in life has been ordained by powers far greater than himself which he has no right to impugn. Democracy, however, as we have known it in the western world, has grown out of a spirit of irreverence for the establishment and existing institutions which engendered demands for their reform.

§   *Social-Cultural Deterrents to Development*

Turning now to other deterrents to economic development in the underdeveloped areas of the world, social-cultural factors frequently have reinforced the depressive effects of an obdurate environment. It is not uncommon to find institutions in underdeveloped economies which restrict the mobility of both capital and labor, and while these may be explained in terms of the special problems of subsistence, they nonetheless inhibit growth. For example, the extended family, an important form of family organization in traditional China, India, and other countries in Asia and Africa, tends to restrict initiative and the desire for material self-improvement. The gain an individual might obtain through productive ingenuity may be dissipated throughout the collectivity of the family which indeed may become broader, encompassing more distant relatives, the greater the gain turns out to be. An important institution for providing a rudimentary social security system in conditions of subsistence, the extended family further may interfere with the optimal utilization of labor. To the extent that it controls jobs through a family enterprise, it may lead to the employment of persons whose only qualification is membership in the family. Apropos of this last point it can be parenthetically observed that the slower pace of French relative to British development in the nineteenth century was in part attributable to the persistence of the family firm in France which was more concerned with maximization of the security of the family than the accumulation of real assets or the reduction of costs through improved efficiency.[3] Moreover, while making western comparisons, it has frequently been noted that the British system of primogeniture, restricting the right of inheritance to the first-born son, compelled the other sons in families with landed wealth to seek their own careers in order to support themselves. Primogeniture had the effect of reducing the size of the family which looked to the land for support. In contrast, French inheritance laws allowed each son a share of the estate. Whether in France or India, the extended family grouping has debilitated the strength of the forces making for economic growth. It may well be the case, as W. Arthur Lewis has observed "that as a community grows more wealthy, its family concept narrows," but in a state of underdevelopedness the rationale for the extended family persists.[4]

More serious than the extended family are the class structures which impose restrictions on the freedom of action of individuals, reducing both vertical and horizontal mobility and limiting the sources from which entrepreneurial and other types of skill can be drawn. The most extreme case, of course, was the caste system among the Hindus of India, which made the lower castes pariahs who were restricted to specific occupations. Though forbidden by law, the vestiges of the caste system still inhibit economic activity in some parts of India. As one writer has recently reported, "In Malabar, rent-receiving landlords could not, as a rule, effectively reinvest their income in agricultural operations because of taboos discouraging both their personal participation in cultivation and close physical contact with cultivating castes."[5]

Less extreme class systems also inhibit productive activity and investment. Feudal landowners, disdaining work and their own societies, may live conspicuously abroad, thus dissipating a potential investment surplus. Or if at home, they may "purchase more land; or invest in urban house property (very noticeably in Arab countries); or lend to impoverished cultivators at high rates of interest."[6] These "impoverished cultivators" are exploited as well by high rents, especially in those parts of the world where the population explosion has made land increasingly scarce. Consequently they too often have little incentive to make agricultural improvements because they would retain such a small proportion of the resulting increases in output.

Between the feudal landowners and the impoverished cultivators there typically exists a wide chasm. An underdeveloped economy has not yet filled up the middle ranks of society with the technical, administrative, and professional groups who can bridge the gap between the very rich and the very poor. The class structure is likely to be polarized between a small elite whose wealth is held in land and a large peasantry whose subsistence existence is essential to the perquisites of the former. The middle classes being so attenuated, they cannot serve the function of moderating the divisions and conflicts implicit in the social structure. The agrarian elite, therefore, feels too much threatened by the potential or latent hostility of the lower classes to sponsor reforms which, while designed to alleviate their straitened conditions, might awaken aspirations for social change.[7]

In addition to the extended family and the class structure, religious institutions and beliefs often limit the mobility and optimal utilization of resources for growth. Notwithstanding our earlier discussion about the important role the Dissenters played in the industrial development of England, religion generally may be accounted a conservative force which inhibits growth. With its non-material, other-worldly concerns, it does not direct energy and interest to the corporeal stuff of economic growth. Certainly in the western world the rise of per capita income has been accompanied by the fall of religion so that it seemingly occupies a fairly remote corner in the lives of many people. One seldom hears of economic transactions not being consummated because of the religious scruples of the parties involved. In the underdeveloped countries, however, religious belief is more likely to constitute a way of life with taboos and proscriptions affecting economic conduct. Thus the Hindu cannot experiment with the sacred cow in order to improve the breed because this would involve the killing of the weaker strains. More significantly, the mysticism and asceticism of Hinduism promotes a deprecatory attitude toward business, private gain, money, and in general the activities on which growth depends. The Yogi can be neither a commissar nor a capitalist. To the extent that the Yogi is a symbol of the aspirations of Hindus in India the accumulation drive is weakened. In Mohammedan countries the inferior status of women prevents them from participating fully in the activities of the community, thus reducing the number of women who are educated and capable of performing semi-skilled, skilled, and professional services for the economy. Moreover, the fasts required of orthodox Mohammedans conflict with the demands of a modern economy for a vigorous, punctual, and disciplined labor force. In parts of Africa cattle are reserved for religious ceremonial purposes and may not be used as beasts of burden.

§　*Economic-Demographic Deterrents to Development*

The social-cultural deterrents to growth we have been discussing create a traditional state of mind which would not be particularly responsive to positive growth conditions even if these conditions prevailed in the underdeveloped economies.

The economic-demographic deterrents raise problems for the most forward-looking of growth enthusiasts. Subsistence income itself, as pointed out in earlier chapters, poses grave difficulties, for in order to raise aggregate output the rate of investment must increase. But if the economy is using most of its current output for consumption, it will have little left over for investment. It will be difficult enough to maintain its stock of assets, let alone increase them. While it may well be the case that there is hidden unemployment in a subsistence economy in the inefficient utilization of labor in agriculture and in the service occupations, the appropriation of this reserve of labor for the construction of capital cannot easily be accomplished. Aside from the mobility restrictions previously discussed, the movement of workers from the agrarian sector of an economy to an industrial sector requires investment in social overhead capital—transportation, housing, education—which cannot be expanded readily in the face of competing demands for capital. Though the marginal product of labor in agriculture may be zero and positive in industry, the transfer costs in the short run may dissipate the gain to the economy from moving workers from one to the other.

Not only does subsistence make it difficult to raise the rate of saving but it also debilitates the labor force and restricts its efficiency. Dietary standards typically are not high enough to provide labor with the energy and strength requisite to vigorous work and for building up resistance to disease. It has been estimated that for the year 1954–55 the per capita intake of calories and protein per day was for India 1,840 and 50 grams, for Peru 2,080 and 54 grams, for Egypt 2,390 and 69 grams, whereas for the United States it was 3,090 and 92 grams, for Australia 3,040 and 91 grams, and for Norway 3,140 and 91 grams.[8] As these figures show the average worker in the poor economy simply does not get enough to eat, and this is a cause of his low productivity. The subsistence economy is thus caught in a vicious circle difficult to break out of: income is low because workers are unproductive, but workers are unproductive because income is low.

But this is not the end of it. If one adds the demographic characteristics of the underdeveloped economy to the picture, the economic problem is compounded. Both the birth rate and death rate tend to be higher in the underdeveloped than in the developed economy. For example, in 1955 the birth rate per thousand population in the United States was 24.6 and the death rate 9.3. In Sweden the figures were 14.8 and 9.4, the United Kingdom 15.4 and 11.7, France 18.4 and 12.0, and Belgium 16.7 and 12.6. In contrast, the birth and death rates for some economies with low per capita income were as follows: Ceylon 37.9 per thousand and 11.0 per thousand; Guatemala, 51.7 and 18.5; India, 30.5 and 12.7; Mexico, 46.4 and 13.1; Puerto Rico, 34.8 and 7.1.[9] The fact that the death rates in the latter countries are only slightly higher than the death rates in the former reflects the impact that scientific and medical advances in the western world have had on mortality rates everywhere. The much greater discrepancy in birth rates reveals the minimal influence in the underdeveloped societies of the urbanization complex which brought the birth rate down in western societies. In other words, the death rate is more responsive than the birth rate to the various factors which reduce them. If this continues to be the case, then it is quite possible that economic growth will be aborted by an increase in population. For an increase in output which induces a proportionate increase in the rate of population growth does not raise per capita income.

The pattern of birth and death rates in the underdeveloped economies creates a population age structure which further complicates the economic outlook. Because of the high death rate, life expectancy at birth is relatively low and in consequence the population is relatively young. In 1955, male life expectancy at birth was 32 in India, 35 in Egypt, and generally for Asia, Africa, and Latin America less than 40, while in the United States and Canada it was 66, England 67, and Norway 69.[10] For the same year, the percentage of population below the age of 15 was 40 in Asia, Africa, and Latin America, and 25 and 23 in the United States and the United Kingdom respectively. This means that on the average the working life of the individual in the underdeveloped economy is short in comparison to that of the individual in the developed economy. Indeed, he is removed from the labor force by death when by western standards he is just approaching his most productive years. Moreover, a not insignificant proportion of such a society's investment, time, and energy is necessarily devoted to raising children for a premature burial, an activity hardly enhancing the opportunities for growth.

It should be noted that the demographic problems of today's underdeveloped countries are not simply a repetition of the problems faced by the developed economies when in the past century they set out upon the road of industrialization. It is true that the birth and death rates in Britain, for example, were higher at the beginning of the nineteenth century than they are now and that in the process of growth death rates fell more rapidly than birth rates, giving rise to a great increase in the rate of population growth. But the magnitude of the birth rates in Britain and elsewhere in Europe was not so great then as it is today in the underdeveloped economies. In fact there is some evidence indicating that Britain and Europe were more responsive to economic conditions. As far as one can tell from the available evidence, the birth rate in northern Europe during the greater part of the eighteenth century was in the neighborhood of the low 30's per thousand. This compares with a birth rate of over 40 per thousand in the typical underdeveloped economy. With regard to changes in the birth rate, it seems to have been the case "that poverty was a major cause of family limitation and that it was the poor who often restricted the size of their families."[11] Thus in periods of bad harvests or declining wages there was a tendency both for marriage to be postponed and for established families to be less fecund. To the extent that this tendency prevailed in Britain and Europe in the eighteenth century, it reflected a kind of behavior markedly different from that in many underdeveloped economies today. Rather than being the consequence of customs, institutions, and values independent of economic phenomena, family size apparently was partially related to the level of income. In other words, prior to the industrial revolution in Britain some people were calculating their life's chances in terms of economic indicators, a type of rationality which subsequently gave wings to the industrialization process.

§ *The Handicap of a Late Start: (a) Population*
Growth and the Demonstration Effect

The natural-geographical, social-cultural, and economic-
demographic deterrents to growth in the underdeveloped
economies would be severe under any historical circumstances.
They become especially forbidding when they exert their influence in late stages of the world sequence of industrialization.
This becomes all too clear in connection with the demographic
problem just discussed. The population explosion has been
thrust upon the underdeveloped societies by the accumulation of
mortality-reducing commodities in the advanced economies.
Thus India's death rate has been declining since the nineteenth
century and the prospects are excellent for a continued decline
from the level of 12.7 per thousand attained in 1955. More than
ever India has to run in order to stay where it is because population is increasing so rapidly. Institutions and values affecting
family size which were consistent with the economic needs of the
community when the death rate was much higher now have
become debilitating. The exogenous influence of the older industrialized economies has released a tide of babies who may
have little opportunity for anything but a semistarved existence.
    The premature growth of population is all the more difficult
to absorb because of the demonstration effect which transmits
from the developed economies to the former aspirations for a
standard of life which is patently beyond its capacity to produce.
The newspaper, radio, and movies can create an image of a way
of life very much different from the traditional static existence of
the subsistence society and to many individuals confined to the
latter it may seem superior. As observed in an earlier chapter,
the demonstration effect may stimulate productive activity,
thereby increasing the rate of growth. Presumably this happens
in the United States where lower income groups are besieged on
all sides, day in and day out, by the lure of consumer affluence.
But in the United States, which has long since attained self-sustaining growth, the labor force is disciplined to the requirements
of work in a complex, modern economy, and, moreover, can

acquire from the constantly increasing stream of output the goods which in fact will raise its standard of living. Though the worker may not be able to buy the Cadillac or sports car that his favorite movie star drives, he can work for the extra income neeed to buy a Ford or second-hand Oldsmobile. In the underdeveloped economy, the increments to output are not yet great enough to permit the standard of living of the masses to keep pace with the aspirations the advanced economies may create.

Thus Daniel Lerner reports that in Lebanon, which has high per capita income by Middle Eastern standards, the respondents interviewed in connection with his study of *The Passing of Traditional Society* "suffered from 'relative deprivation.' Constant exposure to modern achievements led them to deprecate their standard of living vis-à-vis the West, rather than celebrate it relative to other Eastern Countries."[12] In Egypt he found that "by far the most discontented of the four groups [professional, white collar, worker, farmer], the workers are disturbed by the discrepancy between their desires and their resources."[13] In a discussion of the political problems of India, Myron Weiner asserts that "in Rajasthan, for example, one of the poorest states in India, the level of discontent is not so great as in areas where there is less poverty but greater consciousness of that poverty. The gap between the consciousness of reality and expectations is greatest in the cities where Western education and influence have intensified expectations."[14]

§ *The Handicap of a Late Start: (b) the Weakening Industrialization Impulse*

If the advanced economies have brought about a rate of increase in the growth of population in the underdeveloped economies and, at the same time, have heightened the material consciousness of many of their inhabitants, they have not been as successful in transmitting the industrialization impulse to the latter. Indeed, the high standard of living and the continued growth of the former seem to make the transfer of economic activity through trade and markets more difficult than it was in the nineteenth century. During the period of British-centered growth, the expansion of the output of manufactured goods in England engendered a proportionate increase in the demand for minerals, foodstuffs, and agricultural raw materials which provided a strong stimulus to the exploitation of resources in countries like the United States and Australia. Moreover, in order to facilitate the growth of the output of primary resources, Britain committed a large part of its investment surplus to the construction of the social overhead capital—railroads, harbors, and so on—needed to market them. In short, during the nineteenth century output, trade, and capital movements worked hand in hand as transmitters of industrialization. The canals and railroads made it possible to market grain raised in Illinois and Wisconsin in Europe, and this established the structural foundations necessary for a variegated growth in the United States.

Now, however, the growth of output in the advanced economies does not give rise to a proportionate increase in the trade for the output of the primary-producing economies which lie largely in the underdeveloped sectors of the world. For one reason, as income continues to rise in the former, the demand for foodstuffs lags behind. The income elasticity of demand for chocolate, for example, at high levels of income being relatively low, the demand for Ghanian cocoa does not grow along with the income of the economies in Western Europe and North America. For another, the technological change so crucial to the growth of the advanced economies has led to the substitution of synthetic for natural resources. Innovations in the chemical industry have created nylon, orlon, and other manufactured fibers, the demand for which is competitive with the demand for natural fibers. Plastics have taken markets away from natural rubber. For still another, as the advanced economies grow, the service sector, a relatively light consumer of primary products, expands relative to the manufacturing sector, a relatively large consumer. Finally, one should note that even in the manufacturing sector technological change has made possible economies in the utilization of natural materials.[15]

From the point of view of the underdeveloped economies

the weakening of trade as a transmission belt of industrialization manifests itself as a balance-of-payments problem. Their demand for the output of advanced economies is relatively greater than the demand of the latter for their output, thus creating circumstances in which imports grow relative to exports. In the absence of external aid, therefore, the level of exports which an underdeveloped economy can attain establishes an upper limit to growth within the existing system of international specialization and trade.

§   *The Handicap of a Late Start: (c) Technological Choice*

Because of the continuing process of technological change which accompanied the industrialization of the western economies, the underdeveloped economies have a wide range of technological choices before them when they come to consider ways and means of stimulating economic growth. From some points of view this is undoubtedly advantageous. They do not have to allocate resources, which they can ill afford, to pioneering technological change. They can adapt techniques whose properties are well known. But the difficulty is that the choice of techniques is almost too broad. We have noted that when confronted with this situation in 1928, the Soviet Union decided to expand capital intensive outputs in emulation of the American economy. This, however, imposed strains on the economy's saving capacity and on the capabilities of a labor force which was long in numbers but short in skills. The temptation for the latecomers to growth to utilize the latest and most dramatic types of technology apparently is hard to resist and while there may be some long-run advantages in doing so, in the shortrun it may add little if anything to current output. Ethiopia, for example, has purchased two Boeing 720B jet aircraft. It is difficult to see what economic advantages Ethiopia will derive from these planes. Not only will the planes be of little use within the Ethiopian economy because of the relatively short distances involved, but they will not stimulate the growth of a local labor force skilled enough to operate and maintain them. It might well have been more appropriate for Ethiopia to purchase secondhand DC3's and DC6's, being discarded by the advanced economies taking the lead in the development of the jet age, and use them for promoting mobility within Ethiopia and for training mechanics and pilots. Capital expenditures would have been minimized and the economy would have received more direct benefit.[16] Better still, Ethiopia might have used the funds spent on aircraft to improve its roads and railways. Brazil is considering the possibility of building an atomic reactor. Though it has good supplies of fissionable materials, the economics of atomic energy are not yet so clear that it can afford to bear the costs of developing this source of energy. Further, one might cite the Aswan Dam in Egypt as a project made possible by modern technology which may well absorb too much of Egypt's labor skills and take too long to mature for the orderly development of the Egyptian economy.

§   *The Handicap of a Late Start: (d) Barriers to Migration*

The handicaps of a late start in industrialization already discussed necessarily exacerbate the welfare problem and therefore are likely to render the maintenance of domestic order peculiarly difficult during the incipient stages of modernization. While the traditional social controls implicit in religious values, social conventions, and family organization may be losing their effectiveness as they come in contact with the wealth of the industrialized world, the social controls of that world may not yet have become fully internalized in the working population. In consequence, one might expect evidences of discontent—absenteeism, tardiness, malingering, stealing, strikes, riots, vandalism—to be widespread.

Unlike the western world in the nineteenth century, able to dissipate some of the discontent of the incipient stages of industrialization by encouraging emigration, the undeveloped economies must cope with discontent and disorders without such help. The past growth of world population has led to the preemption of most of the land in the northern middle latitudes which absorbed such a large proportion of migrating European population in the late nineteenth and early twentieth centuries. The United States has now raised the bars against immigration and its quota system discriminates against just those countries which are feeling the pressure of population growth most severely—India, Egypt, Ceylon, China, and generally the non-Caucasian countries of the world.[17] While there is still open land in Latin America, notably in Brazil and Argentina, it never has exerted the attractive power in population movements that the open lands of the United States did. The natural conditions for settling the interior are more rigorous and hazardous than they were in North America and the land more difficult to obtain and more costly to improve. Though historically there have been migrations within Asia—notably out of China, India, Pakistan, Japan, and Korea to Malaya, Burma, Ceylon, Vietnam, Laos and Cambodia, Thailand, Indonesia, and Manchuria—in recent years these movements have almost ceased. Though improvements in transport technology have greatly reduced the cost and time of travel, the opportunity for the population of the underdeveloped economies to move to the developed economies is negligible. It is even difficult to move from one country to another within the underdeveloped areas of the world. Thus countries now experiencing the discontents arising from an expansion of the appetite for consumer goods greater than the growth of the capacity to produce them, no longer can minimize the contingent control problems by exporting population.

§ *Problems of State-Centered Growth*

The deterrents and handicaps to development that have been examined prevented the forces of autonomous growth which transformed western economies in the nineteenth century from effecting similar transformations of the underdeveloped economies. They also suggest that in the twentieth century the state will have to play a more prominent part in development than it did in the previous century. And, indeed, confirming evidence is not hard to come by. One country after another has established planning departments, economic bureaus, or development commissions which are charged with the responsibility of drawing up its economic balance sheet and outlining its path of future growth. Five-year plans have proliferated, and while these vary widely in scope and purpose, it is not unreasonable to assert that state growth in the twentieth century, inspired in part by the successes of the Soviet economy, is responsible for the actual or hoped-for advances of the underdeveloped economies, just as in the nineteenth century autonomous growth, stimulated by the achievement of the British economy, was responsible for the advances of the western economies.

Before inquiring into the policies the newly developing economies have devised for constraining labor in the interests of economic growth, we must make some general observations about the role the state is likely to perform. It must be emphasized at the outset that the state is not a panacea which guarantees a solution to all the problems left unsolved in the period of autonomous growth. Its performance can be no better than the people who control the instruments of the state. Many of the conditions we have discussed not only inhibit autonomous growth, but prevent the creation of a class of professional and administrative personnel who are able to carry out governmental policy with maximum efficiency. The circumstances that spawned calculating and maximizing entrepreneurs in the western world also gave rise to Weberian bureaucrats, men skilled in administering hierarchical structures according to rules and regulations that minimized the burden of corruption and malfeasance in the duties of public office.

In the underdeveloped economies, limited investment in education keeps literacy rates low: this also makes it difficult to train a class of civil servants capable of administering the public policies appropriate for a developing society. More basic than the lack of able governmental personnel, the cultural characteristics of underdeveloped economies, as well as the fact of subsistence and poverty, may lead to corruption and venality in government that subverts the most rational and well-intentioned economic plans.[18] If there is one complaint common to all foreign-aid programs, it is the charge that the resources made available to underdeveloped economies too often line the pockets of local officials. The ubiquity of the problem is pointed up, oddly enough, by the frequency with which India is cited as the one example of the underdeveloped economy with an indigenous administrative class that can carry out developmental policy with minimal corruption.

If the difficulties of forming efficient government jeopardize the chances of realizing the objectives of economic plans and programs, the conflicting demands imposed upon the state may, in the first instance, prevent the drawing up of optimal economic plans. This point must be developed at some length because it is of considerable importance in assessing the character of the political systems which are likely to emerge in the underdeveloped economies.

The newly independent states of the world almost without exception have not taken over political systems whose members are bound together by a strong sense of nation or by some other principle of consensus. In many of the countries in Africa, the boundaries of state were drawn according to the requirements of the imperial nations of Europe without regard to the ethnic and tribal characteristics of the indigenous populations. In Pakistan, the recognition of the importance of a unifying value such as religion led to the separation of the constituent parts of the state. In Indonesia, the state holds sway over a fragmented area consisting of three thousand islands populated by sixteen major ethnic groups speaking ten major languages.[19] In all the newly independent states, subsistence income and traditional values have perpetuated parochial attitudes and outlooks which everywhere characterize people of little formal education. Even if the new state does have a glorious past from which people might glean their mutuality and common origins, illiteracy makes it difficult to communicate the relevant symbols, while years of imperial domination may have depreciated the value of these symbols. The great contributions of ancient Arab civilization to scholarship, for example, may not mean much to contemporary Arabs in view of the subsequent subordination of that civilization to the Turks and later to the countries of western Europe. This means that the leaders of newly independent states not only must try to stimulate economic development but they must build a political community as well.

It may be gratuitous to observe that states did not labor under this dual necessity during the period of western industrialization. In most cases industrialization took place within countries which had had a continuous political existence antedating its period of accelerated economic growth and whose population had some sense of shared values. The growth of nations preceded the growth of economies. It is sobering, however, to note how long it took for nations to evolve and even more sobering to contemplate the costs incurred in the process. The parochial values of feudal Europe were replaced by the national values of modern Europe only after centuries of personal and autocratic rule, dynastic and religious wars, and imperialistic conquests which at once provided the raw material of history and the symbols facilitating the formation of nations. England, France, Germany, and the United States all became nations in the context of a world whose alleged or real hostility brought about the subordination of individual values to national purposes. England as a nation evolved out of the Hundred Years' War as the United States evolved out of the American Revolution, and France, Germany and other continental nations out of the wars of the French Revolution. It would not be an easy task to measure the costs of these wars and revolutions, but they surely were a charge on the scarce resources of economies which diverted them from other uses more appropriate for economic development. In other words, it does not seem unreasonable to suppose that the use of resources for building nations is inconsistent with the use of resources for building economies. Such were the historical circumstances of western development, however, that this kind of inconsistency was minimized by the emergence of nations prior to those innovations and technological changes which made industrialization possible. Indeed, it may well be the case that in some unfathomable manner the articulation of a people's political purpose in nation was a necessary condition for the onset of invention.

The building of modern political communities in the underdeveloped economies is no less important than it was in the western world in previous centuries, but the costs of nation-building have, in a sense, risen. It was suggested earlier that projects such as the Aswan Dam and jet airlines might not be the best use of resources for stimulating economic development. Yet it is not inconceivable that dramatic kinds of investment like these perform an important function in making citizens of newly independent states conscious of themselves as members of a national group with great achievements to their credit and still greater challenges before them. It has been observed that the cathedrals of France built in the Middle Ages, which can hardly be said to have expanded productive capacity, may have fulfilled a similar purpose for the French.[20] All states allocate resources to the creation of unifying symbols. In this connection one may expect that however new states determine their investment priorities, they will support an army or navy which, in the light of the colonial conditions from which they have recently been emancipated, is an especially important symbol of national independence, purpose, and integrity. Moreover, the use of the military by charismatic leaders, as in India, Egypt, or Indonesia, in the conduct of foreign policy may be viewed as part of the arduous task of generating, or imposing, the consensus from which nations rise. Thus the exigencies of building nations may draw resources away from uses with a higher economic payoff.

This brings us now to the issue with which we are particularly concerned. Given the dual demands of polity and economy, will the state in the newly developing economies pursue policies for facilitating the adjustment of the labor force to the requirements of industrialization that lie closer to the totalitarian controls of the Soviet Union or the permissive controls of western economies? Or, to put it another way, will these economies subordinate the protest function of working-class organizations to the necessity of obtaining commitment to the discipline of routinized industrial labor? While it cannot be alleged that the prospects for democracy turn on the answers to these questions, they do at least raise issues which cannot be ignored in assessing the democratic outlook. We shall therefore seek a clue to the answers in a brief examination of the position of labor in contemporary India and Egypt. We have selected these countries because they are committed neither to the "communist camp" nor the "western camp" and are beset by serious problems of underdevelopedness they wish to solve while continuing their independence of both camps. Though they may not be bellwethers for all underdeveloped economies, their experiences are a crucial portent for the independent nations.

§ *Labor in India*

Of all the underdeveloped economies, India has, with little doubt, received the most attention from the western world. Governmental trade and financial missions, scholars from the universities, and research teams from the philanthropic organizations have flocked to India in quest of the solution to the enigma of underdevelopedness. The great interest in India is not hard to understand. It was the first colonial nation in the British empire to achieve independent status in the Commonwealth after World War II and thus symbolized the aspirations of the colonial people everywhere for independence. Moreover, next to China, it was the most populous country in the world, with some 340 million inhabitants in the year of independence, 1947. Furthermore, in contrast to China, it has become the preeminent example of a society consciously trying to develop its economic potential without adapting the totalitarian political order of Soviet Russia. Though struggling for years to exorcise the incubus of British imperial domination, the leaders of the Indian independence movement nonetheless absorbed enough of the democratic values of British society to believe that democratic institutions were the appropriate form of political organization for India. It is no exaggeration to say that India and China have entered upon a momentous competition whose outcome is fraught with significance for the future of democracy. For if India should fail to keep pace with the production performance of China, many nations at present caught in the vicious circles of subsistence may conclude that totalitarian political methods are requisite to economic development.

When one turns to an examination of the position of labor in the Indian economy, one first notes the small proportion of the population and labor force working in the modern sector of the economy. In the early 1950's there were about 7 million workers employed by manufacturing, mining, construction, utility, transportation, and communication firms out of a total labor force of approximately 140 million. Of these 7 million workers, only about 2 million were organized in trade unions.[21] Yet it would be quite wrong to depreciate the role of workers and trade unions in the development of India. As it were, the workers are at the growth points of the Indian economy and their conduct may have an impact on development out of all proportion to their numbers. Organized workers are concentrated in the mining, transport, and manufacturing industries located in the urban areas of Kanpur, Jamshedpur, and Calcutta in the Ganges Valley of East India and of Ahmedabad and Bombay in the western coastal plain. They are therefore in a position to localize and focus the discontent arising in the process of industrialization. And, as we have argued, it is precisely in the cities that one would expect the demonstration effect to strike hardest at the traditional values that hold down and contain the expectations of people living in subsistence conditions. Furthermore, among Indian leaders who are familiar and sympathetic with the socialist literature of protest engendered by western industrialization in the previous century, there is no lack of willingness to respond to the discontents and demands of workers.

So far has the dissemination of working-class organizations been accelerated in the contemporary age that, at a stage of economic development when there were few if any effectively organized nation-wide unions in the western economies, in India there are no less than four national federations claiming local union affiliates: the All-India Trade Union Congress (AITUC); the United Trades Union Congress (UTUC); Hind Mazdoor Sabha (HMS); and the Indian National Trade Union Congress

(INTUC). This proliferation of federated unions reveals at once both the permissive intent of Indian policy-makers regarding labor and the danger of permissiveness in a society initiating the early stages of industrial development in the mid-twentieth century. These unions are divided by issues which are not unlike the divisions which grew in the labor movement of the western world during the relatively permissive conditions of the nineteenth century. AITUC is the oldest of the four, antedating Indian independence, but because it was captured by the communists during World War II it proved to be an unsatisfactory medium to maintain liaison with the labor movement when the Congress Party assumed responsible control and direction of the Indian government. Therefore the Congress Party lent its support to the founding of INTUC in 1947, and in the following year made it the Indian representative of labor in the International Labor Organization. At about the same time HMS was organized by trade union leaders who were anticommunist but as socialists did not like the close identification of INTUC with the Congress Party and the government. In 1949 UTUC was formed by labor leaders who disliked the antipolitical position of HMS and wanted to stress the revolutionary role of trade unions in the transformation of India Society. In terms of the traditional political spectrum, UTUC lay somewhere between the communist AITUC on its left and the socialist HMS on its right. These kinds of splits in the labor movement could only occur in a society which permitted its citizens the latitude to discuss, advocate, and organize political and social action.

While one can admire this liberal commitment of the leaders of the Indian political community, one can have reservations about their effect on development, given the underdeveloped state of the Indian economy. In the western economies the doctrinal disputes of the socialist left were moderated or muted by the gathering strength of the trade union branch of the labor movement and its vested interest in bargaining for advantages that rising per capita income made possible. But the Indian economy has not yet grown enough to afford the basis of a strong independent union movement. Local unions are financially weak both because workers can ill afford the payment of dues and because of the turnover of the labor force not fully committed to industrial employment. Moreover, the illiteracy and ignorance of the masses as well as their debilitated physical condition have prevented the development of working-class leaders in the trade unions. In the United States, for example, union leaders typically rose from the ranks of the workers, but in India union leaders typically are drawn from the middle classes. Thus the workers are led by men whose interests often are not so much centered in the problems of the plant and local community as in the political issues which confront the nation. Schooled in the great western tradition of dissent and perhaps disgruntled by their inability to find a position in the Indian civil service commensurate with their educational attainments, labor leaders are not unwilling to use trade unions to embarrass the government or to further their pet political nostrums. Certainly the Indian labor scene has not infrequently been beset by the kind of violence, as in the general strike in Bombay, Calcutta, and Ahmedabad in 1956, which destroys the foundations of the orderly labor relations essential for growth. But the political motivation of some of its leaders aside, Indian trade unions have been militant in seeking wage and welfare benefits for their members and have not hesitated to call strikes against firms resisting their demands. Around the period of independence the unions were especially active as they attempted to redress the loss of real income suffered by industrial workers during the war years. The numbers of disputes and working days lost through strikes rose precipitously, reaching a peak in 1947.

The militancy of the labor movement confronted the new Indian government with a mean dilemma. The work stoppages could not be ignored. Yet the government could not make an open assault on the unions. To proscribe them as Bismarck did the Socialist Party in Germany in the late nineteenth century, to obtain injunctions against their activities as business firms did in the United States, or to transport their leaders to overseas colonies as the British government did on occasion in the first half of the nineteenth century, would belie the very purpose of the Congress Party. By resisting foreign domination and the imperial system the Congress Party symbolized justice and the aspirations of Indians for an equitable life. Moreover, the hostility of many of the party's leaders, not least of all Nehru, to the private employer whether British or Indian, was not un-important in stimulating the militancy of the trade unions. But having taken over the direction of the Indian government, the Congress Party could no longer press the claims of labor without regard to their consequences for the social-economic goals of Indian society.

The solution of the Indian government to the dilemma was to pass a series of legislative acts which, on the one hand, in the Industrial Disputes Act of 1947, required employers and em-ployees to submit their disputes to industrial tribunals for arbitration and to refrain from striking pending the decision, and, on the other, in the Factories Act of 1948, introduced the 48-hour week and established health and safety standards de-signed to protect the worker's welfare. The government entered labor-management relations as a strong third party and at the same time set up formal welfare standards to which obdurate and conservative private employers were supposed to conform. The restrictions on the freedom of action of the unions were counter-balanced by the imposition of legal restraints on the discretion of employers in fixing the terms of employment. Thus industrial peace and social justice were hopefully geared to the require-ments of the Indian economy for growth.

It is, of course, too soon to know whether the conflict be-tween the consumption and welfare demands of the workers and the growth requirements of the economy has been resolved or only temporarily mitigated. The consumptionist thrust of organ-ized labor has been weakened by the institutions of compulsory arbitration and, according to the first and second Five-Year Plans, the government has no intention of abandoning the program, though there is by no means universal satisfaction with the manner in which it works. The unions in India are not as free in the conduct of their affairs as the unions in the western economies. Nor are they as restricted as the unions in Soviet Rus-sia. Because they have developed prematurely and often depend for support on an unstable and not fully disciplined laboring class, the unions have had to be constrained by the government in the interests of the plans for development. Because the leaders of the dominant political party in India were inspired by the twin objectives of the welfare state and democracy, they have not been willing to deprive the unions completely of their independence. Whether the present balance between constraint and freedom can be maintained depends upon the success of the Indian economy in attaining the goals projected for it in the Five-Year Plans. If large enough increases in output are forthcoming annually to give substance to the welfare enactments of the state and to provide a margin for discernible rises in real wages, then the labor movement may mature within the existing institutional context. Indeed, it is possible to conceive of collective bargaining, as distinct from compulsory arbitration, becoming more effective with the growth of a labor force with a firmer commitment to the industrial community and a greater capacity for playing an active and positive role in the affairs of unions at the plant and firm level.

But suppose that income does not rise at the requisite rate or that an induced increase in the rate of population growth absorbs the increase in output, what then? If India lived in isolation from the rest of the world, one might shrug this question off. But it has before it not only the example of the mature western world, but, more significantly, the Chinese economy. If the Chinese economy should succeed where the Indian economy fails, it would lend support to the views of those—for example, the communists in AITUC—who believe that in order to stimulate growth in an underdeveloped state the controls of government must subordinate the total activity of society to the objectives of planning. Unions along with the private sector of the economy would then very likely lose what independent status they have under the present system. For it would be very difficult to gainsay the argument that the price of such independence is too high if it only perpetuates a condition of subsistence, especially if coupled with the pledge to be more solicitous of individual freedoms when the requisite level of income has been attained.

However India finally resolves the conflict between consumption and welfare on the one hand, and growth on the other, the democratic potential that high income contains may never be released or may be manifested only in forms that are unfamiliar, and maybe even uncongenial, to the western observer. Of the Chinese or Soviet turn we need say no more; in the chapter on the Soviet economy, we spun out the tenuous set of circumstances which might cause rising per capita income to loosen the firm grasp of a totalitarian regime on the conduct of its citizens.

If, however, India continues on its present course and finds that income rises fast enough to assuage the demands and needs of labor and still provide for further growth, it most surely is not necessary that political institutions evolve as they did during the industrialization of the western world. For even under the moderate regime of Nehru the state plays a greater role in development than the state did in the nineteenth century, and it is not at all clear why or how the benign influence of rising income will curb and democratize the exercise of its authority. It will be recalled that in the west in the nineteenth century where industrialization took place largely through the initiative of private individuals acting in a private capacity, opposition to established nondemocratic regimes became increasingly effective in obtaining political reform, one, because its preeminent role in development gave it a strong moral claim to constitutional rights, and two, because its mass basis threatened the existence of the old order. Note, however, that in the case of Germany, where the problems of development were intertwined with the problems of unification, the state retained strong powers vis-à-vis the political rights of the people and that, though democratizing forces were clearly at work, it was hardly a democratic state on the eve of World War I. In other words, to the extent that there are forces external to the economy that seem to justify authoritarian state action, it will be that much more difficult to deprive it of its prerogatives. Under these circumstances, individuals who otherwise might press hard for democratic reforms may concede that there are objectives more appropriately attained under authoritarian leadership.

In India it is not just economic problems that preoccupy the state. It has to create a nation, a task which in Britain and the United States, as we have noted, had been accomplished without conscious direction well in advance of the industrial revolution. Divided by religious and linguistic differences and varying cultural traditions and regional customs, India must try to carry forward a national revolution at the same time that it attempts to revolutionize the economy. On the one hand, the strong role of the government in development may minimize the growth of an effective opposition to government. Dedicated to welfare principles, the government has enacted legislation ostensibly designed to curb the antediluvian conduct of private employers. It has aided and abetted the growth of INTUC so that there is more or less an official agency in the labor movement which can represent its policies and also keep it informed of the state of working-class morale. To anyone fired with enthusiasm and filled with fervor for the cause of labor, it may well appear to be much the most practical thing to work with the Congress Party rather than oppose it, particularly if the enthusiast is aware of the limitations that underdevelopedness imposes on welfare programs. On the other hand, the lack of consensus inherent in the social, religious and cultural divisions of India may require that political leadership possess enough of a charismatic quality and that a political party be a strong enough symbol of national purpose to become the focus of incipient national unity. If Nehru and the Congress Party perform this function, one party rule may be indispensable. But when and how will an opposition capable of assuming the responsibilities of office, which after all is a necessary condition for democracy, develop? This question must remain unanswered, but it is nonetheless worth asking. For if India does achieve some success in raising the standard of living of the people and in heightening their national consciousness, it will be because of the success of Indian leaders in transmitting their own aspirations to the inert masses, and their very success may make them reluctant to release their hold on the political mechanism which made their achievements possible.

§ *Labor in Egypt*

Since 1952 the government of Egypt has both supported the welfare claims of workers against employers and established stringent regulations controlling the scope of union activity.[22] In that year a revolution brought to power a military junta committed to improving the social and economic condition of the people through agrarian reform and industrialization. As one might expect, the industrial labor force, small though it was, numbering some 650,000 in 1952, was more than normally affected by the expectations of a better life that the revolution created. But because the workers were concentrated in the urban areas of Alexandria, Cairo, and Port Said where their collective strength might be organized and used against the government, especially if their aroused expectations were not satisfied, the government acted to establish a framework of labor organization which would at once secure the loyalty of the workers and prevent them from forming unions hostile to it.

In a legislative act of 1952, the government defined the nature of the relationship between workers and employers by prescribing many conditions which in the normal procedure of labor relations in the western world would be subject to negotiation in collective bargaining; for example, "the manner in which employees are to be paid, employer responsibility for the health and safety of workers, probationary employment period, lay-off and discharge procedures, vacation allowances, work assignments, disciplinary measures, and even the provision of housing and meal services."[23] The revolutionary junta thus professed its concern for the workers by limiting the discretion of employers in matters which in a capitalistic system, and in the prerevolutionary Egyptian regime, were strictly the prerogative of private employers. The state achieved at one stroke what the trade unions in the west achieved only after years of struggle. This type of protective legislation, of course, was a manifestation of the weakness of organized labor in an underdeveloped economy and also of the difference in attitudes on questions of labor and welfare between the present and previous centuries. It did not occur to western governments in the nineteenth century to specify the conduct of employers in such fine detail; even hours legislation had to overcome adverse judicial interpretations or inadequate inspection and enforcement. Not only had the industrialization of the western economies imparted to the underdeveloped economies a strong desire for economic development, but also a greater sensitivity to the position and rights of labor in the process. But therein lies the difficulty, of course, for being more sensitive to these rights did not bring about the circumstances which gave them economic substance. So while apparently strengthening the forces of labor, the Egyptian government took care that organized labor did not acquire the kind of independence which might have jeopardized its own plans for the development of Egypt.

Even before the Revolution of 1952, the government controlled the organization and operation of trade unions. In some areas, most notably agriculture and government, unions were expressly prohibited. Elsewhere they were encouraged but within a framework of relatively tight controls. Union leaders and representatives had to come from the ranks of labor. Egypt thus hoped to avoid what has come to be a problem for India, the capture of trade unions by dissident intellectuals and lawyers who use them for political purposes to embarrass the regime and neglect local issues of concern to the workers. But by prohibiting outside leadership, the government weakened the effectiveness of the local unions, because they could draw only on men whose energies already were spent on full-time employment. Moreover, strikes were proscribed and the unions were not allowed to participate in religious or political activities. Their meetings were subject to police control and all their records were open to government inspection. Most of these controls were continued by the military junta in 1952, though the bar against the organization of agricultural workers was rescinded. Clearly the purpose of the present regime, as of its predecessors, is to confine union activity to the social-economic problems of firm and industry and prevent the emergence of a nation-wide group capable of rallying political opposition.

The governmental controls of labor relations in Egypt appear to lie closer to the totalitarian pole of the policy spectrum than do those in India. The conditions of labor-management relations in the plant and the conduct of unions are prescribed in greater detail and there is less opportunity for workers to seek their ends independently of the government. One can therefore raise all the questions here that were raised in connection with India.

If there is no effective opposition to the regime being generated in an industrialization process sponsored by the regime itself, what will induce it to shed its powers? In Egypt the internal pressures for democratization which may affect the leadership are certainly weaker than in India. The latter at least professes a strong commitment to the values of democracy in the western liberal tradition and could conceivably restructure governmental relationships in order to give added weight to individual preferences without external threats to its tenure of power. It is less clear that this could happen in Egypt. The rise of Nasser and the fall of Naguib in the military junta brought the messianic force of Arab nationalism to the fore. As a symbol of this force, the state is coming to have a rationale apart from the individuals over which it rules. Moreover, since Arab nationalism does not respect the frontiers which demarcate states in the Middle East, it tends to be perpetually involved in external conflicts. As threats to its mission, these conflicts feed the government the substance of the propaganda with which it incessantly rallies the population. Israel, in particular, is the cause célèbre serving the useful function of sublimating domestic discontents. Opposition to such a regime, if it appears at all, may come not so much from the society at large, but from within the ranks of the governmental elite, from those who have control over the coercive instruments of state power, for example, military leaders or propaganda ministers. But changes in government arising from opposition of this sort are "palace revolutions" rather than fundamental constitutional changes in the political order.

§   *Political Development in the Nineteenth and Twentieth Centuries*

Democratic political organization emerged in the nineteenth century on the heels of an industrialization process which had demonstrated the capacity of autonomous individuals to change the economic environment radically and accordingly reinforced demands for change in the political and social environment. In one country after another in the western world limitations were imposed on the prerogatives of nondemocratic rulers who felt that it was more prudent to yield in some degree to popular pressures than to stand pat. Not all countries traveled the same road to democracy, nor did they all get equally far. Britain moved gradually towards democracy with few deviations from the trend which first became apparent in 1832. France followed a violently fluctuating course whose turning points were marked by revolution and reaction. Germany never got as far as either France or Britain, but after the liberal fiasco of 1848 and the machinations of unification were behind it, it seemed to be making headway until interrupted by the holocaust of World War I. As for the United States, it never had to travel the road, for it was created at the destination. The nineteenth century was indeed the democratic age in both Europe and its offshoots in North America.

It is far from certain, however, that the countries undertaking industrialization in the present century will experience the same kind of metamorphosis in their political institutions. Because of the deterrents to growth which have prevented autonomous development in these countries, the impulse for industrialization must come from the center of political power and spread outward into society, rather than, as was the case in the west during the nineteenth century, coming from society itself. And because knowledge of the industrialization of the west has given the leaders of underdeveloped economies a consciousness of the potential of economic development, they are reluctant to leave their economic destiny to the unconscious forces of the market. Not only are they inclined to manage investment, but the labor force as well. Faced by subsistence problems made increasingly relentless by the very success of the mature economies, they do not have the time to experiment with the permissiveness of *laissez-faire*. They must impart to society the growth-generating characteristics that it now lacks or suffer the agonies of economic retrogression with its attendant social disorders. They must try to contain any forces that threaten to nullify the gains of economic growth. Thus India and Egypt, for example, have exerted an influence on the labor movement much greater than was necessary in the industrialization of the west.

So far as an independent labor movement is important in giving depth to the forces demanding the democratization of political institutions, it may be said that such forces in the underdeveloped economies are weak. Since the labor movement more often than not is the creature of government, it does not have as strong a moral position from which to seek the reform of government as did the labor movement in the nineteenth century. While this does not mean that democracy is impossible in the undeveloped economies, it does mean that it is unlikely to emerge as it did in the western world where economic growth triggered the democratic potential implicit in its ideological and social background. Since in the twentieth century the government must play a more active role in shaping society, the question of whether democracy will emerge or not depends a great deal more on the beliefs, attitudes, and values of those who control government. With more powerful means at their disposal to manipulate society than were available to rulers in the nineteenth century, they are less susceptible to threats to their tenure of power which arise in society. Daniel Bell recently has proclaimed the end of ideology, at least in the United States.[24] Perhaps in the newly developing world the future of democracy depends on an ideology which fixes the goals of individual autonomy firmly in the minds of those who have it within their power to shape the political community as they already are shaping the economic order.

Chapter 10

Growth, Freedom, and Democracy in the Twentieth Century

THE DISCUSSION in the previous chapters can be briefly summarized. On *a priori* grounds we argued that while democracy was not compatible with economies at early stages of development, it might be compatible with economies at late stages of development. We then examined the circumstances of the nineteenth century industrialization which resulted in the democratization of political processes in the western world and went on to cast doubts about the viability of these circumstances in the twentieth century. The purport of the analysis was to raise the possibility that a unique configuration of historical conditions relating to the availability of natural resources, the mobility of population, ideology, and the locus and sequence of development, accounted for the emergence of the democratic political order. In short, we examined some necessary conditions for democratic political development which seemed to be more clearly operative in the nineteenth than in the twentieth century.

In this concluding chapter we should like to point up and

reemphasize some of the problems and dilemmas raised by the analysis. We shall have no solutions to offer. At most we can hope that an awareness of the dilemmas will make western people more forebearing and tolerant of the policies nonwestern societies use in trying to break out of the grip of political and economic underdevelopedness.

Looking first at western experience in the nineteenth century, one cannot underscore too heavily the fact that the emergence of democratic political institutions represented a victory of society over the state. The extension of the franchise and the reform of the representative organs of government were responses to pressures and demands generated by autonomous individuals who were seeking the fulfillment of private goals and expectations. Especially important in their conduct, of course, was the maximization of economic values which led to the creation of the industrial order with all its attendant strains and discontents. Partly because of prevailing philosophy or ideology and partly because of the limited technological means available to government for controlling behavior, individuals were given considerable freedom to work out ways and means of assuaging these discontents. In consequence, institutions capable of giving depth and focus to the demands for political reform proliferated in society.

Not surprisingly, then, freedom in the western world came to be associated with the democratization of political processes. But note the character and meaning of freedom. In contrast to what Isaiah Berlin has called positive freedom, the nineteenth-century western world maximized negative freedom—the absence of external restraints to the realization of one's desires.[1] Even as governments were liberalizing their constitutions, they were keeping their hands off the expanding realm of private economic activity. The very success of industrialization induced them to leave those responsible for it alone. So impressive was the burgeoning industrial world and so persuasive were the ideologies that explained and rationalized it that the individual in society came to be viewed as self-sufficient in the sense that his problems, noneconomic as well as economic, could be solved outside the state in institutions of his own making. It therefore was prudent to minimize the restraints that the state imposed on him.

§ *The Age of the Common Man and the*
Decline of Laissez-Faire

In the twentieth century democracy cannot be nourished on the extension of negative freedom, not least of all because of the heightened or new consciousness of mankind which characterizes the present era. The twentieth century has been rightly called the age of the common man. However much nations today may differ in their national purposes and ideological values, they are in agreement on one thing: it is for the welfare of people that societies exist. The day is irrevocably past when the common man could be viewed as a pawn in the service of kings or as a beast of burden beholden to the desires and whims of a ruling elite. Moreover, nations no longer can justify imperialistic ventures on grounds of manifest destiny, the white man's burden, the right of conquest, or some other doctrine of immanent superiority. The ideas of the eighteenth-century Enlightenment have so completely captured the imagination of mankind that the general welfare has become a necessary arbiter of individual and national conduct.

It is perhaps unnecessary to observe that the elevation of the general welfare in the modern world does not mean that individuals and nations are so motivated. Aside from the difficulty of really knowing what it is, the general welfare often is a convenient cover concealing naked self-interest. The pretensions of the modern corporation to enlightened statesmanship are a far cry from the public-be-damned attitude of Cornelius Vanderbilt, but it certainly cannot be argued that the former has foregone the private objectives of the latter. While the United States may saturate its actions in the Far East or Latin America with the heady wine of ethical imperatives, few people are so naïve that they believe these are the prime reasons for those actions.

Nonetheless, the coming of age of the common man represents an explicit recognition of the importance of anyone and everyone, regardless of station or class, in the general welfare. Perversely enough, however, the position of man in the modern *Weltanschauung* makes it more difficult for government to leave him to his own devices and his own salvation. Simply because man is the measure of all things, governments must take cognizance of situations where he does not seem to be achieving or obtaining the well-being that is his due. Governments cannot now callously disregard the condition of man. But that is what the doctrine of *laissez-faire* as formulated in the nineteenth century called for.[2] Even though society may not have been economically capable of providing for the destitute and unemployed at very satisfactory standards, it still required "due toughness of bowels," in Carlyle's phrase, to insist that they fend for themselves or that, at the most, the state only provide them with the most meager subsistence.

If, moreover, the advocate of *laissez-faire* was apprehensive about the exercise of state power, even for the purposes of the general welfare, he seemed quite unconcerned about the abuse of private power, as in the relationships between employers and employees. The highly articulate and sophisticated rationale of *laissez-faire* surely only appealed to those who did not have to bear the brunt of it. And indeed there is ample evidence that those who were left to the tender mercies of the market were outraged by the neglect that liberal philosophy condoned. Now modern ideology, whether it be democratic or communist, has destroyed the panoply that once protected the callous attitude. Class structures and attitudes may prevail everywhere, but they no longer are held to be manifestations of the innate superiority of some people to others and the justification of the discriminatory treatment of the "lower orders." Where class exists, it is a source of embarrassment, something to be explained away, denied, or hidden from view.

Not only is there a heightened ideological consciousness of mankind in the contemporary age, but there is also a greater realization of the potential benefits of economic development. It is therefore all the more difficult to leave individuals alone when present circumstances prevent development from taking place.

The success of the west in achieving self-sustaining growth puts before the underdeveloped world a prospect, a vision, if you will, of a solution to problems which the one has taught the other no longer to believe insoluble. If western methods of economic organization are not congenial to the leaders of underdeveloped economies, western rationality, which enjoins the conscious and efficient application of means to ends, is. These men want to do something about the impoverished conditions in their country. They are in a hurry, and they are not inclined to wait for the spontaneous generation of growth.

Moreover, the mere fact of western development tends to compel underdeveloped nations to seek consciously for a solution to their problems. The population explosion alone is sufficient cause. As the result of expanding output in the west and of innovations affecting standards of medicine and sanitation, population in the underdeveloped economy frequently increases ahead of output, thus endangering the fragile social equilibrium on which it has traditionally depended. Institutions capable of maintaining domestic order at one level of population may disintegrate, or operate ineffectually, at higher levels of population. The injunction to be patient and not hurry along a process that under any circumstances takes time may fall on barren ground when it is thought that the conditions in one's country are deteriorating and its problems are becoming more compelling. It is one thing to leave people alone when their prospects are bright; it is quite another when these are dim.

§ *The Inappropriateness of the Liberal Tradition for Twentieth-Century Development*

The circumstances of growth today in the underdeveloped world are thus not so propitious for the acceptance of negative freedom as they were in the western world of the nineteenth century. People are, as it were, too conscious of themselves and their destiny. Where in eighteenth-century Britain, Parliament could pass enclosure acts whose objectives were limited to the improvement of conditions for experimentation in agriculture, in the twentieth century countries contemplating agricultural reform do so in the context of overall growth objectives. Agriculture is not an end in itself, but part of the mosaic of industrialization the pattern of which has been gleaned in the history of the west. While the dispossessed peasant in eighteenth-century England had to make out for himself with minimal support from the state, the peasant in the twentieth century, similarly dispossessed, may be destined for employment in a factory yet to be built. Because the underdeveloped economy comes late in the sequence of development, its leaders can conceive of prospects and objectives which may have only the vaguest connection with the preferences and conduct of individuals. What naturally, therefore, suggests itself is positive programs for achieving the former rather than negative action in deference to the autonomy of the latter.

The liberal tradition depended upon the congruence of individual preferences and the social welfare. That there could be no divergence between the two was more or less taken for granted since individuals were thought to be the best judge of what was in their own interests. Accordingly the community or society could never take precedence over individual preferences through the collective determination of the social welfare. Our analysis of industrialization in the nineteenth and twentieth centuries impugns the universality of the liberal tradition by implying that the conditions supporting its fundamental assumptions in the one period do not necessarily hold in the other period. Let us be sure that there is no mistake in our meaning. What we are saying is that in the nineteenth century it may have been correct to insist that individuals knew what was in their best interests, but in the twentieth century in the circumstances of underdevelopedness this may no longer be the case. Needless to say, this assertion is completely and totally repugnant to liberal philosophy. In casting doubts on the self-sufficiency of the individual it raises the specter, not just of governmental restraints on individual conduct, but of extensive control of his behavior.[3]

One cannot pass off liberal fears in this regard lightly. The worst tyrant is he who loves mankind too much, for if he thinks

he acts for man, he may coerce him into being free with righteous persistence. Because of the industrialization of the western
world, political leaders in underdeveloped economies have a picture of social welfare from which they can reasonably argue individuals will receive great benefit. But if individual conduct in
these countries now will not lead autonomously to the achievement of this welfare position, then they might have to be taken
in hand and led forward *in their own interests*. Unlike the
Roman tyrant who seized control of the imperial scepter by sub-
verting the Praetorian Guard and perhaps murdering or exiling
hostile senators, the contemporary political leader does not look
upon the people simply as a source of tribute for his personal
aggrandizement. Rather he is likely to view them as interrelated
parts of a complex engineering problem in human behavior,
which must be solved for their benefit as well as his own. Where
the liberal would then deplore the resulting encroachments on
freedom in the negative sense, the political leader would promise
the freedom that comes with the creation of a viable and growing
economy. And if the liberal should ask him what right he has to
impose collective welfare on individuals whose preferences revealed nothing more than a desire for continuation of the "life
of a happy savage," he might well answer that the west had made
such an existence impossible.

However much we may have exaggerated the inappropriateness of the liberal tradition for twentieth-century development, it
cannot be gainsaid that in the underdeveloped economy today
government is playing a much more important role than it did
in the nineteenth century. Whether planning total economic
activity as in China or facilitating the construction of social overhead capital as in India, government tends to play the part that
in the nineteenth century was played by private entrepreneurs.
More significantly from the viewpoint of the discussion in this
chapter, expanded governmental activity has taken place by and
large within one-party political systems which attenuate the opportunity for the emergence of effective opposition. Either opposition is proscribed as in totalitarian China or is so divided
and split that one party dominates the governmental and political process. As we have tried to make clear in previous chapters,

there are cogent economic reasons for believing that limitations on political activity are essential for development at the early critical stage. For if there should be too strong a political manifestation of the consumptionist demands of the population, the growth objectives of the accumulators, on whom the future of an economy depends, might well be jeopardized. One-party rule then may be viewed as a political technique for keeping opposition within the limits necessitated by the requirements of economic growth.

Thus we come back to the ineluctable and unwelcome question which the analysis in this book poses: How can societies which are being made ready for economic growth by the state develop the autonomy and independence with which to shape and control the institutions of the state? Imperfect though the democratization of political processes may have been in the nineteenth century, private citizens mustered their strength in organizations which not only set limits to the scope of state power, but reformed it as well. Now, however, the impulse for reform comes from the state which has reason to believe that it knows better than private individuals what is in their best interests. To put the question the other way round: Can one expect a state which has taken society in hand to devolve voluntarily some of its collective powers upon society in democratic reforms? The answer of history to this question is not very reassuring. In the twentieth century the further spread of democracy depends precisely on this kind of "internal" democratization.

§   *The Conflicts of Growth, Freedom, and Democracy*

For the western nations which trod the path of democratization in the nineteenth century, the obstacles now obstructing that path for the new nations of the twentieth century raise peculiarly vexing problems. The new consciousness of mankind compels nations to justify their actions and policies in the court of world opinion. Not surprisingly, western nations, and especially the United States, attempt to universalize the virtues and values which their historical traditions and experiences have taught them to respect. Thus freedom and democracy have become ideological slogans which are incessantly put forward in defense of American policy. Furthermore, their inverse, slavery and totalitarianism, are frequently invoked in attempts to stigmatize the policies of communist nations. We have in consequence come to view the future of the world as hanging on the outcome of a struggle between good and evil.

The difficulty with such a moralistic interpretation of world affairs is that it threatens a country with a curious kind of schizophrenia in the sense that it fails to recognize the disparity between the moral categories it espouses and the underlying reality that it is trying to influence. Freedom and democracy have real substance for western nations because they have managed to get beyond the stage of economic growth where these values had to be restricted without the loss of those institutions which eventually fostered their development. Growth, freedom, and democracy now appear to be consistent with one another, though it is not impossible to imagine the margins of one being extended so far that it encroaches upon the margins of the others. But the underdeveloped economies confront circumstances which restrict their opportunities to maximize these objectives simultaneously. If they are to grow economically, they must limit democratic participation in political affairs and perhaps some kinds of economic freedom as well. How, then, can the moral significance of American experience with the problems of political and economic organization at high levels of income be meaningful to countries whose experience is limited to the problems of subsistence income?

It is too glib and easy to assert that if men must choose between freedom and bread, they are spineless and lack the dignity befitting human beings unless they come down strongly on the side of the former. It is not convincing, in other words, to insist that in fact freedom is a universal value that can be maximized independently of economic well-being. The immortal declamation of Patrick Henry is not likely to be made on an empty stomach. Moreover, to insist that western freedom is paramount in the face of underdevelopedness overlooks its ambiguous origins. It only has been in comparatively recent times that freedom has been a widely consumed value in western nations. The life of the average citizen in Britain, Germany, and even in the United States at early periods in the natural history of industrialization was very much confined by the exigencies of subsistence. Though free of the restrictions imposed by a purposeful state seeking to accelerate the rate of economic growth, he frequently found himself in circumstances where he suffered from the exercise of private power. Now that rising national income has brought with it increased leisure and greater equity in market relationships, it is easy to forget the long time it took to give freedom substance and a broad base.

No more than freedom can democracy be considered apart from the growth of income. To make free elections and majority rule the measure of a nation's moral worth when it scarcely produces enough income to subsist is to reveal one's ignorance of the historical genesis of democracy in the west. That is to say, it is to apply tests to nonwestern nations that the western nations themselves did not pass when they were at a comparable stage of economic development.

The dilemma posed for the western nations by the conflict of economic growth and political values is, of course, all the greater because they are in competition with nations which deny the existence of the dilemma. Unrestrained by concern for individual preferences or by a belief in parliamentary political institutions, the communist nations look to comprehensive governmental controls and planning as the appropriate means of industrializing the underdeveloped economies. Whatever the future shape of society may be, they subordinate all values to this single objective. Since they place such great emphasis on economic growth they seem to stand on the side of the forces of change, especially in contrast to the western nations with their greater sensitivity to the values and individual preferences represented in the existing order of society.

We do not intend to offer solutions to the problems facing the old democracies because of the disparate stages of political and economic development in which the various nations of the world find themselves. Still less do we propose a pious and sententious profession of faith in the capacity of democracy to triumph in the end over all obstacles. On the other hand, it would require clairvoyance of a rather high and presumptuous order to assert the end of the democratic age. Our analysis does not lead to the conclusion that democracy is impossible in the twentieth century. Rather it suggests that what in chapter 1 we called the macrocosmic conditions are less favorable for the emergence of democracy than they were in the nineteenth century. To that extent the prognosis for any particular nation must turn more on the performance of the microcosmic conditions. If circumstances no longer stimulate autonomous economic growth in society, the future of society depends on the inclinations, preferences, and values of the men who are responsible for the fortunes of state. Not only do they have to take the initiative in accelerating economic growth, but in forming the political community as well. One can only hope that Lord Acton's famous aphorism about the corrupting influence of power does not apply universally. To paraphrase Winston Churchill, never before has the history of democracy depended so much on the actions of so few.

Notes

Notes to Chapter 1

1. See Everett E. Hagen, *On the Theory of Social Change,* Homewood, Illinois, 1962, pp. 36–52; David C. McClelland, *The Achieving Society,* New York, 1961, pp. 1–35.

Notes to Chapter 2

1. J. L. Talmon, *The Rise of Totalitarian Democracy,* London, 1952.

2. C. Crane Brinton, *The Jacobins,* New York, 1930.

3. Karl Marx, *The Civil War in France,* New York, 1933, p. 42.

4. The literature of welfare economics is extensive, but the following will acquaint the interested reader with some of the problems the subject raises, William J. Baumol, *Welfare Economics and the Theory of the State,* London, 1952; Kenneth E. Boulding, "Welfare Economics," *A Survey of Contemporary Economics,* Vol. II, ed. by B. F. Haley, Homewood, Illinois, 1952 pp. 1–34; Maurice Dobb, *Political Economy and Capitalism,* London, 1937, pp. 127–184; E. J. Mishan, "A Survey of Welfare Economics, 1939–1959," *The Economic Journal,* LXX, June, 1960, pp. 197–265; Melvin W. Reder, *Studies in the Theory of Welfare Economics,* New York, 1947; Tibor Scitovsky, "The State of Welfare Economics," *American Economic Review,* XLI, June, 1951, pp. 303–315.

5. Cf., Kenneth J. Arrow, "A difficulty in the Concept of Social Welfare," *Journal of Political Economy,* LVIII, August, 1950, pp. 328–346; *idem, Social Choice and Individual Values,* New York, 1951; William H. Riker, "Voting and the Summation of Preferences: an In-

terpretive Bibliographical Review of Selected Developments During the Last Decade," *American Political Science Review*, LV, December, 1961, pp. 900–911.

6. For a rigorous "economic" analysis of the problem and implications of decision-making in political systems see Anthony Downs, *An Economic Theory of Democracy*, New York, 1957. See also Albert O. Hirschman, "Models of Reformmongering," *Quarterly Journal of Economics*, LXXVII, March, 1963, pp. 236–257.

7. Voting procedure here refers not to the electorate, but to the representatives of the electorate.

8. Skeptical readers might wish to pursue this point in the writings of Professor Frank H. Knight. See especially *The Economic Organization*, Chicago, 1933 and *The Ethics of Competition*, New York, 1935.

9. This may be recognized as a crude invocation of the principle of diminishing marginal utility which, strictly speaking, is applicable only to the increased consumption of one commodity, while all other commodities are held constant. Nonetheless, intuitively it seems reasonable to apply the principle to the growth of aggregate income and consumption. If it were not valid, the increasing proportion of aggregate expenditures devoted to advertising and marketing in a high-income economy such as that in the United States would be difficult to explain. The problem of production may not be solved as Professor Galbraith argues in *The Affluent Society* (New York, 1958), but he surely is right in emphasizing the frivolous and nonessential nature of much current consumption.

10. In a somewhat related vein Anthony Crosland has noted the diminishing pressure of class conflict in a high-consumption society. "In such a society, as poverty disappears, so does the driving pressure towards economic conflict. Any desired consumption-good becomes more and more easily accessible; and economic envy is diminished. Leisure increases relative to hours of work, and the importance of consumption factors relative to that of productive relationships. The 'service' grows relative to the manufacturing population, and technical and non-manual relative to unskilled manual labour; and the outlines of distinct economic classes become increasingly blurred." C. A. R. Crosland, *The Future of Socialism*, London, 1956, p. 255.

Notes to Chapter 3

1. The evidence with regard to the sources of economic growth shows that technological change, or increasing efficiency in the utilization of resources, is considerably more important than increases in the quantity of inputs. See, for example, Solomon Fabricant, *Economic Progress*

and Economic Change, 34th annual report of the National Bureau of Economic Research, New York, 1954, pp. 3–18.

2. The question of investment criteria is a good deal more complex than indicated in the text. Of all the phases of economics, capital theory is perhaps the most difficult and obscure because of ineluctable theoretical problems involved in the treatment of time. Those who are interested in these problems in the context of economic development may find the following references useful: A. E. Kahn, "Investment Criteria in Development," *Quarterly Journal of Economics,* LXV, February, 1951, pp. 38–61; W. Galenson and H. Leibenstein, "Investment Criteria, Productivity, and Economic Development," *idem,* LXIX, August, 1955, pp. 343–370; R. C. Blitz, "Capital Longevity and Economic Development," *American Economic Review,* XLVIII, June, 1958, pp. 313–329.

3. Cf., M. Fleming, "External Economies and the Doctrine of Balanced Growth," *Economic Journal,* LXV, June, 1955, pp. 241–256; P. N. Rosenstein-Rodan, "Problems of Industrialization of Eastern and South-Eastern Europe," *Economic Journal,* LIII, June–September, 1943, pp. 202–211; Tibor Scitovsky, "Two Concepts of External Economies," *Journal of Political Economy,* LXII, April, 1954, pp. 143–151; A. A. Young, "Increasing Returns and Economic Progress," *Economic Journal,* XXXVIII, December, 1928, pp. 527–542.

4. See Clark Kerr, John T. Dunlop, Frederick H. Harbison, and Charles A. Myers, *Industrialism and Industrial Man,* Cambridge, Mass., 1960 for an analysis of the role of entrepreneurial or industrializing elites in economic development, especially as it affects the relationships between labor and management.

5. Max Weber, *The Protestant Ethic and the Spirit of Capitalism,* translated by Talcott Parsons, New York, 1948.

6. David Riesman, *The Lonely Crowd,* New Haven, 1950. Inner-directedness may have been an especially important characteristic of entrepreneurship at early stages of development before the process of invention and innovation had been institutionalized in the large firm. The individual entrepreneur then had to rely largely on his own resources.

7. W. Arthur Lewis, "Economic Development with Unlimited Supplies of Labor," *The Manchester School,* XXII, May, 1954, pp. 139–191.

8. W. W. Rostow, "The Take-off into Self-sustained Growth," *Economic Journal,* LXVI, March, 1956, pp. 24–48.

9. For further discussion of the problems of, and empirical evidence about, capital-output ratios see V. V. Bhatt, "Capital-Output Ratios of Certain Industries: A Comparative Study of Certain Countries," *Review of Economics and Statistics,* XXXVI, August, 1954, pp. 309–319; Evsey D. Domar, "Interrelation between Capital and Output

in the American Economy," *International Social Science Bulletin,* VI, No. 2, 1954, pp. 236–242; William Fellner, "The Rate of Growth and Capital Coefficients," *Long-Range Economic Projections,* Studies in Income and Wealth, Vol. 16, National Bureau of Economic Research, Princeton, 1954, pp. 275–331; R. W. Goldsmith, "The Growth of Reproducible Wealth of the United States of America from 1805 to 1905," *Income and Wealth,* Series II, Cambridge, 1952, pp. 247–318; L. R. Klein and R. F. Kosobud, "Some Econometrics of Growth: Great Ratios of Economics," *Quarterly Journal of Economics,* LXXV, May, 1961, pp. 173–198; S. Kuznets, "Long Term Changes in the National Product of the United States of America since 1870," *Income and Wealth,* Series II, Cambridge, 1953, pp. 29–241; W. Leontieff and associates, *Studies in the Structure of the American Economy,* New York, 1953; K. Martin, "Capital-Output Ratios in Economic Development," *Economic Development and Cultural Change,* VI, October, 1957, pp. 24–31.

10. In part the rapid growth of output in the Soviet Union is attributable to the emphasis planners have placed on activities characterized by low capital-output ratios at the expense of activities characterized by high capital-output ratios. Thus the industrial and manufacturing sectors of the Soviet economy have been given greater weight than the housing and transportation sectors, which typically absorb a large volume of resources before yielding increments to output.

11. It is probably not uncommon for investment in public facilities to provide satisfactions over and above the output or service increases it facilitates. The massive interior of Pennsylvania Station in New York and the garish Moscow subway presumably satisfy something other than transportation wants. In Argentina, the General Pistarine International Airport, constructed during the Peron regime, was much larger than the anticipated air traffic from foreign countries could possibly warrant, yet to Argentinians it seemed to be an important symbol of Argentina's economic status.

12. Howard S. Ellis, "Accelerated Investment as a Force in Economic Development," *Quarterly Journal of Economics,* LXXII, November, 1959, pp. 485–495; John Strachey, *Contemporary Capitalism,* London, 1956, p. 197; Harvey Leibenstein, *Economic Backwardness and Economic Growth,* New York, 1957, pp. 94–110.

13. This proposition is correct if welfare is measured solely in terms of the current output of consumer goods. If, however, welfare is measured in terms of the pattern of consumption over time, then it may not be valid. For it is conceivable that people might be willing to have their subsistence reduced now, if they thought it would lead to the expansion of consumable output tomorrow. In addition to the difficulties mentioned in the text previously, problems of this sort involving time preferences and intertemporal comparisons make the concept of welfare in economics all the more elusive.

14. Cf., Maurice Dobb, *Soviet Economic Development Since 1917*, New York, 1948, pp. 1–33.

15. Noneconomists will find a lucid exposition of the index number problem in Robert W. Campbell, "Problems of United States–Soviet Economic Comparisons," *Comparisons of the United States and Soviet Economies*, Joint Economic Committee, Congress of the United States, Washington, 1959, Part I, pp. 13–30.

16. James S. Duesenberry, *Income, Saving and the Theory of Consumer Behavior*, Cambridge, Mass., 1949.

17. Schumpeter coined the word "immiserization" with this observation: "this is probably the best way to render the word *Verelendung*, which is no more good German than that English monster is good English. It is *immiserimento* in Italian." *Capitalism, Socialism and Democracy*, 3rd ed., New York, 1950, p. 22.

Notes to Chapter 4

1. It surely is not fortuitous that since the end of World War II generals have played such an important role in the governing of the underdeveloped economies. In one country after another the army has seized control of government either as the revolutionary custodian of a progressive movement for modernization as in the United Arab Republic, or as a caretaker regime pledged to rid civilian administrations of corruption and inefficiencies as in Turkey. These countries plus Iraq, the Sudan, Burma, Pakistan, and South Korea, of course, do not make up the whole of the underdeveloped world, but enough of it to suggest that the army is now performing a different and more complex function than it did in the developing economies of the European community of nations in the nineteenth century.

2. See, for example, Veblen's analysis of the development of Germany in the latter part of the nineteenth century in *Imperial Germany and the Industrial Revolution*, London, 1915. Also, E. Ames and M. Rosenberg, "Changing Technological Leadership and Industrial Growth," *Economic Journal*, LXXIII, March, 1963, pp. 13–31.

3. Cf. Marvin Frankel, "Obsolescence and Technological Change in a Maturing Economy," *American Economic Review*, XLV, June, 1955, pp. 296–319.

4. What is at issue here is the treatment of time referred to in footnote 2 of Chapter 3. For very short periods of time, the stock of resources of an economy as well as the tastes of the population are fixed. Maximization of economic welfare, then, involves allocation of these stocks to uses which best satisfy consumers with given tastes. Over longer periods of time, however, neither the stocks of resources nor tastes are fixed and the allocation of resources appropriate to the

shorter time period may no longer yield maximum welfare. The crucial question is: What is the appropriate time period for planning the allocation of resources? Should economic policy maximize net output for ourselves, our children, or our grandchildren? Theoretical economics has no answers to these questions which is to say that the decision turns on the goals or values that society is trying to achieve.

5. M. Fleming, "External Economies and the Doctrine of Balanced Growth," *Economic Journal*, LXV, June, 1955, pp. 241–256; A. O. Hirschman, *The Strategy of Economic Development*, New Haven, 1958; Bert F. Hoselitz, "Balanced Growth, Destabilizers, and the Big Push," *World Politics*, XII, April, 1960, pp. 468–477; Harvey Leibenstein, *Economic Backwardness and Economic Growth*, New York, 1957; Ragner Nurkse, "The Conflict between 'Balanced Growth' and International Specialization," *Lectures on Economic Development*, Istanbul, 1958, pp. 165–182, reprinted in *Equilibrium and Growth in the World Economy*, edited by G. Haberler and R. M. Stern, Cambridge, Mass., 1961, pp. 241–259; Goran Ohlin, "Balanced Growth in History," *American Economic Review*, XLIX, May, 1959, pp. 338–353; Tibor Scitovsky, "Growth—Balanced or Unbalanced?" *The Allocation of Economic Resources*, M. Abramovitz, ed., Stanford, 1959, pp. 207–217.

6. There has been considerable discussion about the role of cottage industry in development, particularly in light of the fact that, though in western economies the factory system displaced domestic industry as the most important form of manufacturing, small industry has persisted until the present day. We do not mean to suggest that there is no place for small industry in development, but rather that it is unlikely to provide the stimulus to industrialization. See Henry Aubrey, "Small Industry in Economic Development," *Social Research*, Vol. 18, September, 1951, pp. 269–312; Bert F. Hoselitz, "Small Industry in Underdeveloped Countries," *Journal of Economic History*, XIX, December, 1959, pp. 600–618; A. J. Jaffe and K. Azumi, "The Birth Rate and Cottage Industries in Underdeveloped Countries," *Economic Development and Cultural Change*, IX, October, 1960 (Part I), pp. 52–63.

7. The literature of socialism is vast, indeed prolix. We are therefore all the more indebted to G. D. H. Cole for his monumental *A History of Socialist Thought* which distills from this literature the essential doctrinal development of socialism. Of the five volumes, the last of which Cole did not live to see through the press, volume III, *The Second International, 1889–1914*, Part I, London, 1956, and volume IV, *Communism and Social Democracy*, Part I, London, 1958 are most germane to the discussion in the text. Each volume contains an annotated bibliography which provides an excellent guide to socialist literature. Of Lenin's writings the most relevant is *What Is to Be Done? Selected Works*, Moscow, 1934, Vol. II, pp. 27–192.

Notes to Chapter 5

1. John M. Keynes, *The General Theory of Employment, Interest, and Money*, New York, 1936, pp. 333-371.

2. For a discussion of British income data prior to the industrial revolution see Phyllis Deane, "The Implications of Early National Income Estimates for the Measurement of Long-Term Economic Growth in the United Kingdom," *Economic Development and Cultural Change*, IV, November, 1955, pp. 3-38.

3. T. S. Ashton, *An Economic History of England: The 18th Century*, London, 1955; idem, *The Industrial Revolution, 1760-1830*, London, 1948; W. H. B. Court, *A Concise Economic History of Britain from 1750 to Recent Times*, Cambridge, 1954; Paul Mantoux, *The Industrial Revolution in the Eighteenth Century*, translated by Marjorie Vernon, Rev. ed., London, 1928.

4. Witt Bowden, *Industrial Society in England Toward the Close of the Eighteenth Century*, New York, 1925, pp. 51-69.

5. For an attempt to quantify the role of Protestant dissenters in the industrial revolution in Britain, see Everett E. Hagen, *On the Theory of Social Change*, Homewood, Illinois, 1962, pp. 294-309.

6. In the struggle to make a commercial success of Watt's steam engine "practically a new industry had to be created, together with its personnel and equipment. A body of highly specialized workmen, fit for difficult work which demanded muscular strength, intelligence and great steadiness of hand, were needed to replace the occasional engineers of former times—locksmiths, tinsmiths, and millwrights. Cylinders of geometrical accuracy, properly fitted pistons, gears as accurate as those of a watch, had to take the place of the rough and often ill assembled parts which made up the earlier machines and which were often the cause of their failure." Mantoux, *op. cit.*, p. 329.

7. "The austerity of the ironmasters, whether cause or effect of their sectarianism, affected every side of their lives. Successful themselves, they were intolerant of what might appear weakness or inefficiency in others; and though their charities were numerous there was little of the milk of human kindness in their constitutions. At that time, more than any other, industrial leadership demanded men of an autocratic mold; and, individualists as they were both by nature and circumstances, they resented any attempt on the part of the workers to determine, in any measure, the conditions of their working life. In more than one, indeed, there was developed something approaching contempt for the aspirations of labour." T. S. Ashton, *Iron and Steel in the Industrial Revolution*, London, 1924, pp. 225-226.

8. In *The History of Trade Unionism*, London, 1894, Sidney and Beatrice Webb point out the familial characteristics of the eighteenth-century firm which preserved a community of interests between work-

ers and employers. "Their occasional disputes with their employers resembled rather family differences than conflicts between distinct social classes. They exhibit more tendency to 'stand in' with their masters against the community, or to back them against rivals or interlopers, than to join their fellow-workers of other trades in an attack upon the capitalist class (P. 39)."

9. Before the emergence of the factory system in the textile industry, the distinction between domestic workers and entrepreneurs was not clear cut since the former, when they had sufficient capital, often performed the functions of the latter. Cf. Neil Smelser, *Social Change in the Industrial Revolution*, Chicago, 1959, p. 110.

10. It is not difficult to think of significant exceptions to the proposition that the entrepreneurial middle classes were inept political advocates. By all accounts Francis Place was a singularly effective politician operating behind the scenes in the campaigns to reform the Parliament prior to 1832 and Place was every bit the self-made man. Cf. Graham Wallas, *The Life of Francis Place, 1771–1854*, London, 1908. Similarly, in the years following 1832, particularly during the struggle to repeal the Corn Laws, one could not ask for more formidable political combatants than Cobden and Bright who were nothing if not Manchesterian to the core. Cf. John Morley, *The Life of Richard Cobden*, Boston, 1881 and G. M. Trevelyan, *Life of John Bright*, New York, 1913. Yet all three of these men of the middle classes were really professional politicians, the latter two, indeed, being MP's, who in the years of their most important political activity were not functioning industrialists or men of commerce or trade. To repeat, the men who devote their lives to industry are not likely to be the ones who can spell out the social significance of their work in a manner persuasive to society at large.

11. Cf. C. R. Fay, *The Corn Laws and Social England*, Cambridge, 1932.

12. Utilitarianism, like its close relative Fabianism of the late nineteenth century, was a peculiarly English institution and it would be stretching the truth to imply that it was widely embraced by the industrial middle classes early in the industrial revolution. The Radicals in the first part of the century who propagated the message of Jeremy Bentham were a small band who undoubtedly exerted an influence in English politics out of all proportion to their numbers. Yet James Mill, Francis Place, Joseph Home, John Stuart Mill, and their colleagues formulated, and acted upon, ideas which were in the ascendancy in nineteenth-century Britain. As early disseminators of ideas that subsequently came to have wide currency in Britain, and generally in the Anglo-American world, it is not surprising that they did not initially have widespread support.

13. A. Toynbee, *Lectures on the Industrial Revolution in Eng-*

land, London, 1884; J. L. and Barbara Hammond, *The Village La-bourer, 1760–1830,* London, 1911; *idem, The Town Labourer, 1760–1830,* London, 1920; A. L. Bowley and G. H. Woods in articles on wages and prices which appeared intermittently in the *Journal of the Royal Statistical Society* from 1898 to 1906; J. H. Clapham, *An Economic History of Modern Britain,* Vol. I, *The Early Railway Age, 1820–1850,* Cambridge, 1926.

14. T. S. Ashton, "The Standard of Life of the Workers in England, 1790–1830," *Capitalism and the Historians,* ed. by F. A. Hayek, Chicago, 1954, pp. 127–159.

15. E. J. Hobsbawm, "The British Standard of Living, 1790–1830," *Economic History Review,* 2nd Series, X, August, 1957, pp. 46–69. Also see Colin Clark, *The Condition of Economic Progress,* 3rd ed., London, 1957, pp. 208–218; Phyllis Deane, "The Industrial Revolution and Economic Growth: the Evidence of Early British National Income Estimates," *Economic Development and Cultural Change,* V, January, 1957, pp. 159–174; W. Woodruff, "Capitalism and the Historians: a Contribution to the Discussion of the Industrial Revolution in England," *Journal of Economic History,* XVI, March, 1956, p. 1–17.

16. W. Arthur Lewis, "Unlimited Labour: Further Notes," *The Manchester School,* XXVI, January, 1958, footnote p. 21.

17. The vitriol which Carlyle exuded in his prose is hard to forget as, for example, in the following condemnation of the Poor Law Amendment Act of 1834: "That this Poor-Law Amendment Act meanwhile should be, as we sometimes hear it named, the 'chief glory' of a Reform Cabinet, betokens, one would imagine, rather a scarcity of glory there. To say to the poor, Ye shall eat the bread of affliction and drink the water of affliction, and be very miserable while here, required not so much a stretch of heroic faculty in any sense, as due toughness of bowels. If paupers are made miserable, paupers will needs decline in multitude. It is a secret known to all rat-catchers: stop up the granary-crevices, afflict with continual mewing, alarm, and going-off of traps, your 'chargeable labourers' disappear, and cease from the establishment. A still briefer method is that of arsenic; perhaps even a milder, where otherwise permissable. Rats and paupers can be abolished; the human faculty was from of old adequate to grind them down, slowly or at once, and needed no ghost or Reform Ministry to teach it." *Chartism,* London, 1840, p. 17.

18. J. S. Mill, *Autobiography,* New York, 1924, p. 162. In the third edition of *The Principles of Political Economy,* 1852, Mill wrote: "Hitherto it is questionable if all the mechanical inventions yet made have lightened the day's toil of any human being. They have enabled a greater population to live the same life of drudgery and imprisonment, and an increased number of manufacturers and others to make fortunes. They have increased the comforts of the middle class. But

they have not yet begun to effect those great changes in human destiny, which it is in their nature and in their futurity to accomplish." Quoted by Colin Clark, *op. cit.,* p. 218.

19. W. H. B. Court, *op. cit.,* pp. 124–125.

20. Neil Smelser attributes the welfare problem not so much to physical conditions in the factories which he thinks were improving, in the textile industry at least, following the Napoleonic Wars, as to the changes in the structure of the family occasioned by industrialization and urbanization. "Growing urbanization was gradually weakening community ties. Changes in spinning technology were undermining the spinner's economic authority and forcing on him assistants to whom he was not tied by kinship or community." *Op. cit.,* p. 278. And on the subject of cruelty to children he observes, interestingly, that "as long as cruelty was an adjunct of parental authority and discipline, it remained a legitimate means of socialization. When these parental controls began to weaken, the automatic safeguards over the appropriate use of beating began to weaken . . . cruelty . . . was becoming a problem because its social environment was changing." *Ibid.,* p. 279.

21. The point perhaps needs to be emphasized that entrepreneurs did not exclude welfare considerations from their purview out of meanness. Rather the logic of the capitalist system compelled them to restrict the factors they considered to those which could be articulated in revenues and costs. Otherwise they courted financial disaster.

22. Arthur Young, *The Farmer's Tour through the East of England,* London, 1771, IV, p. 361.

23. Joseph Townsend, *A Dissertation on the Poor Laws by a Wellwisher of Mankind,* London, 1786, pp. 39–40.

24. Thomas Rainborowe, *In the Army Debates at Putney,* October 29, 1647.

25. The suspension of Habeas Corpus, the prohibition of public meetings and the suppression of the Corresponding Society were brought on by the outbreak of hostilities with France in 1793. These measures effectively restrained reform movements for the duration of the war. The reaction in England against Jacobinism and the radicals of the left was not dissimilar to the reaction in our own day of American society to communism. Both societies felt sufficiently threatened by an ideology to sacrifice political freedoms to the requirements of security.

26. William Lovett, a London artisan, founded the London Working Man's Association and subsequently was a leader of the so-called "moral force" school in the Chartist movement. The author of the People's Charter—universal manhood suffrage, equal election districts, no property qualifications for candidates, annual parliaments, secret ballot, and payment of members—published in 1838, he opposed the

"physical force" school within the movement which received the great part of its support in the northern industrial communities.

27. "Thus in the 1790's the need for protecting the conditions of labour was becoming more critical because of the advancing technology; paradoxically, however, the societies for protecting labour, far from blossoming to maturity, were shrouding themselves under the cloak of the more popular friendly society movement." Smelser, *op. cit.*, p. 320.

28. The most notable instances of capital punishment took place during the repression of what the Hammonds called "The Last Labourers' Revolt," a series of uprisings of agricultural workers in 1830 against farmers and landowners occasioned by unemployment in the southern counties. In restoring order the newly elected Whig government, through Lord Melbourne at the Home Office, hanged 9 persons as well as transporting 457 others. J. L. and Barbara Hammond, *The Village Labourer, 1760–1832*, London, 1911, pp. 240–324.

29. See F. C. Mather, *Public Order in the Age of the Chartists*, Manchester, 1959.

30. Cf. Graham Wallas, *op. cit.*, pp. 289–323.

31. The London Mechanics' Institution was founded in 1823 through the efforts of Thomas Hodgskin, Dr. George Birkbeck, Francis Place, and others. At the outset there were two different points of view among the founders with respect to the function of the institution, the one seeing it as a working class organization through which socialist doctrine could be spread, the other as a technical training school based on an acceptance of orthodox political economy. The latter view prevailed since it represented the position of those who provided the major portion of funds for the Institution. Cf. G. D. H. Cole, *A Short History of the British Working Class Movement, 1789–1937*, London, 1937, Vol. I, pp. 85–87.

32. Arthur Redford, *Labour Migration in England, 1800–50*, London, 1926.

33. Although it falls outside the period with which we have been concerned in the text, a report of the Massachusetts Bureau of Labor asserting that strikes in the Fall River textile industry in the 1870's were largely brought on by British workers who were accustomed to defending their rights through union action gives circumstantial support to this point. Charlotte Erickson, *American Industry and the European Immigrant, 1860–1885*, Cambridge, Mass., 1957, pp. 62–63.

34. The first hours legislation in Britain was passed in 1802 and was intended to limit the discretion of factory owners employing parish apprentices, many of whom were exploited with long hours of labor and miserable living conditions. The sponsor of the bill was the older Robert Peel.

Notes to Chapter 6

1. Quoted by Louis Hartz, *The Liberal Tradition in America,* New York, 1955, p. 5. I have not been able to locate the exact reference in Tocqueville's work, but "born free" is an apposite phrase for suggesting his views about the origin of freedom in America. See, for example, *Democracy in America,* the Henry Reeve text revised by Francis Bowen and further edited by Philip Bradley, New York, 1945. "The chief circumstance which has favored the establishment and the maintenance of a democratic republic in the United States is the nature of the territory that the Americans inhabit. Their ancestors gave them the love of equality and of freedom; but God himself gave them the means of remaining equal and free, by placing them upon a boundless continent." Vol. I, pp. 290–291.

2. Frederick Jackson Turner, *The Frontier in American History,* New York, 1920. For a recent discussion of the role of natural environment and economic abundance in American development see David M. Potter, *People of Plenty,* Chicago, 1954.

3. This is not meant to imply that there was a fundamental consensus in matters of economic and political policy. The Civil War belies such a preposterous notion. Sectional differences in economic and political interests were manifest at the foundation of the Republic and these eventually put the union to the ultimate test of survival. But the Civil War was not fought on ideological or philosophical issues. It was not a class war. The individualism for which America was noted did not depend on its outcome, though undoubtedly it was given greater scope following the victory of the north.

4. In *The Declaration of Independence: a Study in the History of Ideas,* New York, 1956, Carl Becker pointed out that the ideas Thomas Jefferson articulated in the Declaration of Independence were so much part of colonial America that they were considered to be self-evident and therefore did not need to be proved.

5. For a magnificent discussion of the impact of early American political experience on Europe see R. R. Palmer, *The Age of the Democratic Revolution, a Political History of Europe and America, 1760–1800,* Princeton, 1959.

6. Davis R. Dewey, *Financial History of the United States,* 11th ed., New York, 1931, pp. 1–32.

7. Quoted by Charles A. and Mary R. Beard, *The Rise of American Civilization,* revised ed., New York, 1933, Vol. I, p. 379.

8. See Saul K. Padover, *The Mind of Alexander Hamilton,* New York, 1958, p. 11.

9. The Beards, *op. cit.,* p. 358.

10. Letter to William Stephens Smith, November 13, 1787, *The Papers of Thomas Jefferson,* Princeton, 1955, Vol. 12, p. 356.

11. As Tocqueville observed of the United States, "There is one country in the world where the great social revolution that I am speaking of seems to have nearly reached its natural limits. It has been effected with ease and simplicity; say rather that this country is reaping the fruits of the democratic revolution which we are undergoing, without having had the revolution itself." *Op. cit.*, Vol. I, p. 13.

12. See for example, Louis Hartz, *Economic Policy and Democratic Thought, Pennsylvania 1776–1860*, Cambridge, Mass., 1948.

13. The initial legislative act authorizing the construction of the Erie Canal was passed in 1817 by New York. As sections of the canal were completed they were pressed into use. 1825 is the date by which the whole length of the canal was finished.

14. U.S. Bureau of the Census, *Historical Statistics of the United States, Colonial Times to 1957*, Washington, D.C., 1960. Series A 34–50, p. 9.

15. *Ibid.*, Series A 195–209, p. 14. Urban areas include all places with population of 2,500 or more.

16. *Ibid.*, Series D 36–45, p. 72.

17. *Ibid.*

18. *Ibid.*, Series F 10–21, p. 139. The terminal dates in this instance are 1859 and 1899 and data are valued at 1879 prices.

19. *Ibid.*, Series F 1–5, p. 139. The income data for years prior to 1921 are given as annual averages covering five-year periods and do not extend further back than 1869.

20. Between 1860 and 1910 average money wages in industry doubled, while the cost-of-living index increased by about 50 per cent. *Ibid.*, Series D 573–577 and Series D 603–617, pp. 90–92 and Series E 157–160, p. 127.

21. *Ibid.*, Series C 88–114, pp. 56–59.

22. See Seymour M. Lipset and Reinhard Bendix, *Social Mobility in Industrial Society*, Berkeley, 1959, pp. 70–71, 104–107, for a related sociological view of the impact of mobility and migration on the structure and attitudes of the American labor force.

23. No one has written more perceptively about the problems of the immigrants than Oscar Handlin. See, especially, *The Uprooted*, Boston, 1952.

24. "Through most of this period the labor unions either barred the foreign-born from membership or made no effort to organize them." *Ibid.*, p. 81. See also, Charlotte Erickson, *American Industry and the European Immigrant, 1860–1885*, Cambridge, Mass., 1957, pp. 106–136.

25. Cf. Daniel Bell, "The Background and Development of Marxian Socialism in the United States," *Socialism and American Life*, edited by Donald D. Egbert and Stow Persons, Princeton, 1952, Vol. I, pp. 215–405. Vol. II, edited by T. D. Seymour Bassett is an invaluable

critical and descriptive bibliography of the literature of socialism. See also Ray Ginger, *The Bending Cross*, New Brunswick, New Jersey, 1949.

26. For studies of the American labor movement see Selig Perlman, *A Theory of the Labor Movement*, New York, 1928; Frank Tannenbaum, *The Labor Movement; Its Conservative Function and Social Consequences*, New York, 1921; Norman J. Ware, *The Labor Movement in the United States, 1860–1895; A Study in Democracy*, New York, 1929; Samuel Yellin, *American Labor Struggles*, New York, 1936.

Notes to Chapter 7

1. Karl Marx, *The Eighteenth Brumaire of Louis Bonaparte*, London, 1852, p. 5. Recent translations of this passage, though capturing its meaning, have done less than justice to Marx's style. Thus the Foreign Language Publishing House in Moscow in a 1951 edition of selected works of Max renders it this way: "Men make their own history, but they do not make it just as they please; they do not make it under circumstances chosen by themselves, but under circumstances directly encountered, given and transmitted from the past."

2. See Everett E. Hagen's analysis of the authoritarian personality in *On the Theory of Social Change*, Homewood, Illinois, 1962, pp. 123–160 for an attempt to dig more deeply into the causes of authoritarian systems.

3. J. H. Clapham, *The Economic Development of France and Germany, 1815–1914*, 4th ed., Cambridge, 1936, p. 82.

4. *Ibid.*, p. 85.

5. *Ibid.*, p. 153.

6. For analyses of the role of the state in American and German development see H. G. J. Aitken, ed., *The State and Economic Growth*, New York, 1959, pp. 4–25, 189–200.

7. Clapham, *op. cit.*, p. 278.

8. William H. Dawson, *The Evolution of Modern Germany*, New York, 1908, p. 238.

9. Clapham, *op. cit.*, pp. 281, 283, 285.

10. *Ibid.*, p. 305.

11. Already at the outset of the industrial revolution in Germany, German writers were concerned about the position of workers in industrialized communities. Far from being pleased by the prospects of repeating British experience, they hoped that what they considered the "excesses" of Manchesterian liberalism could be avoided in the economic development of Germany. The concern of the German historical and institutional economists with the *Arbeiterfrage* and the role of the state in solving it was as great as the confidence of the English classical economists that the state could only make it worse.

12. Clapham, *op. cit.*, pp. 289–295.

13. Writing in the last year of his life, 1895, Fredrich Engels noted the electoral success of socialist parties in various European countries and also the increasing strength of the military establishment because of innovations in the design of rifles and other weapons. He suggested that socialist parties would do better to seek their ends through legal means—the vote—than by leading insurrections of workers in urban communities. Except in unusual circumstances, these were bound to fail in the face of a determined military force. See the introduction by Engels to Karl Marx, *Die Klassenkämpfe in Frankreich, 1848–1850,* Berlin, 1930, pp. 17–36.

14. Theodore S. Hamerow, *Restoration, Revolution, Reaction; Economics and Politics in Germany, 1815–1871,* Princeton, 1958, pp. 56–74.

15. Cf. G. D. H. Cole, *Socialist Thought—Marxism and Anarchism, 1850–1890,* A History of Socialist Thought, Vol. II, London, 1954, pp. 237–266.

16. Appendix IV—Programme of the German Workers' Party—to Karl Marx, *Critique Of the Gotha Programme,* New York, 1938, p. 89. The *Critique* was not published until 1891, having been suppressed at the time it was written in the interests of maintaining the harmony of the German socialist movement. Subsequently it became important in the Bolshevik doctrinal lexicon because it contained propositions with respect to the distribution of income in socialism that gave respectable doctrinal paternity to the inequalitarian wage policy adopted by the Communist Party after the start of the five-year plans.

17. William H. Dawson, *German Socialism and Ferdinand Lassalle,* London, 1888, pp. 251–252. The security of the upper classes when the lower classes begin to demand political, social, and economic changes in society to improve their condition is always a matter of considerable concern to the upper classes. The best of all worlds from their point of view is one in which people accept their status in society as something that is God-given and cannot be altered. Invidious comparisons, therefore, which invite envy and dissatisfaction with one's lot are a threat to the security of the well-to-do. Thus in England at the time of the French Revolution we find William Paley giving this gratuitous counsel to working men who, he feared, might be induced to follow the example of their revolutionary French peers: "The wisest advice that can be given is, never to allow our attention to dwell upon comparisons between our own condition and that of others, but to keep it fixed upon the duties and concerns of the condition itself." And if the condition itself were pretty grim, he assured the workers that "some of the necessities which poverty . . . imposes, are not hardships but pleasures. Frugality itself is a pleasure. It is an exercise of attention and contrivance, which, whenever it is successful, produces satisfac-

tion." William Paley, *Reasons for Contentment*, London, 1793, pp. 4–5, 11.

18. Cf. Cole, *op. cit.*, pp. 264–265.

19. Eduard Bernstein, *Evolutionary Socialism: A Criticism and Affirmation*, translated by Edith C. Harvey, New York, 1909.

Notes to Chapter 8

1. The recovery of the Russian economy during the 1920's was in part achieved at the cost of the depreciation of the assets that the revolutionary regime inherited from the Tsarist regime. That is to say, the growth of net output during the 1920's was not so great as the growth of gross output.

2. The most precise statement of historical materialism by Marx may be found in his preface to the *Critique of Political Economy*, Chicago, 1904. For a rigorous analysis of this statement see John Plamenatz, *German Marxism and Russian Communism*, London, 1954, pp. 18–35. Also see Karl de Schweinitz, Jr., "On the Determinism of the Marxian System," *Social Research*, Vol. 29, Spring, 1962, pp. 37–49.

3. Of all the critical evaluations of Marx that his work evoked perhaps the most interesting and judicious is that of Joseph A. Schumpeter. As conservative as Marx was radical, Schumpeter nonetheless had great respect for Marx's attempt to wed theory and history and treated him with consummate impartiality as a serious scholar of social evolution. See *Capitalism, Socialism, and Democracy*, 3rd ed., New York, 1950, pp. 1–58.

4. V. I. Lenin, *Imperialism, the Highest Stage of Capitalism*, New York, 1939.

5. Actually this statement is not quite correct. As any reader of Marx and Engels' *Communist Manifesto* realizes, the founders of the communist movement had high praise for capitalism relative to the stage of development preceding it. Its role in revolutionizing the forces of production and making possible higher development in socialism lent a certain progressive aura to capitalism. Nonetheless, the emphasis placed on the exploitation of workers as the rationale of the capitalist market, especially when contrasted to the presumed release from such exploitation in socialism, induced in socialists an unyielding market phobia.

6. Cf. Alexander Baykov, *The Development of the Soviet Economic System*, New York, 1947, pp. 1–48; Maurice Dobb, *Soviet Economic Development Since 1917*, New York, 1948, pp. 82–124.

7. For discussion of the economic controversy during the period of the New Economic Policy see Dobb, *op. cit.*, pp. 177–207; Alexander Erlich, "Preobrazhenski and the Economics of Soviet Industrialization," *Quarterly Journal of Economics*, LXIV, February, 1950, pp.

57–88; *idem., The Soviet Industrialization Debate. 1924–1928,* Cambridge, 1960.

8. Cf. David Mitrany, *Marx against the Peasant,* Chapel Hill, N.C., 1951.

9. Karl Marx, *Capital,* Kerr edition, Chicago, 1906, Vol. I, pp. 784–848.

10. See W. W. Rostow, *The Stages of Economic Growth: A Non-Communist Manifesto,* Cambridge, England, 1960. Though Professor Rostow did not succeed in formulating a theory of development which in any sense is comparable to the theories of Karl Marx or Joseph Schumpeter, he did coin suggestive rubrics for different stages of development which are convenient to use in discussions of development.

11. Cf. Isaac Deutscher, *Soviet Trade Unions,* London, 1950.

12. The literature in English on the operation of the Soviet economy by this time is very large. In addition to the work of Dobb and Baykov already cited, for comprehensive discussions of the system one may consult Robert Campbell, *Soviet Economic Power—Its Organization, Growth, and Challenge,* New York, 1960; Alex Nove, *The Soviet Economy,* New York, 1961; Harry Schwartz, *Russia's Soviet Economy,* 2nd ed., New York, 1954. Particularly useful are a series of papers published by the Joint Economic Committee, U.S. Congress, *Comparisons of the United States and Soviet Economies,* Washington, 1959.

13. Cf. Abram Bergson, *The Real National Income of Soviet Russia since 1928,* Cambridge, Mass., 1961; M. Bornstein, "A Comparison of Soviet and United States National Product," *Comparisons of the United States and Soviet Economies,* U.S. Congress, Washington, 1959. Part II, pp. 377–395; Gregory Grossman, "National Income," *Soviet Economic Growth,* A. Bergson, ed., Evanston, Ill., 1953, pp. 1–23; D. Hodgman, *Soviet Industrial Production 1928–51,* Cambridge, Mass., 1954.

14. D. Hodgman, "Industrial Production," *Soviet Economic Growth,* A. Bergson, ed., Evanston, Ill., 1953, pp. 225–244.

15. For a discussion of the impact of Soviet education on Soviet citizens see Urie Bronfenbrenner, "Challenge of the 'New Soviet Man,'" *The New York Times Magazine,* August 27, 1961, pp. 21, 78–79.

16. The rationality of central economic planning is an issue which evoked a long controversy between socialists and nonsocialists. At the outset it was concerned with the practicability of a socialist system but with the rise of the Soviet economy the emphasis shifted to the possibilities of maximizing consumer satisfaction in the allocation of resources where these are controlled by central authority. See F. A. Hayek, ed., *Collectivist Economic Planning,* London, 1935; Oskar Lange, *On the Economic Theory of Socialism,* Minneapolis, 1938.

17. On what has been called the informal operations of the Soviet firm see J. Berliner, *Factory and Manager in the USSR*, Cambridge, 1957; D. Granick, *Management of the Industrial Firm in the USSR*, New York, 1954.

18. F. D. Holzman, *Soviet Taxation—The Fiscal and Monetary Problems of a Planned Economy*, Cambridge, 1955, pp. 1–103.

19. D. Hodgman, "Soviet Monetary Controls through the Banking System," *Value and Plan*, G. Grossman, ed., Berkeley, 1960, pp. 105–131.

20. In the spring of 1961 the Soviet government made its criminal law more severe by extending capital punishment to the following economic crimes: stealing state property, black market dealings, embezzling, forging banknotes.

21. The difficulties of autonomous communication in a totalitarian regime were revealed quite clearly by a recent Russian emigré and graduate of Moscow University in his response to a question about the extent to which students criticized the regime amongst themselves: "From 1951 to 1954, practically all of us showed to the world a completely Communist face. You confined any critical views of the regime to your closest friends and even then unpleasant things sometimes happened. The danger of arrest and deportation was immediate. At times I thought: I am, if not a completely isolated person, perhaps a real white raven among the flock of good and orderly black crows. And I remember once theorizing to myself: Perhaps you think the way you do because of the generations of faulty bourgeois background behind you. I was, frankly, very surprised to discover in 1955 and 1956, after the 'Thaw' began, that there were a great number of other small circles of friends, thinking in much the same way, who had been cut off from each other." "The Voice of a Dissenter," *Harper's Magazine*, May, 1961, p. 127.

22. See P. J. D. Wiles, "Rationality, the Market, Decentralization and the Territorial Principle," *Value and Plan*, G. Grossman, ed., Berkeley, 1960, pp. 184–205.

23. Richard Lowenthal is sceptical of the possibilities of evolutionary or gradual change in the Soviet political system, given the Communist Party's monopoly of power. "As the victory of First Secretary Khrushchev over his rivals following Stalin's death has shown, the party machine is still capable of successfully resisting pressures from various sections of Soviet society, including the pressure of the managerial bureaucracy inside the party. But it could not preserve its monopoly of power without maintaining the basic political and ideological goals which alone legitimate its rule. That is not to say that such monopoly must last forever—only that it is more likely to be broken in the kind of open contest with new social forces that occurs during a succession crisis than to disappear gradually by a process of con-

tinuous 'mellowing.' " "Communism and Nationalism," *Problems of Communism,* XI, Nov.–Dec., 1962, p. 42.

24. *The Economist,* for example, argues that Krushchev is symbolic of the transisition from Stalinist despotism to the society of the new generation whose members "better educated than their elders" are likely to demand "a less arbitrary, less secret, and more rational style of government." September 1, 1962, p. 752. Mr. Crankshaw believes that "the atmosphere, the mood, and the physical conditions of life in the Soviet Union today are all very strikingly different from what they were under Stalin—so much so that it is impossible to believe that they can ever revert to their old state." *Khrushchev's Russia,* Baltimore, 1962, p. 99. These optimistic views, however, are not unanimously held. Professor Hook, for example, has little confidence that the Khrushchev regime has permanently put behind it the stifling oppressive conduct of the Stalinist regime. "All it requires is a nod from Khrushchev to set the apparatus of repression in train again with its grisly consequences." "Revisionism at Bay," *Encounter,* XIX, Sept., 1962, p. 64. And Professor Gerschenkron has recently written that "the [Russian] dictatorship must be as it is or not be at all. Its long-run changeability appears limited indeed." "The Changeability of a Dictatorship," *World Politics,* XIV, July, 1962, p. 604.

25. Michael Kaser, "The Reorganization of Soviet Industry and Its Effects on Decision Making," *Value and Plan,* G. Grossman, ed., Berkeley, 1960, pp. 213–234.

26. Alec Nove, "Revamping the Economy," *Problems of Communism,* XII, Jan.–Feb., 1963, pp. 10–16.

27. Alex Nove, "Prospects for Economic Growth in the USSR," *American Economic Review,* LIII, May, 1963, pp. 541–554.

Notes to Chapter 9

1. Daniel Lerner reports in his study of traditional society in the Middle East that many peasants had difficulty in interviews with "role-playing" questions such as: If you were put in charge of a radio station, what kinds of programs would you like to put on? or, Suppose that you were made head of the government. What are some of the things you would do? "My God! How can you say such a thing?" gasped one shepherd. Daniel Lerner, *The Passing of Traditional Society,* New York, 1958, pp. 69–70.

2. David Riesman, *The Lonely Crowd,* New Haven, 1950.

3. David S. Landes, "French Business and the Businessman: A Social and Cultural Analysis," *Modern France,* E. M. Earle, ed., Princeton, 1951, pp. 334–353.

4. W. Arthur Lewis, *The Theory of Economic Growth,* Homewood, Illinois, 1955, p. 113.

5. Thomas W. Shea, Jr., "Barriers to Economic Development in Traditional Societies: Malabar, a Case Study," *Journal of Economic History*, XIX, December, 1959, p. 509.

6. Doreen Warriner, *Land Reform and Development in the Middle East*, 2nd ed., London, 1962, p. 7.

7. Reforms affecting land tenure and ownership, agricultural credit, and marketing arrangements have been common in the underdeveloped economies in the years since World War II, but these reforms have seldom been pushed by traditional agrarian elites. The initiative for such reforms is most likely to be taken by nationalist revolutionaries like Gamal Abdel Nasser, *ibid.*, pp. 10–54. Land reform has taken place slowly in Latin American countries, despite the prodding of the Alliance for Progress, precisely because agrarian elites are so often entrenched in strong political positions.

8. Food and Agricultural Organization, *Yearbook of Food and Agricultural Statistics, 1955*, Rome, 1956, Part I, Table 80, p. 294. The data for Australia, Egypt, and India are for 1953-54, and for Peru 1952.

9. The United Nations, *Monthly Bulletin of Statistics*, X, July, 1956, pp. 6–10.

10. *Idem, Demographic Yearbook, 1955*, New York, 1955, Table 32, pp. 740–749.

11. John T. Krause, "Some Neglected Factors in the English Industrial Revolution," *Journal of Economic History*, XIX, December, 1959, p. 532.

12. Lerner, *op. cit.*, p. 210.

13. *Ibid.*, p. 230.

14. Myron Weiner, "India's Political Problems: the Longer View," *The Western Political Quarterly*, IX, June, 1956, p. 288.

15. Cf. Ragnar Nurkse, *Equilibrium and Growth in the World Economy*, edited by Gottfried Haberler and Robert M. Stern, Cambridge, Mass., 1961, pp. 282–336.

16. I am indebted to Hans Heymann, Jr. for calling my attention to the anomaly of an economy as underdeveloped as Ethiopia investing in equipment as advanced as jet aircraft. On the problem of capital and maintenance costs in economic development see R. C. Blitz, "Maintenance Costs and Economic Development," *Journal of Political Economy*, LXVII, December, 1959, pp. 560–570.

17. During the spring of 1962 the restrictions on immigration were dramatized by the flight of population from China to Hongkong. Impelled by poor economic conditions to leave China, the refugees so overtaxed the facilities of Hongkong that many had to be returned. Since the U.S. immigration quota for Chinese is so small—105 per year—and since Chinese immigrants must be sponsored by American residents, the United States could do relatively little, under existing

law, to relieve Hongkong of the burden of handling a large influx of Chinese peasants.

18. See, for example, Everett E. Hagen's analysis of the problems of development in Burma in *On the Theory of Social Change*, Homewood, Illinois, 1962, pp. 432–470.

19. Gabriel A. Almond and James S. Coleman, eds., *The Politics of the Developing Areas*, Princeton, 1960, p. 78.

20. Bert F. Hoselitz called my attention to the role that cathedral-building might have performed in the creation of the French nation.

21. Charles A. Myers, *Labor Problems in the Industrialization of India*, Cambridge, Mass., 1958, pp. 1–13. Throughout this section I have drawn heavily on this immensely informative volume.

22. In this section I have relied on Frederick H. Harbison, "Egypt," *Labor and Economic Development*, Walter Galenson, ed., New York, 1959, pp. 146–185.

23. *Ibid.*, p. 151.

24. Daniel Bell, *The End of Ideology*, New York, 1960.

Notes to Chapter 10

1. Isaiah Berlin, *Two Concepts of Liberty*, Oxford, 1958.

2. Perhaps the best—certainly the most gruesome—example of the callousness bred by *laissez-faire* was the English Government's handling of the potato famines of 1846–48 in Ireland. So profound was the Government's belief in *laissez-faire* that it fully intended, at the outset at least, to let the laws of supply and demand solve the problems of famine and plague caused by the disastrous destruction of successive potato crops. Cecil Woodham-Smith, *The Great Hunger*, London, 1962, pp. 54–93.

3. Hans Meyerhoff has suggested that the liberal dichotomy between society and the state no longer is consistent with the predominant values of the contemporary age. "Organization and rational efficiency, economic power and military supremacy, internal strength and stability, preservation of law and order, peace of mind and security, hierarchy (status), harmony, and integration within the organism, whether it be society or the individual—these and other 'survival values' (in Paret's language) have become the dominant value symbols of our age." "Plato Among Friends and Enemies," *Encounter*, XVII, December, 1961, p. 50. Meyerhoff's observation squares with our view expressed in the text that the initiative for development and change is passing from individuals to the state. Since the autonomy of the individual in society is so basic to the liberal tradition, it is not surprising that there has been hostile liberal reaction to Platonic philosophy, vide Karl R. Popper, *The Open Society and Its Enemies*, London, 1945, even as the social economic conditions for an organic

concept of society in the state may be becoming more propitious. The inconsistency between the social-economic conditions in most areas of the world and the normative values of American society in particular has been brilliantly analyzed by Robert L. Heilbroner in *The Future as History,* New York, 1959.

Index

Adams, Samuel, 136
Agriculture, 85, 91, 132, 138, 147, 165, 243, 274
   in Russia, 202–3, 211, 220
All-India Trade Union Congress, 257–8, 261
Amalgamated Association of Iron and Steel Workers, 154
American Federation of Labor, 154–5, 156
American Railway Union, 154
American Revolution, 134, 135–6, 137, 148, 254
Anarchism, 154, 190
Anglicans, 42, 124
Anti-Corn Law League, 96
Anti-Socialist Law (Germany), 178, 179, 181, 196
Arabs, 253–4
Aristocracy, 97, 101–2, 123–4, 144, 151, 173, 181, 187–91, 197
Arkwright, Richard, 55, 84, 143
Ashton, T. S., 93, 99, 286n, 288n
Aswan Dam, 250, 255
Attwood, Thomas, 125
Australia, 25, 115, 121, 122, 209, 243, 248
Authoritarianism, 175, 196–9
Autonomous growth, 81, 91, 94–8 passim, 180, 192, 227–9, 234, 251–2

"Balanced growth," 285n
Balance-of-payments, 249
Banking, 91–2, 105–6
Bebel, August, 176, 182
Becker, Carl, 291n

Belgium, 25, 244
Bell, Daniel, 292n, 300n
Bentham, Jeremy, 287n
Berlin, Isaiah, 270, 300n
Bernstein, Eduard, 182, 295n
Bessemer, Henry, 87, 147
Birth rate, 244–5
Bismarck, Otto von, 159, 178–9
"Blanketeers," 113
Bolsheviks, 72, 201–4, 210, 213
Boulton, Matthew, 55, 89
Bowley, A. L., 99, 288n
Brazil, 235, 237, 238, 250
Bright, John, 96, 123, 287n
Brotherhood of Locomotive Firemen, 154
Bukharin, N. I., 203, 204
Burke, Edmund, 110

Canada, 25, 121, 122, 209, 244
Capital, 36, 37, 56–7, 69–70, 91, 95
   and output ratio, 45–7
   scarcities of, 47, 51, 66, 82, 88, 106–8, 127, 132
Capitalism, 34, 41, 54, 55, 72, 264
   and Germany, 168, 176, 181
   and Great Britain 96, 99–108 passim, 112, 120, 126
   and Russia, 191, 193–5, 198, 200, 203, 222
   and the United States, 139, 150
Carlyle, Thomas, 102, 111
Carnegie, Andrew, 55, 154
Ceylon, 224, 251
Chartism, 113, 124–6, 174, 289n
Child labor, 104, 152

China, 18, 235, 237–8, 240, 251, 256–7, 261, 275, 299n
Civil rights, 80, 110, 114, 169
Civil War (U.S.), 144, 145, 146, 147, 157, 291n
Clapham, J. H., 99, 288n, 293n, 294n
Cobden, Richard, 96, 123, 287n
Cole, G. D. H., 285n, 290n, 294n, 295n
Collectivism, 54–5
Combination Acts, 113, 115
Committee of Public Safety, 14
Commons, House of, 7, 80, 97, 98, 118, 124, 135
Communications media, 15, 62, 63–4, 216, 246
Communism, 5, 193, 278 (See also Marxism; War Communism)
Communist Manifesto, 172, 295n
Communist Party, 13, 43, 196–9, 204–7, 212, 216–17, 218, 229
Congress Party (India), 258–60, 263
Congress of Vienna, 159
Consensus, 19–23, 27, 32–3, 34, 180–4, 253
Constitution (U.S.), 148
Constitutional Convention (U.S.), 137
Consumers' goods, 49–51, 54, 100, 220, 226–8
Consumption, 16–18, 43, 52, 101, 103–4, 170, 209, 226–8
   and goals of workers, 56, 170–1
   vs. saving, 41
Continental Congress (U.S.), 139
Corn laws, 123, 287n
Cottage industry, 285n
Court, W. H. B., 102, 286n, 289n
Crompton, Samuel, 84
Crosland, C. A. R., 281n

Darby, Abraham, 87
Debs, Eugene V., 150, 154
Democracy
   and British economy, 79–128 passim
   and freedom, 269–79
   in Germany, 158–86 passim
   and industrialization, 3–11, 59–75
   and labor controls, 59–62

   and rationality, 19–21, 23–4, 34
   and rising income, 225–9
   in underdeveloped economies, 234–68 passim
   in the United States, 129–57 passim
Demography, 242–5, 246–7 (See also Population)
Discontent, 55–7, 64–9, 71, 108–22 passim, 133, 149, 169, 171, 211, 266
Dobb, Maurice, 284n, 295n
Duesenberry, James S., 52, 284n

Economic growth, 34–58, 69, 82, 84, 87, 114, 122, 148
   and capital-intensive methods, 66–7
   deterrents to, 234–56 passim
   and freedom, 269–79
   in Germany, 165–7, 169–70
   and "hump" problem, 67–8, 88–90, 106, 142, 200
   and mercantilism, 81–3
   among pioneers and latecomers, 65–9, 74, 246–51 passim
   and population, 48–9, 82, 244–7, 251
   in Russia, 191, 208, 214–16
   and welfare, 49–55, 98–108 passim, 118, 155
Education, 23–7
Egypt, 243, 247, 250–1, 255, 256
   labor in, 263–6
Enclosure movement, 91
Engels, Friedrich, 99, 294n, 295n
Enlightenment, 6, 84–5, 138, 271
Entrepreneurship, 8–10, 18, 55, 69–70, 98, 143, 190
   in the Mercantilist era, 82–3
   noneconomic influences on, 84–5
   private, 69–71, 90–4, 120–1, 151
   and the rationale of investment, 37–42
Ethiopia, 249–50

Fabianism, 287n
Family, 240, 245, 246

Feudalism, 28–9, 32, 130, 133, 162, 165, 168, 175, 185, 193, 197, 241, 254
Five-Year Plans, 43, 191, 215, 227, 252, 260, 261
France, 4, 6, 7, 79, 138, 159, 162, 170, 240, 244, 254, 267
Franco-Prussian War, 177
Freedom, 269–79
French Revolution, 4, 6, 12, 110, 114, 134, 135, 138, 254
   and Jacobins, 6, 14
Frontier thesis, 121–2, 131–2, 291n

Galbraith, J. K., 53, 281n
General German Workers' Association, 176
Germany, 10, 25–6, 129, 130, 198, 200, 229–30, 236, 254, 259, 262
   and democracy, 184–6
   industrialization in, 158–86 passim, 187
   labor movement in, 171–80, 182–3, 185–6
   and Prussians, 4, 159–60, 162, 163, 165, 177, 196
   railroads in, 164, 165, 166, 170
   Socialism in, 175–80
   and welfare problem, 167–71
Glorious Revolution, 3, 116, 197
Gompers, Samuel, 155
Grand National Consolidated Trades Union, 113, 115
Great Britain, 3–4, 6–7, 10, 25, 42–3, 54, 129, 134, 136, 196–7, 199, 209, 214, 234–6, 240, 244, 267
   and dissenters, 42–3, 241–3
   gentry in, 97, 101–2, 123–4
   compared to Germany, 159, 169, 171, 172, 174
   industrialization of, 61–2, 79–128 passim
   and mercantilism, 82–7, 90, 96–100 passim
   and textiles, 85–9
   compared to United States, 141–2
Greece, 12, 24

Gross National Product, 147, 218–19
Guatemala, 244

Hamilton, Alexander, 137–41
Hammond, J. L., and Barbara, 288n, 290n
Handlin, Oscar, 292n
Hargreaves, James, 84
Harney, George Julian, 125
Hartz, Louis, 291n, 292n
Hayek, F. A., 296n
Haymarket bombing, 154
Heilbroner, Robert L., 301n
Henry, Patrick, 136, 277
High-income economies, 31–4, 44, 59
Hind Mazdoor Sabha, 257–8
Hinduism, 242
Hobbes, Thomas, 110
Hobsbawm, E. J., 99, 288n
Hohenzollerns, 4
Hook, Sidney, 298n
Hoover Mission, 208–9
"Hump" problem, 67–8, 71, 81–90, 106, 142, 200

Ideology, 193, 235, 268, 269, 270, 272, 292n
Illiteracy, 25
Imperialism, 5, 194–5
Imperialism (Lenin), 195
Income, 17, 26–7, 38, 41, 50, 81, 172
   high, 31–4, 44, 59, 108
   low, 43, 226
   national, 44, 105, 215, 227
   per capita, 35–6, 45, 48, 121, 169, 235, 247
   rising, 225–9
   Soviet, 214–16
Index number problem, 51, 284n
India, 85, 89, 234, 235, 240–1, 242, 244, 246, 247, 251, 255, 265, 266
   labor in, 256–64
India National Trade Union Congress, 257–8, 263
Individualism, 90, 120–2, 131–2, 133, 141, 151, 161, 175
Individuals, 9, 57, 69–72, 273–6
   and "totalitarian" democracy, 12–15
   and welfare problem, 54–5

Indonesia, 251, 253, 255

Industrialization
  deterrents to, 44–8, 234–56 *passim*
  in Germany, 158–86 passim
  in Great Britain, 3–4, 79–128 *passim*, 143, 196–7, 199, 234–6, 240, 244, 267
  and "hump" problem, 67–8, 71, 81–90, 106, 142, 200
  "late starters" in, 65–9, 246–51 *passim*
  and Soviet totalitarianism, 187–233 *passim*
  "take off" stage of, 47–9, 67
  and underdeveloped economies, 234–68
  in the United States, 129–57

Industrial revolution, 47–54 *passim*, 84, 235, 286n
  classic, 3, 42, 61–2
  discontents of, 64–9
  in Great Britain, 79–128 *passim*
  in the United States, 132, 146–7

Inequality (economic), 52–3

Inner-directed man, 42

International Labor Organization, 258

Investment, 36–7, 38–42 *passim*, 46, 47, 50–1, 70, 105, 227
  private vs. public 38–40

Investment banking, 91, 105

Israel, 266

Jackson, Andrew, 148

Jacksonian era, 3

Jacobins, 6, 14, 110

Japan, 201, 251

Jefferson, Thomas, 132–3, 135–41 *passim*, 148, 291n

Junkers, 162, 181

Kautsky, Karl, 182

Keynes, John M., 81, 286n

Khrushchev, Nikita, 231–3, 298n

Knights of Labor, 153–4

Labor (as economic factor), 31, 33, 37, 46–7, 50, 55, 93–4, 169, 256–66

Laboring classes, 10, 56, 59–60, 98–9, 108–9, 110–11, 123, 142, 152–3, 163, 177, 193–4, 246

controls upon, 59–75, 168, 178, 210
  and welfare problem, 103–23 *passim*, 148–50, 168

Labor leaders, 74, 124, 125, 127, 171, 182, 259, 265

Labor movements, 55–7, 59–75 *passim*, 113–23 *passim*, 127, 150, 255, 257, 268, 293n
  in Egypt, 263–6
  in Germany, 171–80, 182–3, 185–6
  ideologies of, 108–13, 120–2, 171–2
  in India, 256–63
  in the United States, 152–7
  (*See also* Trade unions)

Labor parties, 72

Laissez-faire, 90, 143, 144, 145, 175, 267, 300n
  and the common man, 271–3

Lassalle, Ferdinand, 175–7

Latin America, 5, 25, 244, 251

Lebanon, 247

Lenin, V. I., 14, 72–3, 191, 194, 195–6, 201–2, 204, 210, 213, 295n

Lerner, Daniel, 247, 298n

Lewis, W. Arthur, 44, 45, 99, 240, 282n, 288n, 298n

Liberal tradition, 12–13, 195, 273–6

Liebknecht, Wilhelm, 176, 182

Lipset, Seymour M., 292n

List, Friedrich, 170

Locke, John, 110, 132, 133, 135, 143, 160, 193

Lords, House of, 7, 97, 117

Lovett, William, 111, 125, 289n

Luther, Martin, 160

Majority rule, 15

Malthus, Thomas, 95

Manifest destiny, 5

Marx, Karl, 6, 16, 54, 111, 158, 172, 176, 182, 191, 193–5, 196, 207, 293n, 294n, 295n, 296n

Marxism, 13, 14, 27, 43, 54, 73, 124, 135, 150, 195
  in Germany, 172, 181, 184
  and "immiserization," 54, 99, 149
  and Russia, 190, 192–9 *passim*, 200–1, 204–7, 214, 230

Mass society, 15–16, 24

Mensheviks, 72
Mercantilism, 81–8 *passim*, 90, 96–8,
  100, 136, 143, 200
Mercantilist era, 82–3
  and textiles, 85–7, 88
Meyerhoff, Hans, 300*n*
Mexico, 244
Middle-classes, 4, 134, 259
  in Germany, 173, 174–5
  in Great Britain, 94–8, 110, 117–
    18, 125, 142, 198
  in Russia, 188–9
  in the United States, 154
Middle East, 236, 237, 238, 247, 266
Migration, 71, 122, 133, 149–50, 153,
  161–2, 166, 169, 250–1, 292*n*
Mill, John Stuart, 102, 288*n*
Ministry of Internal Affairs (M.V.D.),
  222
Minorities, 21
Mortality rates, 48–9, 103, 244–5, 246
Multi-party systems, 22, 196–9
Myers, Charles A., 300*n*

Napoleonic Wars, 6, 103, 106, 111,
  113, 119, 159
Nasser, Gamal Abdel, 266, 299*n*
National debt, 140
National income, 44, 105, 214–16,
  224, 225, 227
Nazism, 14
Nehru, Jawaharlal, 260, 262, 263
New Economic Policy, 203–4, 205–6,
  208, 211, 213, 214
New Zealand, 25
North America, 121, 131, 185, 234,
  238, 267
Norway, 243

October Revolution, 191, 192, 195,
  201, 202, 211
Owen, Robert, 101, 107
Owenite socialism, 113

Paine, Thomas, 110, 135–6
Pakistan, 251, 253
Paley, William, 294*n*–5*n*
Pareto, Vilfredo, 49

Parliament (British), 79–80, 91, 97,
  115, 117, 118, 124–5, 126
Party systems, 22–3, 196–9, 231
Passing of Traditional Society, The
  (Lerner), 247
Paternalism, 112, 178
Peasant revolts, 29, 160
Peel, Sir Robert, 97–8
Per capita income, 35–6, 45, 48, 226,
  235, 244, 258, 262
"'Perfect competition," 17
Peru, 243
Peterloo massacres, 113
Philosophy of Manufacturers, The
  (Ure), 99
Pioneer economies, 65–6, 90
Place, Francis, 118, 287*n*
Planning, 45, 191, 200, 253, 261, 296*n*
  in Russia, 191, 200, 203–6, 208, 211,
    212–14, 218–23, 226–9, 230, 231
Plato, 24
Police power, 62–4, 117–18
Political action, 55–7, 153
Poor Law Amendment Act (1834),
  118–20, 125, 288*n*
Popper, Karl R., 300*n*
Population, 35, 36, 45, 64–5, 71, 88,
  103, 121–2
  as a barrier to growth, 48–9, 82,
    244–5, 246–7, 251
  in Germany, 166, 169
  in Russia, 208–9, 227
  in United States, 132, 142, 147, 244
Portugal, 4
Potter, David M., 291*n*
Powderly, Terence V., 153–4
Preobrazhenski, E. A., 207, 208, 295*n*
Prices, 40, 51, 83, 84, 119, 212
  and controls, 81, 86
Primogeniture, 240
Production (output), 36–40, 43, 53,
  147, 219–20, 226
  and population, 48–9, 82
Profit rates, 56, 95
Propaganda, 63–4, 71
Property, 135
Protestantism, 42, 85, 160
Puerto Rico, 244
Pullman strike (1894), 154, 156

Rainborowe, Thomas, 110, 289n
Rationality, 19–21, 23–4, 34
　and welfare problem, 54–5
Real wages, 213
　and welfare problem, 53–4, 99, 100,
　113, 119, 148
Reichstag, 178–80, 183, 184, 196
Reform Bill (1832), 6, 97, 116–18, 125
Relief, 118–20
Rents, 95
"Report on Manufacturers," 139
Resources, 51, 65, 82–3, 188, 219,
　226–8, 237–8
Revolution of 1848, 172–7
Revolution of 1905 (Russia), 197
Ricardo, David, 95, 123
Richelieu, Cardinal, 159
Riesman, David, 42, 239, 282n, 298n
Robespierre, Maximilien, 14
Rockefeller, John D., 55
Rostow, W. W., 44, 282n, 296n
Rousseau, Jean Jacques, 14
Russia, 4, 10, 12, 13, 15, 43, 72–
　3, 162, 189, 249, 252, 256, 260
　autocracy in, 187–91, 197
　Communist Party of, 13, 43, 196–9
　and decentralization, 225–9, 231,
　232
　industrialization in, 187–233 pas-
　sim
　national income of, 214–16
　planning in, 191, 200, 203–6, 208,
　211–14, 218–29 passim, 230–1
　Revolution of, 14, 192–5, 201
　welfare problems in, 208–11

St. Peter's Field Massacre (1819), 117–
　18
Savings, 41, 47
Scandinavia, 25
Schulze-Delitzsch, Herman, 175
Schumpeter, Joseph A., 6, 284n, 295n,
　296n
Senior, Nassau W., 100
Serfs, 29, 189
Shays' Rebellion, 140
Siemen, Sir William, 87
Slater, Samuel, 143–5
Smelser, Neil, 287n, 289n
Smith, Adam, 81, 90, 95

Social Democratic Labor Party (Ger-
　many), 176
Social Democratic Party (Germany),
　34, 181–3, 196, 201
Social Democrats (Russia), 72–3
Social mobility, 151, 292n
Social security, 120, 240
Socialism, 72, 100, 101, 111, 113, 285n
　in Germany, 175–80, 181–4
　and immigrants, 150–1
　and Russia, 192–6, 199–201
Soviet Union, see Russia
Spain, 4
Spinning jenny, 84
Stalin, Joseph, 211, 232–3
"Standard of Living," 49–50, 67, 171,
　231
State growth, 81, 251–6
State Planning Commission (Gos-
　plan), 212
State and Revolution (Lenin), 191
Status, 28–9, 42, 97, 130
Steam engine, 84, 88, 286n
Stephen, Uriah S., 153
Strikes, 60, 213
Subsistence economy, 28–9, 31, 37, 40,
　46, 48, 50–1, 54–5, 57, 67, 103,
　108–9
Sweden, 244
Switzerland, 14

Taxation, 21–2, 41, 57, 136, 140
Technology, 46, 65–7, 70, 86, 89, 90,
　92–3, 95, 127, 169–70, 190, 230,
　248–50, 254
Ten Hour Bill (1847), 123
Ten Hours Movement, 113
Textiles, 85–7, 88–9, 104, 107, 167,
　170, 190
Third Party Program (Russia), 231
Thirty Years' War, 159, 160
Tocqueville, Alexis de, 130, 291n,
　292n
Tories, 79, 101, 144
Totalitarianism, 12–14, 25, 60–1, 71,
　184, 256–7, 261–2, 265, 277
　and Russia, 187–233
Townsend, Joseph, 109, 289n
Toynbee, Arnold, 99, 287n

Trade unions, 31, 55–6, 59–60, 71, 112, 113–16, 126, 127, 176, 182–3, 198, 263–6
and India, 256–63
and industrial revolution, 72–5, 152–7
and Russia, 198, 210, 213, 218
Trading, 27–34 *passim*
Tradition-directed behavior, 239
Treaty of Westphalia (1648), 158–9
Trotsky, Leon, 206, 210, 211, 212
Turner, Frederick Jackson, 131–2, 291n

Underdeveloped countries, 8, 84, 234–68, 273, 284n
barriers to growth in, 234–56 *passim*
and liberal tradition, 273–6, 277
Unemployment, 118, 119, 120–2, 153, 169, 173, 243
Unemployment compensation, 119
United States, 3, 5, 10, 17, 18, 25, 121–2, 141–2, 162, 199, 209, 236, 243–4, 246, 248, 251, 262, 267, 271
and economic growth, 141–6 *passim*, 215
historical background of, 129–41 *passim*
vs. Germany, 159, 164–6, 235
vs. Great Britain, 141–2
industrialization of, 129–57 *passim*
labor movements in, 152–7
welfare problems of, 148–52, 168
United Trades Union Congress (India), 257–8
Ure, Andrew, 99
Utilitarianism, 50, 96, 119, 120, 287n

Veblen, Thorstein, 284n
Verelendung ("immiserization"), 54, 99, 149

Voting, 19–23

Wages, 52, 55, 95, 119, 169, 175, 176, 212
and controls, 81, 86
Wallas, Graham, 287n, 290n
Walpole, Robert, 6
War Communism, 202–3, 205–6, 210, 213
Washington, George, 138
Watt, James, 55, 84, 89, 92, 286n
Weber, Max, 6, 42, 282n
Weiner, Myron, 247
Welfare, 49–58 *passim*, 133, 274, 280n, 289n
in Germany, 167–71
in India, 260–1
and industrial revolution, 98–126 *passim*
and laboring classes, 103–8
and politics, 56–8
and real wages, 53–4, 99, 100, 113, 119, 148
in Russia, 195–6, 201, 208–11
in the United States, 148–52
Welfare state, 110, 178
Wellington, Duke of, 117
What Is To Be Done? (Lenin), 213, 285n
Whigs, 79
Whiskey Rebellion, 140
Wilberforce, William, 124
Wilhelm II (Germany), 179, 180
Woods, G. H., 99, 288n
World War I, 147, 167, 184–5, 191, 208, 262, 267

Young, Arthur, 109, 289n

Zemstvos, 197
Zollverein, 164